The Professional Thief

The Professional Thief

By a Professional Thief

Annotated and Interpreted by
EDWIN H. SUTHERLAND

Phoenix Books

THE UNIVERSITY OF CHICAGO PRESS

CHICAGO & LONDON

This book is also available in a clothbound edition from

THE UNIVERSITY OF CHICAGO PRESS

THE UNIVERSITY OF CHICAGO PRESS, CHICAGO & LONDON
The University of Toronto Press, Toronto 5, Canada

INTRODUCTION

The principal part of this book is a description of the profession of theft by a person who had been engaged almost continuously for more than twenty years in that profession. This description was secured in two ways: first, the thief wrote approximately two-thirds of it on topics and questions prepared by me; second, he and I discussed for about seven hours a week for twelve weeks what he had written, and immediately after each conference I wrote in verbatim form, as nearly as I could remember, all that he had said in the discussion.[1] I have organized this body of materials, written short connecting passages, and eliminated duplications as much as possible. In this organization I have attempted to preserve the ideas, attitudes, and phraseology of the professional thief. The thief read the manuscript as organized and suggested corrections, which have in all cases been made.

This manuscript was secured about seven years ago. The thief had done no stealing during the five years prior to the writing of the manuscript. Consequently the conditions described in this manuscript are essentially those of the period 1905–25. Names and places have been altered when it seemed to be desirable to preserve anonymity.

This document is a description of the profession of theft as experienced by one professional thief. His experiences were necessarily limited, and his point of view may have

[1] The thief was paid a small weekly wage for this work from funds provided by the Social Science Research Committee of the University of Chicago.

been biased. In order to supplement his experiences and to correct a possible bias, I submitted the manuscript to four other professional thieves and to two former detectives. Without submitting the manuscript, I discussed the ideas and problems with several other professional thieves, with several other representatives of municipal and private police systems, and with clerks in stores. From all these sources I secured oral or written comments. Furthermore, I have brought to bear on these problems all the available published literature regarding professional thieves. Selections from these several supplementary sources are presented in the footnotes in Part I. These footnotes are in all cases presented by me and not by the thief who wrote the text of that part of the book.

In general, these supplementary sources did not even hint at disagreement with the manuscript on fundamental issues. The absence of material in the footnotes which disagrees fundamentally with the ideas and conclusions of the professional thief who wrote the document is even more important than the presence of material which disagrees in details or which merely adds to the information in the text.

The professional thief who described his profession was known as Chic Conwell. He was born in Philadelphia about fifty years ago. His family was in comfortable circumstances. In adolescence he was ushering in a theater, formed an attachment for a chorus girl, married her, began to use narcotic drugs occasionally in association with her, left home, and became a pimp. In that occupation he became acquainted with thieves and through them learned to steal. He worked during subsequent years as a pickpocket, shoplifter, and confidence man. He stole in practically all of the American cities and many of the European cities. He lived in the underworld for twenty years and was thoroughly acquainted with it and with the techniques of many types of professional thieves.

In addition to several short terms in houses of correction, he served three terms in state and federal penitentiaries, with a total of about five years. The first term occurred soon after he became a professional thief and before he had perfected the techniques and connections which give relative immunity to professional thieves. The second imprisonment was a compromise required by the fact that a public official, who was indirectly involved in the same theft, had a more powerful claim for protection than did this thief. The third imprisonment was on a narcotic-drug charge. During the years between these prison terms, he was stealing almost continuously. Subsequent to his release after the third term he worked regularly at legitimate occupations, when he could find work, until his death in 1933, and during this time he did not use narcotic drugs.

Chic Conwell was an attractive person. A friend made the comment: "Chic was a confidence man and a good one. A good confidence man must have something lovable about him." He could have passed readily as a lawyer, a banker, or a merchant so far as personal appearance and casual conversation were concerned. He had the initiative, ingenuity, and abilities that are characteristic of leaders. He was near the top of his profession.

The profession of theft is more than isolated acts of theft frequently and skilfully performed. It is a group-way of life and a social institution. It has techniques, codes, status, traditions, consensus, and organization. It has an existence as real as that of the English language. It can be studied with relatively little attention to any particular thief. The profession can be understood by a description of the functions and relationships involved in this way of life. In fact, an understanding of this culture is a prerequisite to the understanding of the behavior of a particular professional thief. Also, an understanding of this culture is a prerequisite to the development of adequate policies of control of professional theft.

The document in Part I should be read from this point of view. The hypothesis may well be taken that professional thieves constitute a group which has the characteristics of other groups and that these group characteristics are in no sense pathological. Also, the hypothesis may be taken that tutelage by professional thieves and recognition as a professional thief are essential and universal elements in the definition, genesis, and continued behavior of the professional thief. No one is a professional thief unless he is recognized as such by other professional thieves. Tutelage by professional thieves is essential for the development of the skills, attitudes, codes, and connections which are required in professional theft. If this interpretation is valid, recognition and tutelage explain the professional thief in all cases, not in 60 or 70 per cent of the cases.

These hypotheses and other general characteristics and processes which are suggested by the available material are elaborated in the interpretation, which constitutes chapter ix in Part II of this book. In the Conclusion (chap. x) the explanation is made that this study of the professional thief is not to be regarded as a completed description and explanation. It is submitted merely as a basis for further studies of particular aspects of the profession of theft, in the belief that it will provide an orientation and will assist in the definition of problems. Several of the more general problems on which additional work might be done are outlined.

EDWIN H. SUTHERLAND

TABLE OF CONTENTS

PART I. THE PROFESSIONAL THIEF, WRITTEN BY
A PROFESSIONAL THIEF AND ANNOTATED
BY EDWIN H. SUTHERLAND

   I. THE PROFESSION 3

  II. THE MOB 27

 III. THE RACKETS 43

 IV. THE FIX 82

  V. THE THIEF AND THE LAW 119

 VI. STEALING AS A BUSINESS 140

VII. THE SOCIAL AND PERSONAL LIFE OF THE THIEF . 154

VIII. THE THIEF AND SOCIETY 172

PART II. INTERPRETATION AND CONCLUSION

 IX. INTERPRETATION 197

  X. CONCLUSION 229

GLOSSARY

GLOSSARY 235

BIBLIOGRAPHY

BIBLIOGRAPHY 247

INDEX

INDEX 255

PART 1

THE PROFESSIONAL THIEF
By A Professional Thief

Annotated by Edwin H. Sutherland

CHAPTER 1

THE PROFESSION

The professional thief is one who steals professionally. This means, first, that he makes a regular business of stealing. He devotes his entire working time and energy to larceny and may steal three hundred and sixty-five days a year. Second, every act is carefully planned. The selection of spots, securing of the property, making a get-away, disposing of the stolen property, and fixing cases in which he may be pinched (arrested)[1] are all carefully planned. Third, the professional thief has technical skills and methods which are different from those of other professional criminals. Manual skill is important in some of the rackets, but the most important thing in all the rackets is the ability to manipulate people. The thief depends on his approach, front, wits, and in many instances his talking ability. The professional burglar or stickup man (robber with a gun), on the other hand, uses violence or threat of violence even though he may on occasion use soothing language in order to quiet people. Fourth, the professional thief is generally migratory and may work in all the cities of the United States. He generally uses a particular city as headquarters, and, when two professional thieves first meet, the question is always asked: "Where are you out of?"

[1] Each term in the criminal argot used by this thief will be explained in parentheses immediately after the first appearance of the term. A glossary appears at the end of the book. Because of the large number of these words, they are not written within quotation marks.

3

In addition to these four characteristics, professional thieves have many things in common. They have acquaintances, congeniality, sympathy, understandings, agreements, rules, codes of behavior, and language in common.

The professional thief has nothing in common with the amateur thief or with the amateur in any other racket. The professional thief will be in sympathy with the amateur's attempt to steal something but will not be interested in him, for they have no acquaintances or ideas of stealing in common. He would talk with an amateur whom he might happen to meet in the can (police lockup) no longer than necessary to find out that he was an amateur. He might offer advice on how to beat the rap (charge), but this would be very rare, for, in addition to the fact that the amateur means nothing in his life, there is danger in telling the intricacies of the fix to someone who may be loquacious.

The professional thief has nothing in common with those who commit sex crimes or other emotional crimes and would not even be courteous to them if he should chance to meet them in the can.

Sympathy and congeniality with professional burglars and stickups is nearly as close as between thieves in one racket. They are all thieves, and the fact that one has a different racket does not alter this feeling. To professional burglars whom he knows on the street he will tender ideas and spots, not as a 10 per cent man (on a commission basis) but purely out of a spirit of congeniality. He will render assistance to a professional burglar in fixing cases, securing bonds, or escaping from a jailhouse as readily as to thieves in his own rackets.

4

The attitude of one thief toward another or of one group of thieves toward another group is very friendly unless there is some personal enmity existing between them aside from their professional activities. Even though personal enmity existed, one mob (group of thieves who work together) would advise the other, directly or through a third party, of any imminent danger. Regardless of how strong the ill feeling be between two thieves, neither of them would want to see the other pinched, and each would exert much effort to prevent it. A cannon (pickpocket) mob was grifting (stealing in) an "L" station in Boston. A thief who had personal unfriendliness toward them came onto the platform and was leaving the station when he noticed two coppers (policemen), more or less hidden, watching the cannon mob. The thief, disregarding his ill feeling toward the mob as well as the danger of a pickup (arrest on suspicion) from the two coppers, returned to the platform and made known to the mob that they were being cased (watched). He felt that the cannon mob would have done the same thing for him had their positions been reversed. Should a thief happen to notice a store copper watching a booster (shoplifter) or a cannon or any other mob working, he would, if possible without endangering his own liberty, cut into the booster or other mob and advise them of being cased. This procedure is very simple if the coppers do not know you, as you would merely have to brush by the person being cased and by a glance or a single word—such as "Nix!" —make known the danger. This is not a rare occurrence, but one that happens almost every day. Everyone wants to see everyone else get along regardless of his racket.

Not only does one thief warn another thief of danger

but also he avoids doing things which will put other thieves in danger. If a thief were going through a store and saw a booster working, he would not stop to watch the booster because this might cause someone else to look in the same direction and might result in the booster getting pinched. A great deal of trouble is caused by the curiosity of nonprofessional thieves or, in very rare instances, even of professional thieves. Two heels (sneak thieves) had got into the stockroom of a high-class jewelry house, had secured a tray of platinum watches, and were leaving the store. As they got to the center of the main floor a snatch-and-grab (unskilled) booster whom they knew and who knew them spoke to them. They chilled for him (pretended not to recognize him) and kept on going, but he turned around and stared after them. He should have known enough not to recognize and speak to them anywhere that they might be grifting, even if he was not a real professional, and besides he should never have stared after them when they chilled, which in itself was enough to let him know they were hot (in danger). This booster was known in the store and was being watched. When it was noticed that he spoke to the two who were going out and stared at them, the attention of the store copper was transferred to the other two, and he immediately started to cut them off at the door. The heels sensed this at once and reversed and maneuvered back to the stockroom, where they got a chance to clean themselves (get rid of the stolen goods). They were stopped and searched on the way out and warned to stay out of that store. Thus a good score (stolen object) and the opportunity of future success in that store were knocked out by someone who did not know his business.

6

Thieves also give much assistance to other thieves who are in trouble. Personal feelings seldom affect this. Jew Jake, a booster, had for years been bad friends with Little Eddie, another booster. Jake got in the can in Chicago, where he was a stranger and was broke. Eddie heard of it and approached a person who knew the fixer and asked him to find out how much it would cost to get Jake out. The fixer announced $150 as the amount necessary. Eddie turned over the $150 with the statement: "I hate the no-good bastard, but I can't let him lay in the can for $150." If money were needed to spring a man (get a man out of the lockup or prison), the person who was getting the money together would not hesitate to appeal to someone who held ill feeling for the person in the can. A man is in the can, and the money is needed to get him out, and this takes precedence over all personal relations, unless friendly relations have been disrupted by things like burning (holding out part of the stolen goods), or turning in (informing), or attempting to kill. A thief would appear and feel very small if a friend or even a temporary enemy were in the can in need of money in an amount he could spare and he refused to loan it to him. In major cases where a lot of money is needed for a case, subscription papers are taken around to the several hang-outs, and only broke guys do not contribute. This would be regarded as an outright gift. When the money is not secured in the form of a general subscription, it is regarded as a loan, repayable at the first opportunity.

It is very common when a mob is cutting up (dividing the proceeds of) a day's work to suggest sending a part of it to some member of the profession, not necessarily one of the mob, who is doing a bit (prison sentence).[2] This week it will be John Smith in Charlestown, next week Kelly in Dannemora, the following week Brown in San Quentin. In some instances a mob which drops a man will take care of him during his entire bit. This becomes generally known, and his other friends will merely write to him, sending their money to some other thief who is not so fortunate as to have a mob taking care of him. Whenever money is sent to anyone doing a bit, it is purely a gift. Thieves are glad to be able to send it, as it is the only way they have of expressing their friendship and continued memory of him.

Assistance to thieves who are doing a bit or who are in the can is more frequent and liberal than when they are in other trouble. A thief who is not friendly with another, on learning that this other thief is in the hospital or is broke and in need of money, would say, "To hell with him," or "Let him starve." The thief feels that, if another thief is on the street, he is capable of stealing and has no reason to be broke or hungry. Thieves are all professionally united against law-enforcement bodies, which are the only enemies common to all thieves.

Should one mob find some bad features in any spot, they will always advise other mobs of it, as they will also advise them if a spot is lucrative. Should one mob have a bad case and mention the details to some other mob in a different racket, the other mob may give them valuable information as to someone who can handle the complaining witness or can talk to the arresting officer. One thief might inform another regarding a certain spot:

[2] Hutchins Hapgood's thief reported the same practice at the turn of the century (*Autobiography of a Thief* [New York, 1903], p. 127).

8

"The best slant in that spot is on Monday between twelve and two o'clock, but watch out for that big red-headed saleswoman; she is double smart." If, however, a thief has figured a way to beat some spot and intends to continue to beat it by that means, he will not make public how he beats the spot, although he will tell others that he does beat it. No one will ask him how he does it, realizing that, if he had cared to mention his system, he would have done so without being asked.

Thieves, of course, do not like competition from other thieves, but they are tolerant. At times a mob will return after a day's work and offer as an excuse, "Forty mobs were working." This would, of course, reduce the earnings of each individual mob, but this is not taken as a complaint against competitors. Even when other mobs use rip-and-tear (crude) methods that heat up (cause danger in) the spot, they are never complained of or to. It is the spirit of thieves to be tolerant of other thieves and let everyone grift as he sees fit. In smaller cities, however, the local mobs resent outsiders entering their territory, and many cases are known where they advised the local coppers who were protecting the local cannons that out-of-town mobs were working. This would mean nothing more than the coppers chasing the out-of-town mobs or shaking them down (extortion) at the worst.

Codes of ethics are much more binding among thieves than among legitimate commercial firms. Should an outfit have a putup touch (opportunity for theft suggested by an outsider) for 10 per cent, no other outfit would think of offering the putup man 15 per cent for it, although no commercial house would hesitate to outbid a competitor in a case like this.

9

There are few fixed rules of ethics, but there are some common understandings among thieves. One of them is illustrated in the following incident. A man complained that he had been beaten to the con (in a confidence game) for $1,200, and many con men were picked up and shown to the victim. He failed to identify anyone until the coppers coached him to the effect that the only way he could get his money back was to identify someone. It is believed that the coppers suggested a certain mob to him, believing that this mob had plenty of money and would kick in $1,200 rather than fight it. It was the wrongest rap in the world, but they had to come in with $1,200 for the victim and $300 for the coppers to square the case. The thieves knew that another mob had got the money. In an instance of this kind the mob that got the money is expected to make good the money the other mob lays out, and it is very unusual for a mob to fail. So coppers are not a bit particular whom they hang a rap on, so long as they get credit for the case, for the thieves at times even up among themselves in this way.

It is understood that no thief must squawk (inform) on another. The instances where professional thieves have squawked are so rare that no serious consideration of this angle is necessary.[3] Prisoners squawk for one purpose

[3] A professional bank burglar who had read this manuscript commented: "I agree with the author here. I never knew a single professional thief who squawked. A fellow who steals for a living—I mean a man who really steals and does nothing else—would not dream of squawking." On the other hand, professional thieves have turned informers when their protection is threatened, as in the campaign waged by the district-attorney, Van Cise, in Denver (Philip S. Van Cise, *Fighting the Underworld* [Boston, 1936], pp. 252–58). An interesting discussion of the attitude of the juvenile delinquent toward the squealer and of the process by which this atti-

only—to relieve themselves of punishment. Professional thieves have no thought of receiving punishment while in the hands of the fix, and they have no incentive to squawk. Police officials, prosecutors, and others rarely question professional thieves. They have or else haven't got a rap for the prisoner. In either case there is no gain from questioning. If a thief should squawk, the other thieves would not descend to the same plane and squawk on him. They use much better methods. The worst penalty is to keep him broke. This is done by spreading the news that he has squawked, which makes it impossible for him to get into any mob. That is the greatest disgrace and the greatest hardship that can befall a thief.

A professional thief must not squawk on another thief even when he has been beat by the other. He does not like to be beat any better than anyone else, and it is just as easy to beat him. A professional thief reported his experience thus:

I was riding on a streetcar in Chicago when I felt some one put his hand in my prat [hip pocket] clear up to the elbow. I turned and saw that it was Eddie Jackson, whom I knew and who knew me. When he saw who it was, he asked in friendly sarcasm, "What in hell are you doing here? Why can't you stay out of the way?" He led his mob away knowing that there was absolutely no danger from me. Another time I was riding in the subway in New York when I felt a hand in my right prat. I rounded to see who it was. Right behind me was a rabbi-looking Jew with a long beard and a black alpaca coat. He was standing there with his arms folded across his breast, looking very benevolent, and I decided I must have made a

tude is developed is found in Clifford R. Shaw and Henry D. McKay, "Social Factors in Juvenile Delinquency," *Report of National Commission on Law Observance and Enforcement* (Washington, 1931), No. 13, Vol. II, 243–47.

mistake. But a few days later I was over on the East Side and there saw this Jew who was pointed out to me as one of their best mocky cannons. They said, facetiously, that I should feel honored that he tried to beat me. I must have looked like ready money, but I would not have reported him to the police even if he had secured my poke [pocketbook].

Another general rule among all thieves except cannons is that, if one mob comes into a place and finds another mob already at work, it will leave at once. It will do so partly from professional courtesy and partly for safety. The other mob might be already known to the coppers, especially if it is composed of amateurs. The only exception to the rule of not working where another mob is at work is where two mobs, each having confidence in the ability of the other, agree in advance to work in the same place. This is unusual and would happen only when some sale, fashion show, or like event was taking place which made the spot good at that particular time.[4]

[4] Jack Black lists the following as the principal elements in the ethical code of the criminal: (1) Do not hold out property on fellow-criminals; (2) do not for any reason fall down on a job; (3) do not inform the police of the crimes of others; (4) pay your debts to other criminals; (5) don't be a hard loser. These forms of loyalty to another are regarded as necessary because they are all in conflict with society ("A Burglar Looks at Laws and Codes," *Harper's*, CLX [February, 1930], 306–13). Victor Nelson makes the following statement regarding the code of prisoners: "In the old days, when a convict or a criminal was actually a social pariah, shunned by all respectable people, he was forced into a group, the code of which he was obliged, at the risk of his life, to live up to. At present, when laws in general are broken by nearly every one, the sharp dividing line between criminals and honest men has become, like most religious codes or ethical standards, greatly undermined and weakened. . . . . The only criminal who, as a rule, can be expected to live up to the prison code is the gangster (and some few thieves). The gangster is usually a man who has grown up in a neighborhood where rigid adherence to the code was a matter of life and death, so that it is actually a religion with him to be

There are many business maxims and rules, which may be illustrated by the rule, "Never grift on the way out." Two thieves recently went down into southern Indiana. During the week they picked up a whole carload of junk, which must have been worth $10,000, though they would not be able to sell it for more than a fourth of that amount. They stopped on the way back at Fort Wayne to work some more, though they already had a full load. The coppers caught them there, and they had to turn over to the coppers their car and everything they had in it and wire to Chicago for $500 more. The coppers got the car, the stuff, and the money, and the grifters got the debt. Another case, just as bad, occurred to a boosting mob in a department store. The mob had made a touch of a Spanish shawl, worth three or four hundred dollars. The man who was carrying the shawl out saw some nine-teen-cent fingernail files on the first floor near the door. He was foolish enough to pick up one of these for his own use and put it in his pocket. He was seen, got a pinch, the shawl was found, and then he was in bad. This explains the regular rule, "Never grift on the way out." Amateur thieves, when arrested, are frequently found to have two pairs of hose, a dozen handkerchiefs, two pairs

'right.' . . . . He is, of all criminals, the man who most nearly lives up to a code of conduct which he believes right (from his twisted point of view)" (*Prison Days and Nights* [Boston: Little, Brown & Co., 1933], pp. 118–19 [by permission]). In somewhat the same vein an old professional criminal in Chicago is much chagrined at the behavior of young criminals of today; he believes that criminals are going to the dogs, have no morals at all, and do not observe the ethics of the criminal profession. Jim Tully has given a description of the ethics of the yeggs ("Yeggs," *American Mercury*, XXVIII [April, 1933], 391–400). See also the analysis of the mores of the professional criminal in Charles L. Clark and Earle E. Eubank, *Lockstep and Corridor* (Cincinnati, 1927), pp. 144–56.

of gloves—all from different departments or even from different stores. The professional will rarely have more than one score on him when arrested. As soon as he takes off a score, he leaves the store, plants it, and goes back for another.

The distinctions most sought after among thieves are money and proficiency in their chosen lines. These, as a rule, go together. Thieves have the greatest respect for one who can succeed in the most difficult situations, although they recognize that success and failure are largely a matter of luck. All the thieves, for instance, speak about Big Jake who has the reputation of being the only con who beat anyone while in prison. He was a trusty in Joliet and used to run errands outside the walls. One time he was sent to town on an errand for the deputy, and while there he beat some sucker on a confidence game for several thousand dollars. That one thing would have made his reputation for the rest of his life, if it had not been made already.[5]

A thief is not a professional until he is proficient. When a thief is taken on for unimportant tasks by some mob, he is not regarded as a professional. He may develop into a professional in the course of time if he does these unimportant jobs well enough to lead the mob to give him more important jobs. If he does not succeed in the first tasks, he is dropped and gets no opportunity to fill in with any mob even for unimportant tasks. He may then become a beggar, a pimp, a steerer for some gambler, get into the heavy rackets, or try to grift single-handed. If a

[5] A professional forger attained fame in the underworld by passing a worthless check on the authorities of a prison which he visited as a sight-seer.

14

professional who has an established reputation takes on a new racket, he may not be efficient at it. That is about the only condition in which a professional would not be proficient. He would quickly drop the new racket for some other professional racket if he did not become proficient at it in a short time.

The disgraces dreaded by thieves are the opposite of the distinctions, namely, inefficiency and poverty. Inefficiency, likewise, not merely means low success in stealing but also includes violation of any of the rules or codes of professional thievery, such as squawking, or burning his partners.

In addition to these disgraces, certain things furnish thieves an opportunity for razzing their acquaintances. These include petty misfortunes, accidents, and similar things in professional and private life and are not particularly different from other occupations in this respect. More specifically, the ex-thief or ex-prisoner who writes books is razzed. The other thieves think he has gone long-hair or something. They might say, if they should meet him, "The author! Did you ever try to write poetry?" The same thing is true of the ex-thief who makes speeches or lectures. This is a relatively mild razzing and does not imply any loss of confidence in the ex-thief. They know that, if he is a thief, he is not going to say anything to hurt anyone, and, if he is not a thief, he doesn't know anything that would hurt anyone. In the main, the thieves would give the ex-prisoner credit for conning the public out of something when he wrote a book or made a speech and regard it merely as a new racket.

The professional thief lives in the underworld and has sympathetic and congenial relationships there. He is isolated from legitimate society except as he contacts it in his professional capacity, and legitimate society is largely isolated from the underworld. The underworld is an exclusive society because of the danger involved from strangers. Within the underworld communication regarding the law, which is the common enemy, is free. Every crime which is committed gets through to the hangouts in a very short time. It reaches the hangouts before it appears in the newspapers, and it is not in the same form as in the newspapers. The only "crimes" which are exceptions to this are the thefts from jewelry salesmen, generally in the form of a big loss of diamonds. You rarely hear about such stories in the hangouts except as they appear in the newspapers. This indicates that most of the thefts from jewelry salesmen are phony.[6]

Because the underworld is an exclusive society, it is necessary that the stranger be identified before he is admitted.[7] The language of the underworld is both an

[6] The author stated in a conversation that he believed 98 per cent of the reported robberies of jewelry salesmen were "the bunk." The Chicago newspapers of May 20 and 21, 1934, reported that a jewelry salesman had been robbed of jewelry valued at $35,000; later it was reported that he had connived with the owner of a jewelry store on North State Street, for which he worked, to collect insurance on jewelry; two other salesmen were involved in the same transaction. Another illustration occurred in December, 1935, when a jewelry salesman was reported to have been robbed; later it developed that this was a device of an informer for the jeweler's association in order that he might show his efficiency in securing the return of the "stolen" jewels.

[7] O'Connor makes the following statement: "In the so-called underworld when an alien without invitation invades the territory where the mobs congregate, he is known as 'A weed in the garden.' Until proved otherwise, he is given the chill. Cold stares are aimed at him, his every move is openly watched, and he is generally made to feel so uncomfortable that he soon disappears" (John J. O'Connor, *Broadway Racketeers* [New York: Liveright Publishing Corp., 1928], p. 50).

evidence of this isolation of the underworld and also a means of identification. Criminal slang of three hundred years ago is still being used today by criminals, though much of it is completely unknown to the general public. This language is passed from one crook to another by speech and not by writing. A slang dictionary published in England about 1585 had a lot of the same words and expressions we have now, and also a lot of the same rackets, such as dropping the poke, moll-buzzing, crashing windows.

A professional thief can tell in two minutes' conversation with a stranger whether he is acquainted with the criminal underworld and in two minutes more what particular rackets he knows intimately. If a thief were in the can and another person were brought in, the first might ask, "Where were you nailed?" The second might say, "In the shed." It is possible that an amateur might know that "nailed" in that connection meant "arrested," but no amateur would use the word "shed" for railroad station. Not only does the word "shed" help to identify the other as a professional but also the fact that he was arrested there helps to show the rackets which he might have been playing, such as the con game, or the cannon. Additional questions will draw out the technical words used in particular rackets, for each racket has words referring to the objects and actions peculiar to it. The cannon, for instance, has many technical terms referring to the different pockets. The word "prat" originally meant "buttock" but has been used by thieves for several centuries to refer to the hip pocket. Probably few members of the general public have ever heard of the word. Similarly one of the operations in picking pockets is to "prat a man in," which means that one of the stalls backs into a prospect and pushes him around gently in order to get him in a proper position.

Many people believe that these expressions are used in order to conceal the meaning from the public who may be listening in and that they are thus for the purpose of giving secrecy to the conversation. That interpretation is out; there is nothing to it. When thieves are talking in a place where others may overhear, they do not use their slang, for it would immediately attract attention to themselves. They use regular words with inflections or winks which indicate their meaning. For instance, three thieves were riding on a train. One of the mob went into a drawing-room and stole some property. Later the three thieves went into the dining-car and sat at a table for four. The owner of the drawing-room came into the diner and was seated at the table with them. He did not know the thief who had entered his room, and the thief did not know him, though the other two thieves did recognize the owner. So when the owner was sitting down, one thief said, "It is rather warm in here," and glanced at the man from the drawing-room. The other thief immediately knew what was meant. Similarly when the heel is being worked two-handed, the one who is watching will keep up a constant line of talk or blah in order to make the operation seem natural, but the talk does not mean anything. If some danger appears, the one who is watching will say, "Let's go over and get a drink of orange juice," or "I had forgotten this letter my wife gave me to mail yesterday. Let's go out and mail it." The other thief knows that the suggestion to stop and get a drink of orange juice is not merely conversation and also that it is not a bona fide expression of thirst. He knows that it means danger and he acts accordingly.

Sometimes a professional thief is greatly embarrassed when he appears in public with an amateur who does not understand this indirect language of the professional thieves. A professional thief reported the following instance:

I was eating supper in a cafeteria with an occasional thief and drug addict who was a student in a law school. Two coppers were sitting at another table near by. The occasional thief had selected our table and had not recognized them as coppers. They were not in uniform, but a uniform is not needed to advertise to a professional that a copper is a copper. They could not possibly have been anything else. My friend said loud enough so the coppers could hear, "Did you hear what Jerry Myers got?" I knew alright that Jerry got four years, but I was not going to let the coppers know that we were talking about anyone who had received a bit, and I had to hush the youngster up. I could not say, "Nix!" as a thief might have said if the coppers had not been able to hear, for that word in itself would have informed the coppers that we were worth watching, and besides my friend would not have understood what the word meant in that connection. So I said, "I understand the doctor said he got tonsilitis." A professional thief would have sensed danger at once and would have carried on along that line, but my friend thought I must be hard of hearing or else a fool and he started in again, "No, I mean . . . . " but I kicked him under the table and butted in again with some more information about tonsilitis. The police were watching us carefully, and I could not office (warn) my partner by moving my eyes toward them. As soon as I hesitated for a moment on the tonsilitis, he started in again on what Jerry got, so I had to get up and go to the counter for something more to eat. When I returned I picked up his book on Conveyances and looked at it a moment and then asked, "Have you seen the new book on Abnormal Psychology by Dr. Oglesby?" The policemen, who had finished eating some time before, immediately got up and reached for their hats. I nudged my partner to look at them, and as they stretched up you could see that each had a revolver in a holster. They doubtless went away thinking, "Just a couple of harmless university students or professors." My partner now understood why I had interrupted him and skinned his shins, and he asked, "Why didn't you tell me they were here?" I had told him a half-dozen times in language any professional thief would have understood but which he could not understand, principally because he did not have the attitude of suspicion which is the foundation of the indirect method of conversation, but also because he did not give me credit for good sense.

Language is not in itself a sufficient means of determining whether a person is trustworthy, for some people in the underworld are stool pigeons and some outsiders learn some of the language. Another method is by finding out what people the stranger knows. If he belongs to the underworld, he will know some of the important people in the underworld of Chicago, Baltimore, Kansas City, or some other city. It will not take long until a professional thief will find mutual acquaintances if the stranger really is a professional. What he knows about these mutual acquaintances will show whether he is trustworthy. If he knows someone in the local community, it is possible to ask this one about the stranger. He will either say, "He is alright" or else, "He is no good." That locates him so far as you are concerned. In the underworld a person's reputation quickly spreads to everyone, just as does everything that is done. There is no underworld newspaper, but there is complete communication among the members so that everyone knows about everyone else in his particular part of the underworld.

Professional thieves have no policy of recruiting for the profession. They can always secure a sufficient number of partners from among the thieves who are already professionals. On the other hand, a person can become a professional thief only if he is trained by those who are already professionals. It is ridiculous to imagine an amateur deciding to become a pickpocket, con man, pennyweighter (jewelry thief), or shake man (extortioner) without professional guidance. He knows nothing of the racket, its technique or operations, and he can't learn these things out of books.

The members of the profession generally started their occupational life in legitimate employment, although some of them entered other illegal occupations before becoming professional thieves. Few of them came from the amateur thieves who are reared in the slums, for these youngsters seldom have the social abilities or front required of professional thieves.[8] The following are a few of the known cases of origin of professional thieves: Five pimps arrived in New York from Philadelphia with their women. Within a few months one of them filled in for a small part in a smack touch (coin-matching racket), another was a participant in a putup stickup (robbery suggested by others), two were offered small parts in certain touches but refused. Ten years later the first two

[8] There is a good deal of evidence that many pickpockets did have their origin in the slums. See Josiah Flynt Willard, *Notes of an Itinerant Policeman* (Boston, 1900), pp. 34–35; O'Connor, *op. cit.*, p. 31; *Illinois Crime Survey* (Chicago, 1929), p. 1065. On the other hand, there is little evidence available which either supports or contradicts the description of the origin of other types of thieves.

had become capable con men, and one of these had married a wealthy woman and retired from all rackets; the other two were professional thieves in other lines, while the fifth was still a pimp. At about the same time another pimp killed a man because of a woman. During a long stay in jail he became known to professional thieves who were continually in and out of the jail. When he beat the murder rap, he was filled in by a shake mob. He made considerable money in this line and on the sneak. Later he married the daughter of a wealthy family. She stuck with him when her family disowned her, and he continued on the shake. He is now finishing his second bit. Another professional thief started as a salesman in a department store. In some way he was inveigled into stealing merchandise from the store. When he was caught and discharged, he was filled in by a boosting mob. He is still boosting with a wife and sister-in-law whom he acquired after leaving the store. Several bellboys who were stealing everything possible in the hotels where they were employed drifted into the professional ranks when no more hotels would employ them. Their contacts with professional thieves were made while they were disposing of the goods they stole while still employed by the hotels. They became sneak thieves, boosters, and one finally arrived at the status of safe-blower. Two hotel clerks, who came in contact with professional thieves living in their hotels, are among those who came to be professional thieves. Both had put up touches in many hotels where they were employed prior to joining the professional ranks. Both are now hotel prowls (sneak thieves). Several former taxi drivers are now among the professional thieves, making contacts in their capacity as cab drivers.

One turned out to be a con man, another a heel. Waiters in the old saloons, beer gardens, and rathskellers have turned to professional thievery in many instances. They formed contacts with professionals in their capacity as waiters. Several of them are now on the con, one is a heel, several are on the cannon, and two or more are on the shake.

Do not let it be understood that a waiter, cab driver, hotel clerk, or bellboy simply quits his job and, deciding to become a professional thief, immediately becomes one. In all cases the severance of legitimate connections is followed by a period of unemployment, forced or otherwise, hanging around places frequented by thieves and generally known in person by the thieves through previous work. He is first filled in for a day's work on a particular job of no great danger and calling for no particular ability. More often it is purely an act of charity on the part of the mob in order to provide him a little money. This is a most common practice. If he does this unimportant part well, he may be called on later for more important parts, and gradually acquire the expert skill of the professional.[9]

Professional female thieves, in the great majority, are recruited from the ranks of prostitutes, waitresses, cashiers, and kindred hotel and restaurant employees. It is

[9] A confidence man commented: "Any man who hits the big-time in crime, somewhere or other along the road, became associated with a big-timer who picked him up and educated him. Then, if first he had the guts and secondly the ability, he gradually turned into a professional big-time racketeer. But no one ever crashed the big rackets without education in this line." The training given to the pickpocket is described in several places. See Robert Heindl, *Der Berufsverbrecher* (5th ed.; Berlin, 1927), p. 231; Shaw and McKay, *op. cit.*, pp. 232–39.

easily seen how these contacts develop. In rare instances legitimate workers in other lines started by boosting clothes for their own use. They did not respond to the punishment administered when they were arrested and continued boosting. Contacts between feminine amateurs and feminine professionals are much more frequently and easily made than between male amateurs and male professionals. This is because most female thieves start at boosting and upon arrest are placed in contact with professional boosters.

There are few limitations on the types of people who become professional thieves. The very young and the very old are eliminated. Color places certain limitations. There is but one known professional Negro thief who operates with whites, but there are several well-known Negro thieves working in their own mobs. Every racket has Jews in the ranks of operatives, but Jews perhaps specialize a little more on the cannon than any other racket. Chinese pickpockets are rare, and the few who are known operate with others of their own race and more often than not operate on members of their own race. There are two Chinese cannons of note who are very clever and never get a pinch. There are a few Chinese bums who try to work various con rackets on Chinese people but do not try anyone else. Women are found in many rackets. They are naturally exclusive as gun-molls (female pickpockets). They are used occasionally in some other rackets, where they aid the male members of the troupe as steerers or stalls. There are hundreds of troupes entirely female on the boost.

Members of the profession make their exit from the profession in various ways. Some die, some get too old to work and wind up in a home for old people, some develop a habit (drug) and become too inefficient to be professional thieves, some violate the ethics of the profession and are kicked out, some get in bad with the fix and can no longer get protection and are therefore useless as members of a mob, some become fixers in resort cities, some become big shots in gambling, vice, junk, or booze rackets, some get "the big one" (extraordinarily large theft), and some settle down in legitimate occupations without getting "the big one." The legitimate occupations into which professional thieves have gone include detective agencies, cab companies, cigar stores, hotels, farming, manufacturing, and the movies.[10] Some of the female thieves marry persons with legitimate occupations.

[10] Hapgood's thief, finding that few of his former associates were engaged in professional crime when he came out of prison at the end of a four-year term, made some inquiry and learned that they had taken the following exits from professional crime: (1) some had become fences or were engaged in other "sure-thing grafts" with a minimum of risk; (2) some had "gone slack," including those who had become drunkards or drug adicts; (3) some had become stool pigeons or agents of private-detective companies; (4) some had entered semilegitimate occupations, such as gambling, saloon, hotel, bondsmen; and (5) some had entered legitimate trades and remained honest (*op. cit.*, pp. 259–61). Landesco found that few professional thieves had become bootleggers during the prohibition period (*Illinois Crime Survey*, p. 1071). The New York City papers in 1934 reported that several old-time professional thieves who had disappeared for many years were brought back into professional crime by the depression. Richard Fisher ("Diamond Dick"), seventy-seven years of age, had made a reputation in the theft of diamond stickpins but had disappeared until the depression brought him back into the criminal world. An ex-thief in Chicago in 1936 looked up five acquaintances who had been picking pockets in 1930 and made the following report: "Two are working in a gambling house; one is selling narcotics; one is selling 'hot merchandise' and the other is a pimp. Would you place these gentlemen in the category of 'reformed pickpockets'?" Alec ("Whitey") Johnson had become wealthy as a pickpocket, invested his money in real estate,

Professional stealing is not organized crime. There is no organized crime unless we are to call each mob, troupe, outfit, or combination which is grifting together an organization. They are organized in the sense of being together as a stock company but not in the sense the newspapers would have readers believe. "Rings" are confined to the legitimate business world, as the cement manufacturers of Wichita, Germantown, Dover, and Spokane are members of a national association. The thieves in Wichita, Germantown, Dover, and Spokane may know one another, but they are not members of a national association. There is organized beer and booze running, gambling and prostitution, in the sense that a syndicate controls several spots in one city or spots in adjoining cities. This is the only semblance of a "ring," and it is not in the field of crime, for these are not considered crime by the professional criminals, the police, the lawyers, or the courts.[11]

---

was wiped out in the early years of the depression, returned to his early profession, was arrested, and in 1935 committed suicide in jail. Hapgood's thief wrote: "As a general thing I found that guns who had squared it and become prosperous had never been very successful grafters" (*op. cit.*, p. 334).

[11] A confidence man commented on this paragraph as follows: "The author is absolutely right in his assertion that there is no such thing as organized crime as yelped about in the papers. There may be certain mobs operating together; there may be certain people in certain cities who have control of everything and who are thoroughly protected in anything they want to do. But there is no such thing as a connection of mobs from one city to another, or anything like a nationwide hookup of crime. This is a figment of the journalistic imagination."

For a different interpretation of the concept of organized crime, see below, pp. 209–10.

CHAPTER 2
THE MOB

The working group of professional thieves is known as a mob, troupe, or outfit. The number of members in a mob is determined in part by the racket which is being hustled, in part by the angles which are being played, and in part by the circumstances and situation. The cannon (picking pockets) is operated very rarely single-handed, a little more frequently two-handed, most frequently three-handed, and occasionally a fourth man is added. Most of the rackets have not more than three or four men in a mob, and there is no standard number for any one racket. Sometimes a large number of thieves work together in a loose organization in the more elaborate confidence games, using a common pay-off joint or big store (fake gambling club or brokerage office).[1]

Some mobs are permanent, some last for a season, and some only for a trip or two. Many mobs are organized merely to grift a convention for a few days or a resort for a season; when this occasion is ended, the members separate. While the life of most of the mobs is comparatively short, many have grifted intact for years. At least a half-dozen mobs grifting out of Chicago have had no change in personnel for several years, and others have changed only one man.

[1] Thirty-five confidence men were arrested in Van Cise's drive against confidence men in Denver; all were using Blonger's pay-off joint (Philip S. Van Cise, *Fighting the Underworld*, pp. 352–53).

When a mob is organized with the expectation that it will be permanent, it may break up for several reasons. One member may become sick, or his wife may object to him being on the road, or the members may become dissatisfied with the amount of money being made. If a mob consists of two members, and one leaves, the mob is nonexistent. Even if it consists of three members, and one leaves, the others may separate also. But a mob never breaks up because a racket gets too hot (dangerous). In such cases they would merely pack it in (desist) temporarily or grift somewhere else. To break up because of heat would be an admission of defeat, and no thief will admit defeat.

When a mob sticks together for several years, it is because it has been successful in making money. It is not because of loyalty to a leader or because of personal liking for one another. In some mobs the members do not speak to one another socially, but since they make money together their social relations are secondary. A hook (pickpocket who takes the money from the pocket of the victim) who has now retired had a national reputation for being the most arrogant, irritable, cheap, and contemptible of all cannons in social life, but in his business life he was highly thought of, and many cannons sought the chance to grift with him. When not grifting, he criticized every act of every member of his mob. If one of them rented an apartment, bought a suit, or got himself a new woman, this hook always took exception to the taste or judgment of the other. But when grifting he never criticized the action of any member of his mob; if they blew a score (failed in an attempted theft), it was just blowed. On the other hand, a member who criticizes the professional activities, always finding supposed errors on someone's part regardless of whether the score is made or blowed, has trouble getting connected up with any outfit, for it is hard for any such outfit to work together in unity.

An individual thief is likely to shift around a great deal from mob to mob. A very capable hook from Baltimore jockeyed around with one mob and then another, eventually organizing two of his lifelong friends into a mob with him. These three grifted together for years with no thought of anyone being boss or having fall-dough (money to be used in case of arrest). First one and then the other stall (assistant) went into a different line. Then the hook organized a mob, with himself as boss, and demanded fall-dough from the members. This combination grifted together practically intact for several years. The boss then got into the junk (narcotic drug) racket, broke up his mob, got a bit, returned to the cannon when he finished his bit, and at present is hopscotching around from one mob to another. Father Time has crept up on him, and he does not grift with the same regularity and vigor as before, and perhaps that is the reason he does not organize a mob on the same basis as he did earlier. Another hook from Chicago jumped from one mob to another for years and finally got control of several spots to grift right (under complete protection). He organized his own mob, which for years has grifted these spots. But since these spots are good for only about twenty weeks in the year, the mob is intact only during those weeks, during the balance of the year each joining out with another outfit.

Since the mobs of the professional thieves are generally small, there is no formality about joining or separating from a mob. When a vacancy exists in a mob, it may be filled by someone who is suggested by the boss or by one of the other members. Since the weaknesses, capabilities, habits, and idiosyncrasies of all thieves become the general knowledge of other thieves, they know when his name is suggested whether they want him or not. The suggestion of a certain thief to fill in may bring forth the fact that he is a drunkard, lazy, a dope fiend, copper-shy, late for meets, or that his wife wouldn't let him grift on the road, or any of many other characteristics. If the person suggested is unanimously approved, he is asked to fill in.

The thief invited to join out a mob does not always accept the invitation. He might not like their methods, he might lack confidence in the hook's ability, he might not like the personal qualities of some of the members, or he might not like the spot they are going to grift.

A member may be discharged from the mob by the boss, if the mob has a boss, or by the mob acting together. Discharge is for something which affects the welfare of the whole mob, such as drunkenness, lack of ability or of co-operation, and being late to meets. Generally a fault of this sort is talked over by the mob many times before discharge, and the one at fault is given many bawlings out first. The only exception to this is in case of burning, or holding out the amount stolen. In this case the first offense is the last offense. If the mob is organized with a boss, it is the boss's privilege at any time to hand the member the fall-dough he has put up and discharge him. There is no argument and no appeal. A man is fired only if he jeopardizes the others in some way, and no objection would be raised by the other members.

Just as often a member may withdraw from a mob. He may have many different reasons for withdrawing. His wife or other members of the family may be sick, he may not desire to go to a certain place which is contemplated, he may be dissatisfied with the amount of money being made, or he may become angry at the boss or some other member of the mob. If there is a boss and fall-dough, the expression used is, "Give me my fall-dough, I resign." In this event the others would try to cool him off and cause him to withdraw his resignation.

In most cases when members withdraw or are fired, there is no hard feeling on either side. The next week the quitting member may ask for his job back, or the discharging boss may ask the man to join him again. However, the member who was discharged will never ask the boss to put him to work again nor will the boss ask the quitting member to rejoin him. The initiative must be taken by the person who caused the original break. Call it pride, ethics, or what you will.

In organizing a new mob, filling in a vacancy, and dividing the work of a mob which has been organized, the capabilities of the members are considered. Each member does the part at which he is best. Some professionals are outstanding in a particular phase of the racket in which they are engaged. The man who has great capability as a stall might fail miserably as a hook, and the reverse. On the shake (extortion from homosexuals) the steerer is always the same person, and the inside and outside man never change with each other, because the work of each is absolutely different. On the wire and the stock market (two types of confidence games), the inside and outside men may change positions.[2] In rackets where one must show his kisser (face), experience and intelligence are necessary.

When a member of a mob is inexperienced, his partners help him by cutting in and bringing the conversation or the action to its proper place, if they feel that a certain angle is being played too strong or not strong enough. This happens only when an inexperienced man is taken on, and this does not occur often because there are available many men who are fully capable. The inexperienced man would be expected to have acquired a fundamental knowledge of the racket and a theoretical knowledge of its action, and his part at first would not call for much.

In addition to the special abilities which are taken into account, there is a more general capability known as "larceny sense." This term is applied to the thief just as the term "business sense" is applied to the business man. It is an ability to deal with unusual situations in the best possible manner and is acquired in the course of experience. Every thief with good larceny sense will try to figure out every eventuality in taking off a touch. Some thieves are considered to have no larceny sense, while others have plenty of it. The following incident illustrates the operation of this larceny sense, even when it was in error. A booster received an order to steal a certain type of fur coat and went to a store to fill the order. When he entered the elevator, he recognized a woman store detective and gave her credit for recogniz-

[2] A confidence man who read the manuscript commented: "It is very rare for inside and outside men to change roles on the wire. The two roles call for entirely different types of men. The outside man must be a loud, hurrah type who sends the sucker along to the inside man, a quiet, staid individual."

ing him. When the elevator came to the floor on which the fur department was located, he got off and turned to the right, while the detective got off and turned to the left. He walked through several departments before going into the furs in order to see if she were following him. When he felt he was safe, he returned to the fur department and cut into a salesperson. After he had located the coat he wanted, another employee came to the door and told this salesperson he was wanted on the phone. In this store it is very irregular to have an employee called to the phone, and usually the salesperson would request the number to call later. However, this salesperson left the booster alone in the room with the fur coat he wanted in his hands. A situation as easy as this is highly improbable, and the thief's larceny sense warned him that it was too soft and must be phony. Instead of taking the coat or even looking around to see if he was being watched, which would immediately put any watcher on guard, he seated himself and waited for the return of the salesperson. Then he made an appointment to come back later with his wife. As he left the department, he looked around for evidence of his being put up and, upon finding none, decided that he had fallen into one of those spots which are so soft that they look dangerous but really are not. To keep the record clear, it might be added that he returned the following day, at the hour when the salesperson of the previous day was at lunch, and took the coat which had caused him so much apprehension the previous day.

There is not much distinction between members of a mob so far as leadership is concerned except in cannon mobs and not always there. The cannon mob is generally designated by the name of the hook, and it will be said, for instance, that Brown is now on the coast in Manny Gloob's mob. The hook is recognized as leader because he controls the fall-dough, when there is fall-dough, since he is the one most likely to be arrested; also, because he is the one who generally has the right grift, when there is right grift. So the hook generally fills in members for his mob and tells them where they are going and when. At the same time it is recognized that every one of the mob knows as much about the racket as he does, where to grift and where not, when to grift and when to pack in. Therefore, the hook cannot get away with anything out of line. The hook generally has plenty of conceit and will not admit that the stall is his equal. It is very common to hear hooks tell that they supported two or three stalls all summer or that they have been stealing a living for two or three stalls. Actually the work of the stall is as important as that of the hook. The term "boss" is seldom used, and when used it is in a spirit of friendly sarcasm. But the leader of the cannon mob has no problems the other members do not have, except that he is more likely than the others to be arrested. Everything that happens is just part of the day's work, and the only thing the hook gets that the others don't get is glory, and he would have to take that for himself for no one would give it to him. The expenses and proceeds are divided equally, and there is no difference in the financial standing of the members.

There is an approach to the boss idea in the muzzle (extortion from homosexuals). In this racket a mob sometimes uses an amateur who is a kid nineteen or twenty years of age, and such steerers need a boss in the Simon Legree sense. They are not finished thieves and they need to be bawled out, kicked around, and fired. These kids are constantly falling in love, failing to get to work

34

on time, and unconsciously using other means to disrupt a mob. So they must be controlled.

There is no leadership in the boosting mobs. It is a general rule that one thief actually takes the merchandise, while the other protects. But both parts are regarded as of the same importance, and neither one is boss, either sarcastically or otherwise.

In the con rackets there is no approach to the boss idea except that there is a boss in the pay-off joints. In a particular city one may have police protection for the pay-off joints, and he is the boss of the pay-off joints, just as someone else is the gambling boss or vice lord. When a steerer arrives in a city, he approaches the boss of the pay-off joints and asks permission to steer his prospects against one of these joints. This boss is boss of the whole pay-off end of the racket but not of the mob.

The mob has many codes, rules, and understandings, most of which are so general that they apply to the whole profession as well as to a particular mob. One of these rules is that the division of all gains in all rackets is to be even. No one gets more or less than anyone else in the mob. This rule applies only to members of the mob and does not apply to outsiders who may assist the mob in various ways. The owner of a pay-off joint may get 15 per cent of the touch, the putup man gets 10 per cent, and the pawnbroker who works in collusion with the mobs on short con rackets may get a percentage. A second rule is that the nut (expenses) must come off the top of every touch. This means that all expenses must be paid from the gross return before there is division among the members. A third rule is that all loans must be repaid out of the first knockup money, and this is rigidly adhered to.

A fourth understanding is more general, and it involves many different situations. It is sometimes stated "in on the good, in on the bad," and sometimes "in with the touches, in with the falls." If one member of a mob gets a pinch, and the case costs $500, each member of the mob contributes his share of it. If a four-handed mob packs in for the day, three going in one direction and the fourth in the other direction, and if the three members get a score, the fourth man is in on it for his full end. However, if on the way home a member is pinched for something foreign to the mob's activities, he stands the fall personally. Of course, if he didn't have sufficient money to take care of the case, the others would lend him any money needed, but it would not be considered unethical for the others to move on and leave him in the can. If one of the members stands a pinch for activities concerned with the mob, and the outfit can grift for a few days without him, he would, when he got out, receive his full end of every dollar that was made while he was in the can. It was the mob's fault that they didn't get him out. But if he should get a bit, and it became necessary to fill in a man in his place, the new man would naturally get his end, and the one doing a bit would not have a claim, but the mob would as a rule see that he was taken care of and that a piece of money was waiting for him when he came out.

A fifth rule is that the fall-dough held by the mob is to be used for any member of the mob and that it is the possession of the mob. There are few known cases of a boss absconding with this money or gambling with it or losing it otherwise. He would not dare to do this.

A sixth understanding is that the members of the mob are to deal honestly with one another. One of the most heinous crimes in the mob is for a member to burn the others, that is, report that a score showed less than it actually did and hold out the difference.[3] When this occurs, the first offense is the last. Lying is perhaps considered by thieves to be more unethical than it is by the law-abiding.

A seventh understanding is that, if a member voluntarily separates from a mob, he may properly ask to be taken back, but it would not be proper for the leader of the mob to ask him to come back. Similarly if the boss fires a member, the boss may later invite the member to return, but it would not be proper for the member who had been fired to ask to be reinstated.

An eighth understanding is that the member of the mob should not be held responsible for events which he cannot control. Situations arise sometimes where all the larceny sense in the world cannot be of aid. It is what

[3] This injunction against "burning" is of long duration and is evidently an inevitable element in the code of the thief. Yet it is violated with some frequency. David Haggart, a pickpocket in England in the first quarter of the nineteenth century, shows that pickpockets frequently burned their partners but that it was regarded as a serious offense (*The Life of David Haggart* [Edinburgh, 1821], p. 14). Hapgood's thief reported that two of his partners held out a part of the proceeds and that he cut up one of them with a knife for this (Hutchins Hapgood, *Autobiography of a Thief*, p. 221). One of the members of Kid Weil's confidence mob claims that Weil, and perhaps also Buckmeister, turned in only $10,000 when they had actually secured $15,000. A similar crime of holding out $40,000 from a $75,000 theft is reported regarding Samuel Adeska, a member of a confidence mob in London which was headed by Joe Golden, also known as "The Butter Kid." Adeska was captured by the police on a tip from a member of his own mob. In Chicago three pickpockets were found dead —Joe Marzullo in 1933, Clarence ("Red") Harvey in 1934, and Frank Panio in 1935. In each case it was suspected that murder had occurred because of "burning," and a general complaint was made by one pickpocket that thieves were losing their ethics.

the thieves call the "luck of the law." But if a member shows up late for meets on several occasions, that is regarded as his own fault, and he may be discharged for it.

A ninth rule is that one member of a mob should not cut in on another. Each member is given his part to do and is expected to handle his own part, unless it be a case of an inexperienced man who has been taken on for a minor part. If another member should cut in, it would be a reflection on the ability of the first to handle the situation himself and would be resented as such, unless an unusual or dangerous situation arose.

Finally, it is recognized as a responsibility of every member of the mob to do everything possible to fix a case for any member of the mob if the pinch occurred in connection with mob activities.

A mob must be a unit and work as a unit. These rules and understandings have developed primarily for the purpose of preserving the unity of the mob. In spite of the rules and understandings, there are some persons who are hard to get along with and who tend by their actions to disrupt any mob.[4] In such cases the procedure is to have nothing to do with them, especially if the difficulty concerns business rather than social relations. A woman booster, called Mabel, was capable in her work but had difficulty in keeping her partners because she was nervous and excited. A male friend who was an experienced heel, merely to help her make some money, joined her out for

[4] The following characterization of a swindler was made by a fellow-patient in the Government Hospital for the Insane: "Nor can he ever fit in as a member of a working gang of con men, because he is too unstable and undependable in crises" (Ben Karpman, *The Individual Criminal* [Washington: Nervous & Mental Diseases Pub. Co., 1935] p. 278 [by permission]).

work. During the first week, after beating a store for a summer ermine coat and arriving on the sidewalks, Mabel became highly nervous and began to abuse her partner because he did not have a taxicab right there the minute they came out of the store. In situations like that it is best to say nothing, for they could not afford to attract attention. But after they were in the cab and on the way home, the man opened up on her. He told her he was just as anxious to get a cab as she was, that such outbursts as these had caused all her other partners to leave her, and that, if she wanted him to continue to grift with her, she would have to stop all the bawling-out foolishness. She promised to do better and for a few days did so. But shortly after this she started to argue with him while in a store in regard to what articles they were supposed to be stealing, so, after bawling her out, he announced himself as quitting. Shortly after this, while grifting with another girl, Mabel stood a dead-right pinch (arrested in the act of theft). At the time of the pinch she was wearing a wrist watch which had cost $3,500, and the sight of that watch aroused all the larceny in all the coppers. Before the case was finished, it cost her $1,100, though it would not have cost her more than $500 if she had not been wearing the expensive watch. The fixer who took care of the case suggested that someone should beat out her brains with a baseball bat. No one had sufficient interest in Mabel's future welfare to follow the instructions, but it became practically impossible for her after that to get anyone to work with her.[5]

The following incident is .an illustration of perfect co-ordination in meeting an unexpected situation. A prominent actress had asked a professional thief to get her a Spanish shawl from a certain department store in Chicago. The shawls were in one of a row of small rooms, each one connected by open doors with the others and each having a door leading out into the main room of the store. The two heels who undertook the task found the room in which the shawls were located without a saleslady in it at the moment. One heel stood in the middle of the room to watch in three directions, while the other stooped down to the lower drawer in which this shawl was located. He had just stuffed the shawl in his brief case and had closed the drawer when he noticed a pair of woman's shoes on the floor near by, with the toes pointed toward him. He knew they had not been there a few moments earlier and that therefore someone must be in them, and since the toes were pointed toward him, he knew that someone was watching him. So he fumbled with his shoestrings for a moment and then came up. As soon as he saw the saleslady's face, he knew that she was suspicious but also knew that she was not certain. If she had been certain, she would have screamed, or, as frequently happens, would have opened her mouth to scream without being able to utter a sound, or she would have turned very red. Immediately the thief stated, "I am looking for Miss Brown." The saleslady replied, "There is no Miss Brown here." The thief said, "That is the name the saleslady here gave me a couple of days ago. She is a blond lady about thirty-five or forty years

[5] The interpretation of her behavior which was made by a confidence man who had read the manuscript and who was himself a drug addict is: "Undoubtedly she was a junker [drug addict] and this is what caused her excitable actions. While on the subject, I might add, what he at no time states specifically, that at least 90 per cent of boosters are drug addicts and at least 75 per cent of cannons."

of age, and I talked with her in this department. Perhaps I misunderstood the name. If you will take me to the manager of this department, perhaps he can help me locate her, for he turned me over to her when I was here previously." Very reluctantly she took the thief with her to see the manager, looking back two or three times at the drawer and evidently not being able to make up her mind what to do about it. She did not have the wits or experience to control the situation. As soon as they were out of the room, the second thief picked up the brief case from the floor where it had been left, and away he went. The whole thing was then safe, for a search of the thief who was left would not result in any incriminating evidence, and nothing could be proved. The saleslady went into the office to see if the manager would talk with the customer, and when she returned the second thief had disappeared. As soon as the two thieves had opportunity to talk it over, it was learned that the saleslady had come around the corner from the main part of the store and had stepped into the room without opportunity for warning. Any attempt on the part of the stall to cut in after the saleslady appeared would have been a reflection on the ability of the other to handle the situation. The stall stood ready to make a getaway with the shawl as soon as the heel led the clerk away, and it worked out perfectly.

A grifting mob is more or less a single unit. If one member does or says anything, it is always followed out by the others because there is no time, while in action, to discuss any points. Each member's judgment is generally valued sufficiently to follow it, or he wouldn't be with the mob. A cannon mob may be working a get-on (place where many people enter streetcars) and beat the first man just before he steps on the car, the next man after he pays his fare, and perhaps the next one as he gets off. Each of these positions must be decided by the snap judgment of one of the mob. The plan may be changed by a slight signal from any member of the mob. A member of the mob might see a copper on the car and give the signal to let the sucker (victim) go, just as they are ready to beat him.

During his lifetime a professional thief may practice many different rackets. Cannons keep to their racket more permanently than other thieves. Most cannons of today started out as cannons and, with, perhaps, the exception of a few short excursions into other rackets, have always been cannons. A considerable number of cannons have gone into the narcotic racket, but the majority of them, after their first bit, go back on the cannon where the case can be straightened out or on which, at the worst, they get a short jail sentence. Heels and boosters change somewhat from that racket to con rackets. Con men change frequently from one con racket to another. If need be, they can step out on the heel, boost, shake, tap, and other rackets.[6]

[6] A confidence man who had been engaged in the more elaborate confidence games made the following criticism of this statement: "What he says of the change of types of con rackets refers only to the small-time con rackets. The really big guns stick to one racket consistently. The statement that con men step out on the boost is absurd. This would be only the dregs of the profession. No self-respecting con man would think of doing so." Incidentally, the confidence man who made this statement was serving a prison sentence for robbery with a gun and was very much ashamed of it. He had great pride in his previous achievements as a con man but said that anyone could stick a gun in a sucker's belly and get some money and that anyone who did this and landed in prison for it should feel ashamed.

42

CHAPTER 3
THE RACKETS

\The principal rackets of professional thieves are the cannon (picking pockets), the heel (sneak-thieving from stores, banks, and offices), the boost (shoplifting), penny-weighting (stealing from jewelry stores by substitution), hotel prowling (stealing from hotel rooms), the con (confidence game), some miscellaneous rackets related in certain respects to the confidence games, laying paper (passing illegal checks, money orders, and other papers), and the shake (the shakedown of, or extortion from, persons engaged in or about to engage in illegal acts).

All these rackets involve manipulation of suckers by nonviolent methods. For this purpose the skills required in the different rackets differ from one another somewhat. But in all of them the thief must be a good actor and a good salesman in order to manipulate the sucker. The thief who has not been taught these skills cannot be a professional. He may operate on a murder grift, raw-jaw, or rip-and-tear basis, but he cannot use the methods which are used by professionals except when they are working under extra-good protection.

Each of these rackets has many variations in the specific details of procedure. A mob may beat forty men in a day on the same spot in the same racket. Although the principle is the same, there are forty minor variations. Not many suckers could be beaten if every mob approached every sucker in the same stereotyped manner.

Banks, especially, cannot be beaten twice in exactly the same manner. Methods must be devised to meet new situations, sometimes on the spur of the moment. If a con mob becomes aware that a sucker, into whom they are putting the story, has heard or read of the racket, every effort is made to show that this proposition is different from the ones of which he has heard. It is not possible to describe all the variations in the rackets; even if the entire number was described today, it would be out of date tomorrow. Each of the rackets of professional thieves will be described, with some of the variations.

I. THE CANNON

The term "cannon" is used to designate the pickpocket and also the racket of picking pockets. The theory of the origin of this term is that the pickpocket some centuries ago was called a *gonnif*, which is the Jewish word for thief. This term was then abbreviated to "gun"; later someone in a moment of smartness referred to a pickpocket as a "cannon" to designate a big gun, and the term "cannon" then became general. The term "gun" is still used to refer to pickpockets, and the female pickpocket who operates upon men is called a "gun-moll."

A cannon mob usually consists of two, three, or four members, although occasionally a person works the cannon single-handed. The operations involved in picking the pocket of a sucker begin with fanning, or feeling the pockets to determine where the money or pocketbook is located. Fanning may be unnecessary if the sucker has been observed as he put away his pocketbook. Also the sign, "Beware of Pickpockets," is helpful, for whenever a sucker sees this sign he feels the pocket in which his money is located to discover whether his pocketbook is still there, thus relieving the mob of the necessity of fanning him. A second operation is pratting the sucker in, which consists of pushing him around gently in order to distract his attention and in order to get him in a position where his pocketbook can be stolen easily. The members of the mob who do this pratting are called stalls.[1] The third operation is to put the duke (hand) down and extract the poke (pocketbook). The person who does this is known as the hook, wire, tool, or instrument. When his hand goes into your pocket, you never feel it, partly because your attention is being distracted by the stalls and partly because of his manual dexterity.[2] There is generally some method of shading the duke (concealing the hand) when it is thrust into the sucker's pocket. This may be done by another person or by the hook himself, using a coat or newspaper for this purpose.[3] The shading of the

[1] One of the methods used by the stall is to feign drunkenness and to brush or fall against the victim, whose pocket is picked during the resulting confusion.

[2] One of the techniques used by some hooks is described thus: "A pickpocket makes a 'straight hoist' from his toes; that is, if he gets his fingers on a billfold in a hip pocket, he does not use only his arm, but he stiffens his whole body and raises himself on his toes" (Ben Karpman, *The Individual Criminal* [Washington: Nervous & Mental Diseases Pub. Co., 1935], p. 208 [by permission]).

[3] The wire faces the victim when he is picking an inside coat pocket. The duke is shaded, and attention distracted by the "throw," which consists of a newspaper or some other object placed under the chin of the victim. "Anyone that will stand to have that newspaper laid under their chin can be beat and most generally are. . . . . I myself and several others that I have talked to find an 'insider' as easy, if not easier, than a prat poke if the man will stand for a throw" (quoted from the autobiography of a pickpocket, in Clifford R. Shaw and Henry D. McKay, "Social Factors in Juvenile Delinquency," *Report of the National Commission on Law Observance and Enforcement* [Washington, 1932], No. 13, Vol. II, 238).

duke is not necessary if the stealing is done in a crowd where everyone is pushing; this is known as "push grift." The fourth operation is cleaning. When a hook has secured a pocketbook, he generally cleans himself of it to another member of the mob as soon as possible, for he does not want to get a pinch with several pocketbooks on him; this would not only increase the difficulty and expense of fixing the case but also cause the mob to lose all the money in all the pocketbooks. Whenever a hook is tumbled (suspected), he makes every effort to get rid of the pocketbook; he may drop it, throw it away, or stick it in the hand or pocket of the sucker or of some other person near by.[4] When the other members of the mob get a pocketbook from the hook, they clean it and dispose of it as quickly as possible. They may be forced to wait until they have accumulated three or four, and then go to a washroom, hallway, alley, or other private place. It is desirable to keep the pocketbooks off the ground or floor, if possible, for several of them in one place are significant that a cannon mob is working near by. A

[4] The teamwork in the pickpocket mob is illustrated in this statement: "The duke man comes on his [the wire's] left hand and covers the wire's hand while he is at work and covers him from the people standing back and the people on the side. A duke man always keeps his right hand at his side, so when the wire comes away from the mark's [victim's] coat with his purse or roll of money, he always hands it to the duke man. The duke man puts it in his left coat tail [meaning his left coat pocket]. The reason that the duke man keeps his right hand at his side in case of a rumble the wire pulls his hand away and there is always two hands there and the victim is undecided which one it was. The reason that he always goes to his coat tail with the purse in case the victim blows [meaning feels his loss] and turns around and grabs the duke man, the stall and the wire know just what pocket to go to, take the purse out and throw it on the floor. The sucker is always satisfied when he sees his money" (*ibid.*, p. 236).

mailbox is the finest possible place of disposal of empty pocketbooks, and the mob will use that, if one is near by.

If the pocketbook contains negotiable papers, such as drafts, travelers' checks, etc., the cannon mob finds a market for them with another type of thieves who specialize in that line. These thieves will pay 20–30 per cent of the face for travelers' checks issued in the United States and made payable to a man. Few of them will buy drafts, for they are too hard to cash.

Many thieves object to the cannon grift, so far as they are personally concerned. It is too much for them to take the pocketbooks of people who may have four or five children dependent on the money. They have no objection to other thieves who may want to do this. Some cannons prefer the jug touch, which is picking pockets of suckers who are in or are coming out of banks with money which they have just secured. A member of the mob who waits in the bank spots someone who draws several hundred dollars, the mob follows him and beats him at the first opportune moment.[5] This is easy unless he gets into an automobile in front of the bank. If he does that, the only way to get him is to use raw-jaw methods. They crowd around the door of the car, telling him he has the wrong car, or anything else to stop him from getting into the car. They push him around gently until he is relieved of his money. He is naturally incensed when someone tells him he is trying to get into the wrong car, and through his excitement he is entirely off his guard. This method is generally employed only as a last resort by a

[5] A man who had just withdrawn $900 from his bank in Memphis had his pocket picked by a thief who crowded into the same compartment of the revolving door of the bank.

mob badly in need of money or about to leave town, for it causes a great amount of heat in and around the bank. The bank becomes an interested party, and also the Bankers' Association, the insurance company, and the private-detective agency which protects the bank. On this account most cannon mobs are afraid of jug touches, but they yield gratifying returns for the right mobs.

The location of pockets on the person is, of course, a matter of great interest in this racket. Special names are given to the pockets, such as left or right breech (front trouser pocket), left or right prat (hip pocket), tail pit (side pocket), fob (under the belt), and insider (inside coat pocket). A left-breech tool is one who can steal from the left-front trouser pocket, which is unusually difficult. The ability to do this is added to any reference to the cannon as is, might I say, Ph.D. to a student. It means more than being a Phi Beta Kappa. "Do you know little Buttsie, a left-breech tool from Baltimore?" and "He can beat a left breech" are regarded as very complimentary statements.

II. THE HEEL AND BOOST

The heel and the boost are two related types of stealing from places of business. The difference between them is that the booster contacts the salesman, while the heel does not. The booster asks the salesman for some article and then steals what he wants from the articles displayed or from other accessible articles. The heel is a sneak thief who steals what he wants without asking the salesman for assistance. The booster is known to the general public as a shoplifter. Both the heel and the booster are professionals, different from amateur shoplifters, who are

48

known as snatch-and-grab or boot-and-shoe boosters.[6] The professional thief is a good actor and goes about his business as though he had a perfect right to be there doing what he is doing. The stores do not want to run the risk of angering legitimate customers by accusing them of theft.[7]

The methods used by heels and boosters vary with the type of articles wanted, with the time of the year, and with the arrangement of the store. The methods may be illustrated by the procedure used by a heel in stealing men's clothing. The thief walks up the stairs and does not use the elevator. He pays no attention to the greeter who stands in front of the elevator but walks right past him as though he had the most important business of anyone in the store and as though he knew perfectly where he was going and what he was going to do. The clerks see him go past them and pay no further attention but wait on their customers or stand around talking. The thief gets to the back part of the store and, when no one is watching him, takes what he wants. If he wants an

[6] Professional shoplifters are a small percentage of all shoplifters. Anderson reported that 75 per cent of one hundred persons arrested consecutively for shoplifting in New York City were first offenders (V. V. Anderson, "Further Studies of Delinquent Personalities," *Proceedings of the American Prison Association, 1919*, pp. 439–44). Grassberger found that over 85 per cent of the shoplifters apprehended in a large store in New York City were females and that two-thirds of these did not steal as a regular occupation (Roland Grassberger, *Gewerbs- und Berufsverbrechertum in den Vereinigten Staaten von Amerika* [Vienna, 1933], p. 297).

[7] A department store in Chicago made a present of a thousand-dollar fur coat to a woman whom they had accused of stealing a compact and who proved to their satisfaction that she had just purchased it in another store. Such actions by the stores are primarily for the purpose of protecting them against suits for damages but are secondarily for the purpose of protecting them against the development of ill will.

overcoat, he simply folds it over his arm or puts it on, removing the price tags or being sure that they do not show. Another method would be to reach the department by elevator, inform the greeter that he has an appointment there with a friend who wants to buy a suit and, not finding him in the department, state that he will wait at the other end of the department near the window. After looking out the window for a time, he seems to get restless and walks back and forth, occasionally stopping to look at a suit or overcoat. When the coast is clear, he may take an overcoat in the same manner, return to the greeter and inform him that he will not be able to wait longer for his friend.[8] The greeter may have seen this thief in the department several times previously within the week, but he sees too many people to be certain of his recollection. The thief may engage him in conversation while he waits for the elevator to take him and his stolen property away. The greeter in one Chicago store likes to brag about the length of time he has been there, and the thief, with a stolen overcoat over his arm, may say to the greeter: "How do you do, Mr.

[8] This method is confirmed by a clerk in the men's clothing department of a large store in Chicago who made this statement in conversation: "A young man came into the department and said he wanted to wait for a friend who was going to buy a suit. He went across the room from the elevator and sat near a window. Some of us looked at him occasionally, but he was either sitting there or else getting up and looking out the window, or maybe stepping for a minute to one of the racks of suits. Then he went into one of the changing booths for a few minutes. When he came out, after looking out the window for a time, he started down the side aisle toward the elevator. One of the clerks in this department has a special interest in catching thieves and he was suspicious, though the rest of us were paying no attention. He had summoned a man from the protective department and they met this 'customer' near the elevator, searched him, and found that he had two suits of clothes underneath his regular suit."

Green. This makes your twenty-second year here, doesn't it?" The greeter will reply, "No, it is my twenty-sixth." The thief then says, "I remember my father told me you were here when he first became a customer twenty years ago." In another store the greeter has a hobby of leghorn chickens and the thief may start a conversation about leghorn chickens. This seems to make the greeter feel that the person cannot possibly be a sneak thief.

Sometimes the thief creates a disturbance that is meant to distract attention from himself. A heel mob was advised of a spot where the manager of a business took from $2,500 to $3,000 in cash to the bank every morning at a certain time. It was found that the money was kept in the safe and not removed until the manager was ready to start for the bank. Then it was taken out of the safe and laid on his desk while he put on his coat and hat. After some study the thieves decided on a plan. A few mornings later, just as the manager reached for his coat, a slight explosion occurred, and a fire started on the opposite side of the store. The manager rushed across the store to the fire. When he realized the fire was of no importance and thought again of his money it was too late—the money was gone. Fights have been started, women have apparently fainted, children have been knocked down, and other theatrical settings arranged for the purpose of distracting attention from money or merchandise so that a favorable atmosphere for taking off a score will be possible.[9]

[9] The method used by John Coffey, a heel in New York City and Philadelphia, was to go into the toilet room of a department store shortly before the store was to close, wait there until after it was closed, then take an expensive coat or other article and leave the store with the employees.

Occasionally an employee enters into collusion with the heels and boosters, either because of social contacts made on the outside or because they happen to get evidence that he is stealing from the store. In one case an assistant buyer in a New York department store was beating his own firm in a small retail way. Some professional thieves learned about this through social contacts on the outside and developed a system, with his assistance, whereby for a considerable length of time they beat the store in a wholesale manner. When he was let out by the store because of a matter entirely foreign to the stealing, he immediately joined out his thieving associates as an out-and-out booster and has been continuously engaged in such rackets since.

The jug heel is a special type of stealing from banks. One group of jug heels specializes in raising bundles of money from the counters inside the cages up over the glass partitions by means of a stick and string, with a hook or gum or other sticky substance at the end.[10] In many large banks a thief can get in behind the cages, put his cap in his pocket, put on a green eyeshade, stick a pencil behind his ear, and wander around as though he were an employee, thus having relatively free access to

Sometimes he took expensive coats at this time to other departments, hid them there, and then returned the next day for them ("The Autobiography of an Ex-thief," *Outlook and Independent*, CLIV [March 12, 1930], 421–23).

[10] The newspapers reported three large thefts in which this technique was used in New York City banks during 1932–35. In November, 1932, $590,000 in bonds were stolen from one large bank; in December, 1934, the same amount from another bank; and in January, 1935, $1,456,000 from a third bank. Also, it was reported in 1935 that about $11,000 disappeared from a desk in still another bank when a clerk turned to answer the phone.

the cages. Occasionally the jug heel secures the co-operation of a bank employee. In one case of this nature a heel contacted a bank employee in the can (lockup), where the bank employee was held on a domestic-court case of some kind. The thief asked the teller if bank employees ever thought of stealing the bank's money which they handled daily. The reply was, "Everyone of them in every bank every hour thinks of stealing money but doesn't know how." The thief advised the teller that he did not need to go any farther to learn how to steal, for he was now at headquarters. Later the thief met this teller on the street, and a plan was discussed. The teller was given instructions that at a certain hour of a certain day he was to have as much currency in bills of large denominations as possible, in a bundle within eighteen inches of the wicket through which he did business. At that hour the teller received a phone call which took him to the rear of his cage for a few minutes. While he was doing this, the touch came off perfect—an absolutely natural jug heel which showed $16,000. The teller did not know how or when he was beaten until an hour later when he noticed that the bundle of currency was gone. He did nothing unusual until time to check up, when he announced the shortage. The private detectives and city detectives questioned the teller for hours and finally decided that it was a genuine jug heel and that collusion was out of the question. They held him blameless and sent him home. He continued to work for two months. At that time he got $2,500, with a promise of $1,500 later, and was instructed not to spend it in any way that would arouse suspicion. But within two weeks he rolled down to work one morning in a robin's-egg-blue sport-model

Jordan. This immediately aroused suspicion and he was questioned again. He made an explanation of the sources of his money, but, when this was investigated and found to be false, he broke down. The bank officials and protecting agents made him believe the old myth that, if he told the truth and helped them, they would help him. He told everything but fortunately did not know the location of the thieves. Then they helped him—to convict himself. The bank sent him to the penitentiary as an example to the other employees. Incidentally, when he opened up on the mob, it was decided that he had lost all claim to the rest of his end (share) of the touch, and he did not receive the balance due him. The supreme court of thiefdom held this to be good law.

III. PENNYWEIGHTING

The pennyweighter is a professional thief who defrauds jewelers by substituting spurious articles for genuine articles while the genuine articles are being shown to him as a prospective customer. This may be done by one person operating alone or with the co-operation of an assistant who makes the substitution while the first thief engages the attention of the salesman. Though the first person may in this case be suspected, he does not have the genuine jewelry on his person if he should be searched. This racket requires considerable knowledge of jewelry and careful planning of the job so that the spurious jewelry will not be noticeably different from the genuine articles.

IV. THE HOTEL PROWL

The hotel prowl is a thief who steals from guest rooms in a hotel, either by finding them unlocked or else by using different methods of unlocking the doors.[11] This racket may be worked single-handed or with one or two associates. Assistance is occasionally secured from bell-boys or clerks. Bellboys seldom feel it necessary to call in professional thieves when there is any stealing to do; they try to do it all themselves. In a few cases bellboys inform professional thieves that certain guests have left their jewels in their rooms. For this they receive the regular 10 per cent for the putup. Hotel clerks have been more prolific in putting up touches for professional thieves. The most general putup by the clerks is for salesmen of furs, dresses, jewelry, and similar articles. The clerk studies the habits of the salesmen; when the salesman goes on a trip that will keep him away from the hotel for some time, the clerk gives the key of the room to the thief, who takes out the goods by the most advisable methods.[12]

[11] Other methods of securing entrance to the rooms include: the thief stands at the clerk's desk and, when a guest leaves a key on the desk, he places his hat over it and then takes the key and goes to the room; the thief rents a room and has a duplicate key made and later returns to this room to steal from others who may be in it at that time; the thief uses long pliers to turn the key which is left in the lock on the inside of the door; the thief uses a thin instrument which is inserted between the door stop and the jamb to force back the bolt; he may use a skeleton key or an adjustable key. In addition, many people do not lock their doors, not being in the habit of doing so at home; some leave the keys on the outside of the door; sometimes a thief may become friendly with a guest who has an adjoining room, with a door between the two rooms, and secure entrance through this door. If a thief is discovered in a room, regardless of his method of entrance, he may pretend to be drunk, offer the guest a drink, and, when questioned, state that his room number is the one directly below this one, or directly above, or next door (Ludwig F. Grimstad, "Hotel-Room Prowlers, Connivers, and Sneak Thieves," *Saturday Evening Post*, CCVI [June 30, 1934], 30 ff.).

[12] A professional thief made the comment on this: "The author is correct in his statement that the hotel prowlers generally have an 'in' with

V. THE CON

The con, or confidence game, has many angles, but the central principle in all true con rackets is to show a sucker how he can make some money by dishonest methods and then beat him in his attempted dishonesty. For this it is necessary to be a good actor, a good salesman, and have good manners and a good appearance.[13]

There are two principal kinds of con rackets. In the first class are those in which the sucker may be kept keyed up for several days. This generally includes a trip to his bank, which may be in another city, in order to get a sufficient amount of money for the play. The wire (horse race) and the stock market are the two principal con rackets of this nature, and they are known together as the pay-off.[14] The second class of con rackets are called

some crooked employee of the hotel. The only worth-while hotel prowl occurs when the prospect has been cased and is known to be traveling with a quantity of jewelry."

Somewhat related to the hotel prowl is the luggage theft at railway stations. While much of this is petty theft by amateurs, some thieves have developed a professional technique. George Whitney Bates used this method of theft in England for twenty-five years before he was caught. He specialized on luggage which he had discovered contained articles of considerable value.

[13] A professional confidence man wrote: "Not all persons can be good con men. They generally must have a winning personality, shrewdness, agility, like the good things of life, and be too lazy to work for them, and have great egotism. They must, first of all, be good actors. The whole con game is a matter of acting. If they cannot put on this veneer of culture, they cannot make it go. A confidence man must live by his wits."

[14] For descriptions of the methods used in the pay-off see John J. O'Connor, *Broadway Racketeers* (New York, 1928), pp. 167–79; Philip S. Van Cise, *Fighting the Underworld* (Boston, 1936), pp. 258–300; J. Frank Norfleet, *Norfleet: The Actual Experiences of a Texas Rancher's 30,000-Mile Transcontinental Chase after Five Confidence Men* (Fort Worth, 1924), pp. 1–18, 83–112, 236–37, 273–301.

"short con" because they can be played in a very short time, in almost any place, and are designed merely to get the money the sucker may have on his person at the time. There are many types of short-con rackets, including the smack, the money machine, diamond smuggling, dropping the poke, the duke, the lemon, and the foot race.

The first part of the wire racket is to pick out the sucker they want to beat. The mob wants to be sure the sucker has sufficient money and will be willing to use dishonest methods of making more money. In the more elaborate plays the sucker is carefully investigated in advance before time is wasted on him; in those which are less elaborate the mob picks up any likely looking person and tries to get information regarding him as the play develops.[15] Next comes the buildup. The two methods of buildup which are used most commonly are the point-out and dropping the poke.[16] In the point-out a steerer

[15] A confidence man made the following comment regarding the preparations in the pay-off: "The real artists in this field frequently spend from two to six months trailing their intended victim. They learn more of his business and family relations than he knows himself. If the sucker is a Mason, the con artists go through the entire course of training in the Masonic rites and are better equipped to discuss the most intimate details with the prospect than would be an authentic member of the order. The same applies, of course, to the Elks or any other organization. The buildup may require months and involves true finesse."

[16] Joseph ("Yellow Kid") Weil had the reputation of being one of the more astute confidence men. He did not depend on the standardized techniques but developed many methods of his own. In making an original contact with a victim, he frequently made a tentative offer to purchase or sell something. While driving through Indianapolis, he saw a good-looking store. He stopped to see if he could interest the owner in selling the store, and this talk was the initial step in the swindle which followed. He read an advertisement that someone wanted to sell a yacht. He had no use for a yacht but he pretended that he was interested and developed

for the mob, after engaging the prospect in conversation, perhaps on several occasions, points out a passerby (who is really another member of the mob) as a betting commissioner for one of the largest stables in the country and in a position to give advance information on the outcome of races and also as under obligation to the steerer. If the buildup is based on dropping the poke, the prospect and the steerer find a pocketbook containing valuable papers. They return this to its owner (who is actually another member of the mob), and he informs them that he is a betting commissioner for a large stable and in a position to give them advance information regarding the outcome of the races, as a reward for their honesty in returning the pocketbook.[17] The third step is known as the convincer. This is a demonstration of large winnings by following the advice of the betting commissioner. This may be done several times, and the prospect is himself generally permitted to win several hundred dollars and

---

a confidence game on the basis of the relationship which developed. He told a merchant he was interested in buying a large quantity of olive oil, perhaps as much as 50,000 gallons. He told a landscape gardener that he was planning to build a home for jockeys and that the landscaping would perhaps go as high as half a million dollars. Persons approached in this manner are impressed, see a possible opportunity for profits, and are not suspicious of the other activities of the prospective buyer or seller.

[17] An element which is frequently introduced at this point is that the person who is pointed out or located by the lost pocketbook seems to be provoked and suspicious and rather unwilling to meet the prospective victim. Later he explains that he has to be careful to avoid reporters and strangers (see Norfleet, *op. cit.*, p. 278). A confidence man wrote: "No confidence game will work well in the sucker's own town. He is surrounded by too many regular conditions, and there are too many chances for him to get advice. It is necessary to hurrah him for some time. He is taken to dinner, to shows, to night clubs, and is shown a grand time for a while. His feet must not be permitted to touch the ground."

actually put it in his own pocketbook, as a part of the convincer.[18] The fourth step is to get the prospect to the gambling club, known as a joint or store, which is maintained entirely for purposes of confidence games. The betting commissioner informs them that it will be safer and more convenient for them to place their bets in this club and that he will continue to furnish them with information before the club receives it and that their winnings will be absolutely certain. Unless the prospect has larceny in his soul, he will be unwilling to arrange in this way to cheat the gambling club, but seldom does a prospect turn back at this point. The fifth step is to put the prospect on the send. The play is arranged so that the prospect makes a big winning at the club on an I.O.U. Just before the winnings are to be paid to him, the manager comes in and instructs him that the rule of the club is that he must show that he has the amount of his bet in cash as demonstration of his ability to pay in case he had lost. Since he has already won the money, it is merely a question of going to his bank.[19] He returns with the cash, which they generally arrange for him to deposit

[18] When Norfleet was being beaten in Denver, he was permitted to win $3,000, put it in his pocket, and keep it overnight; the next morning he was instructed that he could borrow call money with his $3,000 and that day he won more than $200,000; he had the money stacked up on his arm in bills and was preparing to leave the place when the next step in the procedure was introduced. A convincer of this size is very convincing.

[19] A confidence man wrote: "Someone has to go with him when he goes home for the money, for the sucker seldom has a sufficient amount in his checking account to meet the requirements of the mob. That is the point at which most prospects are lost, for if one wants to borrow $35,000 against his securities, the banker generally inquires why he wants the money and then warns him against it, unless he himself tries to get in on the deal."

in the club. At any rate the money is now available for "the big one." The sixth step is to get all his money away from him. There are many variations in the methods used, but all are based on a natural error and on the confidence which has been created by earlier winnings. One type of error is to instruct the prospect to place everything on a certain horse, which the man already knows has come in second. In racing parlance "to place" is to come in second, but the instruction is given in such form that the prospect thinks it means that this horse will come in first and that he should bet accordingly. Consequently he bets everything he has on this horse to win, and he loses. When the steerer returns (for it is necessary for him to be away when the error is made), the sucker learns that he has lost everything, by his own misunderstanding of instructions.[20] The seventh step is to cool him off, so that he will not go to the police or make a fuss in other ways. The steerer informs the sucker that he himself lost everything by the sucker's error but that he will try to borrow some money and retrieve the losses of both; in the meantime the sucker should go home and await word of further action. This may succeed not only in cooling the prospect off but also in building him up for another play later, for many of these suckers can be beaten an indefinite number of times.

[20] Another method is used in many cases; the steerer receives written instructions as to how he is to place the money, but he loses the paper, depends on his memory, and makes a mistake. Among the less subtle methods are these: a con man under some pretext secures possession of the money and disappears; members of the mob represent themselves as policemen, raid the club, and take possession of all the money as evidence; the victim is given "knockout drops" or some other substance that renders him unconscious.

60

The stock market is played practically the same as the wire, substituting a fake brokerage office for a fake gambling club, and buying and selling stocks instead of betting on horse races. The prospect in this case, also, makes a natural error in buying or selling stock and thus his money is lost.

In both the wire and the stock market the method which has been described involves the use of pay-off joints, which are fake betting places or brokerage offices. These joints are furnished and manned purely to cater to steerers and their prospects, and there is no regular betting or brokerage business going on in them. This joint takes 40 per cent off the top of all touches.[21] When a joint

[21] A confidence man is authority for the information that the first "Big Store" of any consequence was opened by the Gondorf Brothers in New York about 1906. He states, also, that the development of the Big Store in the confidence game is analogous to the merger in the legitimate business world. "The greater part of the upper strata of conland take their marks to the Big Store. The Big Store gets the big scores." Steerers were taking victims from all parts of the United States to Denver during the early part of the decade of the twenties when a Big Store operated there, and during the early part of the next decade to Reno where a Big Store was operated by two local "gambling kings." At least seventy victims were lured to Reno in three years and swindled out of $2,000,000. The method is illustrated by a prospect who was induced to make a trip from Victoria to Seattle, then to Portland, and then to Reno by persons who pretended to be interested in purchasing his ranch in Victoria; while they were waiting for their principal to give a final answer, they played the races, and thus the swindle occurred.

A confidence man wrote this additional statement: "The confidence racket is frequently run on credit supplied by the Big Store. A member of the profession who has used up his own funds but is in good standing will approach the Big Store and tell him he has a good prospect, let us say, in Minneapolis: he feels sure the mark is ripe for the take and will go for sixty G [thousand dollars]. However, it will be necessary to give the sucker a play. He has no funds himself. The Big Store inquires how much will be required to bring the prospect in and trim him, and is told that

is not used, it is called beating a man "against the wall." In this case the prospect never gets into the fake gambling joint or brokerage office but is informed of its existence and of its exclusive character. The steerer informs the prospect that he himself or perhaps even a third man, who is a member of the club, must act as representative.[22]

The short-con rackets are similar to the wire and the stock market in principle and in operation, in cross-fire,

---

twenty-five hundred dollars should cover the necessary expenses. This money is advanced unhesitatingly and is later deducted from the forty or forty-five per cent of the score which constitutes the steerer's end. But the steerer had better be plenty sure that he really has a good, live prospect, and not indulge in fairy tales in order to make a touch of $2,500. He might conceivably get it once but his reputation would be ruined around the fraternity. An honest failure, however, would not react against the racketeer."

[22] Many other swindles have been developed on a rather elaborate scale. The author of this document maintains that these other swindles are not among the rackets of professional thieves and that those who practice these rackets are not professional thieves and are not recognized as such by other professional thieves. On the other hand, a confidence man who had himself specialized in stock-promotion frauds wrote as follows: "Big-scale confidence games include, on the borderline, the stock promotion schemes. For instance, some years ago we started a corporation for tanning leather, with a special process. There was no special process but nevertheless the prospectus described it. We promised two per cent a month and paid dividends out of the capital. We kept on building it up higher and higher, but this always reaches a limit after while. So we shifted to a West Virginia mine and similarly built it up, paying dividends out of capital. After a while, the whole thing falls down. This is not greatly different from much so-called legitimate business. One of the international business executives, for instance, was doing exactly the same thing we were doing, namely, pyramiding his companies and paying dividends out of capital. Also, our stock was one hundred per cent water, while the stock in many so-called legitimate concerns is only ninety or maybe sixty per cent water. No difference in principle."

Joseph ("Yellow Kid") Weil during the later part of his career as a confidence man specialized on stock-promotion frauds and other departures from conventional confidence games. In one case he had a victim

angles, and the part that each man plays. A few of these rackets will be described now.

The smack or match, commonly known as matching pennies, is generally played two-handed; one is known as inside man, the other as outside man. The inside man

---

in tow, to whom he was trying to sell some worthless copper-mine certificates. He had arranged to have a phone call nominally from the president of the Sheridan Trust and Savings Bank to deliver some of these certificates there. He took his victim with him to this bank. As he entered the bank, he asked a man who wore no hat or coat and who was apparently an employee of the bank (but actually a member of the mob) where the president of the bank was; the reply was that the president had just gone downstairs to the safety-deposit vault. They went to the vault where they found a man (presumably the president of the bank but actually Buckmeister, a close associate of Weil's) standing before an open box. The sale of the copper certificates was completed, and the money paid there. After that display it was not difficult to sell the sucker some of the same certificates (Mort King, "The Inside Story of Yellow Kid Weil," *Real Detective Tales*, February, 1931, p. 64). Weil went even farther and rented an empty bank building in Muncie, Indiana, in which the bank fixtures were intact. On days when he wished to make an impression on a sucker, he took him to this bank, which was opened and staffed with cashiers, clerks, and customers for the occasion. It was generally easy to bring a fraudulent transaction to a close in that situation. As soon as the transaction was completed and the victim out of the bank, the doors were closed, the curtains lowered, and the mob dispersed (*ibid.*).

The swindles which are known as "heir castles" should perhaps be included among the major con rackets. Thousands of persons have been defrauded in these "estate frauds" which have been described by William L. Stoddard (*Financial Racketeering and How To Stop It* [New York, 1931], pp. 107–13). The Sir Francis Drake estate fraud is probably the most lucrative of these rackets. The promoters claim that the estate left by Sir Francis Drake, with the accrued interest, amounts now to fifteen billion dollars. Suckers are induced to believe that they are heirs or else induced to invest in the estate with a promise of one thousand dollars for each dollar invested. This fraud was in operation in the United States as early as 1847 and has been almost continuous since that date. Oscar M. Hartzell, leader of a contemporary group which was practicing this swindle, is said to have collected more than a million dollars on it. In April, 1935,

opens the conversation with a prospect by asking for a
match or asking where the aquarium is. After a little
conversation he finds that the prospect is planning to
take the train in three or four hours to some other city,
and he announces that he is planning to take the same
train. Then he suggests that they take a walk and see
a little of the city. On their walk they meet the outside
man, and he cuts in by asking for information regarding
the location of some street. They start a general conversation, and the outside man explains that he also is a
stranger in the city, there for a good time, that he had a

forty-three persons were indicted in Chicago as participants in the fraud.
At the trial many of the victims persisted in believing in the estate and
refused to testify against the swindlers. The persons who practiced this
fraud should perhaps not be regarded as professional criminals, since many
of them were not members of the underworld. In December, 1936, a federal grand jury in Philadelphia indicted twenty-eight persons for fraud in
promoting the Jacob Baker estate scheme; this fraud has been worked for
at least seventy years; more than three million dollars were taken from
three thousand persons in the recent development.

Somewhat similar to the estate frauds is the Spanish prisoner swindle.
Since the time of the Civil War persons in America have received letters
from Spain, purporting to come from a man who is imprisoned for a trivial
offense, who has a hidden fortune which he will share with the prospect
if he will send a thousand dollars to help him get out of prison. There are
many variations of this theme. It is estimated that one hundred thousand
Spanish prisoners have been assisted to get out of prison, but not one
of them has shared his fortune with a prospect, and no one has been
convicted.

The matrimonial swindle involves somewhat elaborate preparations,
but is seldom conducted as an organized racket of thieves. It is reported
by the Associated Press that Nathaniel Herbert Wheeler swindled at least
one hundred and fifty women out of about a million dollars. His method
was to make love to a woman, promise to marry her, induce her to transfer
good property or securities for worthless securities which he provided, and
then disappear.

woman in his room at the hotel who left to get a twenty-dollar bill changed and did not return; he concludes with the explanation that this means nothing to him and in support shows a large roll of bills. Cigars are suggested, and after some banter it is suggested that they match for the right to buy them. As previously arranged the outside man is selected to buy the cigars. This gives the inside man the chance to suggest to the prospect that they cheat the fool before someone else does. He shows that if they match pennies three-handed, with the inside man always showing heads and the prospect always showing tails, one of them will always be the odd man, and they cannot lose. If the prospect agrees (and they always do), the outside man is officed (notified by movement of the eyes) to this effect as he returns with the cigars. The inside man then suggests that they eat lunch, and for this go to a restaurant where there are booths in which they can have privacy. They start matching there for a dollar, gradually raising the amount, with the inside man winning almost all the time. The prospect is not worried because all the money is being won by his friend, and they had agreed to divide when they reach the train. Finally a twenty-dollar bet is made, and as the prospect has only ten dollars left, they know they have all his money. Then comes the blowoff, by which they get rid of him. The inside man tries to slip some money to the prospect, the outside man sees him and starts to raise hell, accusing them of being in collusion to rob him and dashes out with the statement that he is going after a policeman. The inside man is excited and instructs the prospect that they must separate or they will be arrested, and that he will meet him on the train. The prospect never finds the con man on the train.[23]

Another short-con racket is the money-making machine which is supposed to be able to turn out counterfeit money of high quality. The play may be to get the sucker to buy the machine, to rent it, to invest funds to help develop it, or merely to have some money made in it. The prospect who is interested is given a demonstration that the machine can make ten-dollar bills from plain paper; he is given a sample to test, and when he takes it to the bank it is accepted without question. He buys the machine and finds that the only bill in it was a perfectly good bill which had been inserted previously. To make the story stronger, some mobs play up the point that the counterfeiting will never be realized by the government because each note will bear the number of a bill which had been burned up, lost in a shipwreck, or destroyed in some other manner.[24]

The diamond-smuggling racket is usually played on ocean liners. A steerer informs the prospect that he has

[23] Another variation is for the person who seems to be a confederate of the sucker, after winning almost all the money, to pass to the sucker secretly the wallet in which he has been placing all the money he has been winning, with whispered instructions to hold it and meet at the railway station for a division. When the sucker later examines the wallet, he finds that it contains nothing except blank paper. A good description of the match is given by O'Connor, *op. cit.*, pp. 206–11.

[24] Sometimes the victim is induced to provide a certain amount of money which is to be duplicated in the machine or is to be raised to higher denominations. In 1925 a New York diamond merchant provided $56,000, which was apparently placed in the machine; the operator needed more acid and went to the drug store for it but while there telephoned that he had just discovered that he had used the wrong acid in the machine and urged that the machine be opened at once and the money rescued. When

on board diamonds which cost $10,000 in Europe, which can be sold immediately after landing for $20,000, so that a profit of $10,000 can be made if the duty is avoided; that he knows a customs inspector who can be bribed for $1,000 to let the diamonds through but that he has only $500 and, if the prospect will put up the other $500, he will make $2,000 by it. The prospect puts up $500, is given the diamonds as security, the diamonds prove to be glass, and he never sees the steerer again.

Among the short-con rackets, dropping the poke (also known as the pigeon-drop) is frequently used. It has many variations, of which the following is one. A pocketbook is dropped so that a prospect will see and pick it up, generally at the same time a member of the mob reaches for it. Upon examination by the prospect and thief, it is found to contain one bill of large denomination. The thief convinces the prospect that they should divide the bill rather than return it to its owner. The thief is not able to change the bill, so the prospect is asked to take the bill and pay the thief half of the amount or as nearly half as he has in his pocket. The prospect does this and later finds that the bill is confederate money or counterfeit money and that he has lost whatever he paid to the thief. The same idea is carried out in dropping a package from an automobile. The thief talks the prospect into keeping the package, while the thief takes whatever share of its value he can get from the prospect. Upon later examination the prospect learns that he has lost his money

---

the machine was opened, there was an explosion, a puff of smoke, and nothing was found in the machine except charred paper. Of course, the operator had not placed the money in the machine.

as the contents of the package have either been switched or have disappeared entirely.

One of the forms of the duke[25] is an agreement between an inside man and the prospect to cheat an outside man at cards; the inside man will look at the hands of the outside man, signal to the prospect, and the prospect will win. But when the big bet is on, the signals become confused and the prospect loses.

The lemon is an agreement between the inside man, an expert pool player, and a prospect, by which the prospect will win bets on the pool games played by the expert. Through a supposed fluke the expert wins the game which the prospect had bet he would lose, and the prospect thereby loses his money. The foot race was similar to the lemon except that it involved foot-racing rather than pool. Both the lemon and the foot race are now ancient history.

Another short-con racket is to offer to sell to a prospect at a ridiculously low figure some article—perfume, jewelry, furs—which is described by the con man as having been stolen. If the prospect is dishonest enough to buy stolen property and falls for the bargain, he finds when he examines his purchase that it is a very inferior article, which has been switched for the genuine article which he examined or else one on which a label of a well-known brand has been fixed. Some operators play this racket by using pawn tickets instead of articles. The prospect is given an opportunity to purchase for $5 down a pawn

[25] A confidence man in prison writes: "Some years back the duke was called 'the big mitt.' It was played successfully on railway trains and in ninety-nine cases out of a hundred the conductor was 'in.' This is now practically obsolete."

ticket for an article accepted as having a value of $20, which is described as actually worth $50. The prospect thinks he is getting a bargain because the article was stolen. Some of these pawn tickets are counterfeits, and in some cases the pawnbroker is in collusion with the thief and gives a twenty-dollar ticket for a one-dollar article.[26]

In the confidence games the principle is the same— beat a man who is trying to do something dishonest. It is impossible to beat an honest man in a confidence game.[27] But if the sucker is selected properly and the story

[26] Many other short-con games have been played, including the gold-brick, the sick engineer, the glim-dropper, dropping the fiddle, the gaffed chiv, the strap, the string (a variation of the string), the two red aces (a card game), and the match box. Many of these are described by Will Irwin, *Confessions of a Con Man* (New York, 1909).

[27] A professional confidence man, after reading this manuscript, wrote: "The statement that if there was no larceny in a man and if he were not trying to get something for nothing and rob a fellow-man it would be impossible to beat him at any real con racket is unqualifiedly true. This remark is often made by professionals." Another confidence man wrote: "These suckers ought to be trimmed. It is a hard thing to say, but they are a dishonest lot and the worst double-crossers in the world." Another confidence man wrote: "A confidence game will fail absolutely unless the sucker has got larceny in his soul. One of the first questions asked of a prospective sucker after the buildup is developed is, 'Have you larceny in your soul?' This question is asked outright and a 'yes' or 'no' answer is necessary. If he answers 'no' and the mob believes he is telling the truth, he is dropped immediately. If he answers 'yes' they can go on with him. A certain business man, deacon in a church and a respectable citizen, was asked whether he had larceny in his soul and answered: 'No, I would not do a dishonest thing for any reason.' But the proposition was developed a little and involved depriving Jim O'Leary, who was then the biggest gambler on the South Side in Chicago, of his money. The sucker sat and thought several moments, and then said, 'I have always hated gambling. I think it is ruining hundreds of people. I would be willing to go a long ways to injure the gambling business. If this proposition will assist in

put in right, he does not refrain from dishonesty. There is no known case in America of a prospect who, after hearing the story, declined to go farther into the scheme because it was dishonest. Hundreds of men have even embezzled the money of others to use in confidence games, including several prominent bank presidents. The situation is quite different in England, because the aver-

putting down gambling, I am willing to help. And after we get O'Leary's money can't we go down to Hot Springs and ruin some of the gamblers there?' I have never heard of a prospective sucker who turned down a proposition which was built up properly, on the ground that it was dishonest. . . . . Of course, we select our prospects. We look over his bank account, his family life, the way he spends his money. Bankers, for instance, are very good prospects. They engage in a lot of speculative business and anyone who speculates is a good prospect. We try to find someone who is living beyond his means, who has social ambitions, or whose wife has social ambitions which are beyond their income. The banker who is speculating is probably short in his accounts already, and a chance at a big profit will generally appeal to him as a way out of his difficulties."

The method used by the confidence men who swindled Norfleet involved purchase of stock on advance information and was a form of sure-thing gambling, in which he had no possibility of losing, and the other party to the transaction had no possibility of gaining. Furthermore, he knew that, if he participated in this with the representative of the concern (who was actually the confidence man), he would be assisting this representative to violate the orders of the concern for which he was working. These two forms of dishonesty in which Norfleet was willing to participate are described in his own account of the confidence game in which he was beaten, and the thieves report that he concealed other aspects of the techniques. The method used by confidence men in the attempt to swindle Norfleet in Denver does not involve dishonesty on the part of the victim, according to the account Norfleet gives of the technique, although it does involve an effort to get something for nothing (see Norfleet, *op. cit.;* Van Cise, *op. cit.*).

The truth of the assertion that the victim of confidence games cannot be beaten unless he is himself dishonest depends on the definition of "confidence game." It seems to be impossible to make a logical differentiation between confidence games and other dishonest practices. They merge gradually into one another. Study courses for civil service jobs, the puff

age Briton is inherently honest. When he is shown that he can steal something from the outside man with whom he has already had contact he will say, "I don't feel that we should swindle him; he appears to be a nice chap." If, in order to overcome this objection, the outside man acts so that he will not appear so nice, the prospect refuses to have anything to do with him because he does not like him. Con mobs in England are compelled to confine their efforts to American visitors, whose sense of larceny has not been affected by the ocean voyage or the British environment. Even when abroad the average American will not pass up an opportunity to show how smart he is, and in all con rackets he thinks he is getting an opportunity to do this.[28]

The banks cause some of the stories to break down. In a great majority of the banks the depositor who wants to withdraw a large part of his balance at once is questioned, and frequently the withdrawal is delayed. In re-

---

racket, the sale of dentifrices and real estate, and thousands of methods described in the literature of consumers' organizations are like the confidence games except that they involve stupidity on the part of the victim, while confidence games are on the somewhat higher level and involve cupidity on the part of the victim.

[28] "During the war the poor confidence man fell on evil days; there were no American tourists to prey upon" (Basil Thomson, *My Experience at Scotland Yards* [New York: A. L. Burt, 1926], p. 30). Basil Tozer describes the confidence games used by English thieves; almost all of them are petty tricks with no elaborate development of plot based on the desire of the victim to get something for nothing (*Confidence Crooks and Blackmailers* [Boston, 1930]). An American confidence man commented on this: "I don't agree that con games will not work in England. But it is true that the American tourists provide the best prospects. This is partly because they are away from home. Englishmen, also, are more likely to fall for the play away from home."

sort cities many of the victims formerly had their money transferred from the home bank to the local bank suggested by the con mob which had him in tow. These banks were in collusion with the con men, and received a small percentage of the total.[29] In one well-patronized resort city there were five right banks a few years ago. Through the efforts of the bankers' association not one of them is left today. But, if the story is put in strong enough, it is not broken down by the opposition of the bank. Some years ago a man was lugged in Chicago and put on the send for $12,000, the money being transferred from his home bank to a Chicago bank. The Chicago bank became suspicious and notified the police department. The man was taken to the detective bureau, and the gallery picture of each member of the con mob was shown to him, he was told what part each played, and was shown just how he was going to be beaten. But the police could not shake his confidence. They finally locked him up overnight and put him on a train for his home town the next morning. Also the Chicago bank returned his money to his home-town bank. But in a day or two he withdrew the money from his home bank, put it in his pocket, took the train to Chicago, looked up the steerer, and went for the entire amount. Ordinarily, however, the mob tries to keep the sucker from contact with anyone, even his wife and family, from the time he is shown the convincer until he is actually beaten; the steer-

[29] A banker in Los Angeles was convicted as an accomplice of a confidence mob and two respected business men in Denver (Norfleet, *op. cit.*, pp. 224 and 324). One of the banks in Reno was regarded by confidence men as a "right jug." The cashier of this bank disappeared shortly before the trial and was supposed to have been murdered to prevent him from testifying.

er sleeps with him, eats with him, and never permits him to get out of sight except for the few minutes while he goes to the bank.

The con rackets are comparatively safe because the victim has attempted to do something dishonest and been beaten at it, and therefore he is not in a position to make a complaint. When he does make a complaint, little attention is paid to him; also he always lies about it, claiming he was robbed by violence. Even if the mob is arrested, it is easy to secure a dismissal.

VI. MISCELLANEOUS RACKETS

The tap, the hype, and the wipe are somewhat like con rackets in that they are talking rackets, but differ from true con rackets in that they do not have the element of larceny on the part of the prospect. The tap is the sale of advertising space in a journal which is supposedly published by a union of express employees or of freight handlers. A merchant is mildly threatened that, unless he subscribes to certain space in the journal, his shipments might be delayed or destroyed. Sometimes these solicitors, through false representations, get the indorsement of a local union of bona fide employees, for a percentage of the returns. To make it look genuine, the solicitor has the checks made out to the treasurer of the supposed union in Los Angeles, Chicago, or New York. In each of these cities, there is a clearing house for such checks, which takes a 25 per cent cut for the services. At times a dozen solicitors, supposedly representing as many organizations, operate out of each of these cities, having their victims send their checks to these clearing houses. Accounts under each organization's name are maintained in banks by the clearing house to permit the checks to be readily negotiated. This clearing house will always come to the front for one of the solicitors, should he get into trouble.

The hype is a method of short changing cashiers.[30] It is usually played two-handed, in some cases single-handed, and in some cases three-handed. A twenty-dollar bill or a ten-dollar bill, and in hard times even a five-dollar bill, is used to make a small purchase. After the change is counted out, the thief discovers that he has a one-dollar bill and asks that the price of the purchase be taken out of that and that the larger bill be returned. Many angles of cross-fire are used to confuse the cashier at this moment of the transaction so that the original bill together with its change are returned to the thief. This racket is very prevalent. Many mobs are continually making sectional and cross-sectional trips, each one showing considerable financial success. In the event of a tumble the majority of cases are straightened out by an apology for an apparently natural error on the part of the thief. When a pinch does occur in the smaller towns or cities, it is generally serious because, as a rule, many others in the town have been beaten by the same mob and complaints and identifications come pouring in.

The wipe is a racket which is generally used on foreigners by foreign-born thieves. A prospect is looked up and found to be financially O.K. He is cut into with a story that the thief's uncle died and left, say, $5,000

[30] The hype is also known as "laying the note" and "the stingaree." O'Connor (*op. cit.*, pp. 144–50) described it with a technique somewhat different than that presented here. Maurice C. Moore described it as practiced in England, with a technique identical with that described above (*Frauds and Swindles* [London, 1933], p. 5).

74

to be distributed to the needy, and the prospect was suggested as a proper person to distribute it. The prospect becomes all puffed up with pride. The thief then tells him that he must furnish a cash bond before the legacy can be turned over to him for distribution. When he produces this cash bond, he is shown what he believes to be $5,000, and it is given him to deposit. His disillusionment comes when he opens the wipe or package.[31]

The tap, the hype, and the wipe are described as illustrations of these rackets which are similar to the confidence games but do not necessarily involve dishonesty of the victims. Many others could be described, of which some are used principally by professionals, others by amateurs.[32]

VII. LAYING PAPER

"Laying paper" is the term used in a general sense by thieves to refer to the negotiation of checks, drafts, bills of lading, mortgages, etc. It does not include passing currency. The instruments which are included may be com-

[31] This racket is known also as the charity racket. Newspapers frequently contain reports of its operation. The disappearance of the money is generally accomplished by switching packages. It involves no certain dishonesty on the part of the victim, though it is possible that some of the victims anticipate that there may be an opportunity to hold out some of the money.

[32] "I bet I have more money than you" is a confidence racket similar to the tap, the hype, and the wipe. Two or three men, who have struck up an acquaintance with the prospective victim, bet on who has the most money. The victim is permitted to hold his own money and that of the others while the others go to their rooms for more money. After waiting some time, he examines the money and finds that he has been holding a bill or two and a handful of blank paper which has been substituted for the real money which was at first displayed.

pletely forged, indorsements may be forged, they may be counterfeits entirely, or no "improvements" at all may have been made on them. Post-office money orders are referred to as P.O.M.O.'s, or simply M.O.'s, and may be qualified by the word "bad" to designate counterfeit or "good" to designate genuine. The term "hanging paper" is nonprofessional, used by pulp writers and policemen. No thief would ever use the term. A person who is in the bandhouse (work house) for beating an A.&P. store with a four-dollar check would refer to himself as a "paperhanger"; a thief would refer to him as a clown.

Postal orders which are passed are almost always secured by holdups or burglaries of post offices. Since the orders are numbered serially and every post office is notified within seventy-two hours of the serial numbers that are stolen, there is much danger in passing them. If the orders are stolen in Chicago, and the first one cashed in St. Louis, the inspectors center their attention on St. Louis; should the next one appear in Nashville, they feel that the thieves are traveling southward and advise the officers in Memphis, Atlanta, Birmingham, and New Orleans to be on the lookout. Because of this danger, the racket can succeed for a short period only. It is a favorite method of getting a start when released from prison.[33] A

[33] A confidence man who had read this document made the following comment at this point: "The author states that many ex-convicts get hold of stolen money orders and pass them for a starter. I disagree with this. Stolen money orders are a nasty rap, and very few ex-cons go into it. They do, however, like to go into passing counterfeit money and this for several reasons. If they can make the proper connections while still in prison so they know where to go when released, they prefer to take a G-rap [federal prison sentence] than risk return [to the state prison] for violation of parole. Further the penalty is light and the government is not so hot on the passers but concentrates on the makers of the counterfeit bills."

76

bundle of orders can be secured and cashed during the first day or two, then all the remaining blanks can be destroyed so that there will be no incriminating evidence. Some thieves, however, do not destroy the unused orders but plant them or send them to a safe place so they can be used to bargain in case of a pinch. The Post Office Department is always interested in retrieving stolen money orders and even if a thief is arrested for cashing ten orders out of ninety that were stolen, the Department will be receptive to a proposition for a light sentence in exchange for the return of the missing eighty orders.

Travelers' checks are secured by cannon mobs and are sold to a special group of thieves who specialize in cashing them. The thief has to forge identification material and signatures to match the checks. When that is done, there is little difficulty in cashing them, since they are usually in small amounts. This racket, also, can be pursued for a relatively short time in a particular city, as the danger of arrest increases each time a stolen order appears at the clearing house.[34]

Counterfeit mobs are rather distinct from the professional thieves, and there is relatively little contact between them. But professional thieves frequently arrange to purchase counterfeit money and lay it. This does not

[34] A thief who had specialized in laying paper wrote as follows in regard to the description above: "The forgery racket may be worked single-handed but more often is worked by mobs of two or three. It is in my opinion the class of all rackets. It is my contention that to walk into a bank, past the line of bank coppers, and push a forged check through the paying teller's window requires more guts, larceny sense, fast thinking, and finesse than is required in any other racket, to say nothing of a perfect understanding of banking practices and methods and the masterful preparations to eliminate resistance on the banker's part. The author gives an example of laying forged paper in which he says that the layer contacted

come technically within the scope of laying paper. The danger in it is the same as in cashing money orders, and the pursuit the same.

VIII. THE SHAKE

The shake or shakedown consists in securing money by extortion from a person who is violating a law or who thinks he is violating a law. The operator generally impersonates a law-enforcement officer or an agent of one of the supergovernmental bodies, such as a crime commission, the Committee of Fifteen, or any like outfit. The two principal forms of the shake are the muzzle (also known as the mug or mouse and involving homosexuality by the victim) and the income tax.

The muzzle began as a professional racket about 1909 or 1910 in a poolroom at Forty-third and Broadway in New York City, where a group of thieves of every known variety was congregated. They talked over the possibility of making some money from the members of the third sex who were making the Fifty-first Street subway station a rendezvous for their social relations. The origi-

---

two bank officials to get their O.K. on his check. Perhaps this was done, but not by a sane up-to-date mob. If a good layer cannot sell his work at the paying teller's window he clears it through an account which he opens at another bank, and then proceeds after a reasonable time to overdraw the account. Laymen are often heard to say, 'I don't know how a crook can get a check cashed at a bank, I can't even get a good check cashed.' It's all in knowing how, and I've had many good laughs at the alacrity and dexterity with which paying tellers have counted down three or four grand [thousand dollars] in payment of a piece of forged paper."

Joseph Goodney is accused of having defrauded banks of more than a half-million dollars through forged checks, and Dick Barry was a close second (O'Connor, *op. cit.*, chap. ii). A good description of the development of a casual forger into a professional is presented in Roger Benton, *Where Do I Go from Here?* (New York, 1936).

nal application of the racket was very crude. A couple of thieves would wait until they saw two men go into a toilet together and then would break in and, finding a compromising condition, would demand money from the participants purely in the guise of outraged citizens who threatened to call in the police. As the possibilities of the racket became apparent, the thieves developed more finesse and impersonated police officers who would accept bribes to overlook the violation. From this developed the safer angle of permitting the violators to post an amount of cash as a supposed bond for their appearance in court (the violators never appearing). The professional steerer also developed. This was a youthful member of the mob who would steer a victim to a spot where the other members of the mob, impersonating policemen, would find them in a compromising position. In this instance, the compromising does not mean actual violation of law, but merely being together in one toilet room with obvious intention of violating the law; the other members of the mob always appeared before any act took place, or else the steerer stalled or postponed action if the other members failed to appear. In steering against this racket, the highly effeminate, berouged characters would not be used, for it is impossible for them to work as members of a mob.

So much heat developed around the Fifty-first Street subway station that the field was broadened. The steerers worked other subway stations, then all comfort stations, and later the public washrooms in the better hotels. Following this, a mob was organized to go on the road and the first cross-country trip was a great financial success. Since that time dozens of mobs have operated throughout the country, enjoying practical immunity from arrest and making considerable money. Arrests are so rare that when one does occur it is a matter for much discussion among thieves. In order to complain to the police, the victim would admit his part in the action, and few will do that. The fix is therefore rarely necessary in this racket. The amounts secured vary with the financial position of the victims. The top known touch is $35,000 from a Pittsburgh department-store owner, but the losses of a store owner in New York, while not definitely known, are considered to be much more than that. This man was shook down by real coppers, by con mobs, parents, antivice societies, publishers of periodicals, and what not, until some years ago he moved to Europe, where he has since remained. The muzzle is one of the few rackets in which a go-back (second attempt) can be successfully staged. In some instances two or three go-backs on the same man are successful.

The income-tax shake developed later than the muzzle. A couple of thieves go to a merchant, say a jeweler, and tell him they are from the income-tax office, that they believe he has made a false return on his income-tax report, and that they have come to see him about it. Almost every business man has made a short return on his income tax, and almost every one of them will fall for a story of this kind and pay to keep out of trouble. If the store owner is beat by the thieves in this racket, it is because he has been dishonest. It is not necessary for them to know anything about the income-tax business; they need only raise a lot of hell and make threats about what is going to happen to him. Sometimes he pays them to forget about it, sometimes they have to insist on returning to examine his stock. They generally approach him on Saturday morning and arrange to return Sunday to check his property against his duplicate income-tax return. After checking some of his unset diamonds, for instance, they say, "Here it is. You have not declared this. This will be enough to convict you on." If he objects, they say, "We will let the judge decide that. You appear in the district-attorney's office tomorrow morning at ten o'clock. We will take these diamonds with us as evidence." They give him a receipt for the diamonds and that is the last he sees of them.[35]

[35] Many other variations of the shakedown are reported. The badger game, in which a man is compelled to make a payment to mollify an enraged "husband" with whose wife he has been caught, is one of the oldest. A recent variation of the badger game substitutes for the husband a federal officer who threatens action under the white-slave law. In another form, a man buys jewelry, an automobile, or other article, pays for it with a check which has been indorsed over the phone by a responsible firm, then tries to pawn the article immediately; the report is transmitted to the firm which sold the article, which suspects that a bad check has been passed and demands that the purchaser be arrested; he is held in the police station until Monday morning, and, when his check is then found to be perfectly good, he demands extravagant compensation on threat of a law suit. In another case a man who has been a corporation-management expert in Wall Street secures a few shares of stock in a company, examines the financial operations for the slightest breach of legality, and, if he finds anything, threatens the firm with publicity and a lawsuit unless it relieves him of his stock at an exorbitant price.

\If a thief is to make a profession of stealing, it is necessary that he keep out of the penitentiary. The professional thief generally has a record in the Bureau of Identification as long as your arm, but after most of the cases "dismissed" or "no disposition" is entered. This is due to the thief's ability to fix cases.[1]

In order to send a thief to the penitentiary, it is necessary to have the co-operation of the victim, witnesses, police, bailiffs, clerks, grand jury, jury, prosecutor, judge, and perhaps others. A weak link in this chain can practically always be found, and any of the links can be broken if you have pressure enough. There is no one who

[1] The following records of pickpockets illustrate this immunity: Peter E. Shea committed suicide in 1936 at the end of a twenty-year career in which he had been arrested hundreds of times but never confined in an institution for more than a few days. Louis Finkelstein, who had headquarters in Cleveland during his long career, received his first major sentence in 1935 when he was committed to the workhouse for one year; he escaped within two months, with a suspicion that a guard had assisted him. Eddie Jackson, misnamed Eddie the Immune, died in 1932 at the age of sixty-one after a forty-year career in Chicago, during which he had been arrested "thousands of times"; during the first ten years of his career he served only ten days in houses of correction; during the last thirty years he served ten years. Other professional thieves are arrested less frequently than pickpockets, on the average, but are equally immune to punishment. Count Victor Lustig, professional confidence man and counterfeiter, had been arrested nine times in Prague, London, Vienna, Paris, Berlin, and twenty-eight times in cities in the United States before his first conviction in 1936.

cannot be influenced if you go at it right and have sufficient backing, financially and politically. It is difficult if
the victim is rich or important; it is more difficult in some
places than in others. But it can practically always be
done. It is just a question, if you have the backing, of
using your head until you find the right way.[2]

Sometimes the thief fixes his own cases; sometimes he
employs a fixer. He saves some money if he fixes it himself. So, when he is pinched, he generally tries to straight-
en out the coppers without going to the can. This is
pretty easy if it is merely a pickup without any evidence
against him. In hard times a dollar or two or even a drink
may be enough. But, if the copper has made a dead-
right pinch, it is hard to square it with him, for there may
be witnesses who will make trouble, and he loses the
credit of a pinch if he does not take the thief to the can.[3]

[2] A pickpocket in New Jersey made the statement in 1933: "A pickpocket can practically always fix a case if he has money."

[3] A confidence man commented at this point: "Only the simplest of
coppers accepts settlements from strangers, and more often than not
coppers will refuse to deal directly with any thief except the big-timers.
The smart copper does business through the fix and so accomplishes the
dual purpose of protecting himself and keeping the fix in line for further
profitable business." Eddie Jackson gave the following description of the
arrangement he had with the police in Chicago in 1892: "When the fix
was in with the Central Station it worked in one of three ways: One, if
arrested, we could fix the copper on the beat for $10. Two, if the copper
wanted more than $10 we stood for a pinch if it was between the hours
of eight and four (the shift of the fixed officers). Within these hours we
had plenty of time to work the Loop; when pinched within these hours
we would be turned loose at the Station. Third, if we were pinched on
another shift or if a tough complaining witness appeared, then the lawyer
with the writ interceded" (John Landesco, "The Criminal Underworld
of Chicago in the Eighties and Nineties," *Journal of Criminal Law and
Criminology*, XXV [September, 1934], 345).

Also, there are some policemen in almost every city who cannot be fixed in any way. B and O (Byrnes and O'Brien) are the only ones on the Chicago force known to professional thieves who cannot be fixed. When they pick you up, they say, "Hello! Where are you going?" You reply, "It looks like I am going to the can." They say, "You're right." There is no kidding or conversation with them; everything is straight business. In fact, they are so honest that the important people finally decided they were in the way and kicked them upstairs.[4] But when the ordinary copper makes a pinch, you generally kid each other on the way to the can.[5] They ask, "Were you in that job up on Lawrence Avenue yesterday?" You reply, "No, what job was that? I don't know anything about it." They say, "Well, you should have been in it. They beat someone for $25,000." You say, "That's just my luck. I always miss the good things." Then the copper will look down at his overcoat and say, "My overcoat is getting pretty old. I really should get me a new coat." That means he wants $50 or $75, and you

[4] A New Jersey pickpocket stated in conversation in 1933: "B and O in Chicago are well known to pickpockets, and they are honest." An Illinois professional thief, after reading this manuscript, commented: "The author is right in saying that few coppers are strictly up-and-up, although every racketeer has met some who were. In fact, I have had several contacts with B and O whom he mentions and know that they are honest." A retired detective in Chicago commented: "Some policemen will not take money. B and O had that reputation when they were in the central detail. But they were not the only honest ones. There was *another* team at the same time which was honest."

[5] The retired detective in Chicago, mentioned above, stated in 1934: "Eddie Jackson and the coppers were always kidding each other. Eddie and his mob would pass a couple of dicks on the streetcar and would thumb their noses at the dicks, and the dicks would shake their fists back. But they understood each other."

84

say, "I think I could arrange to get a new coat for you from a friend who sells me things at wholesale."

If the thief cannot fix the copper and is taken to the can, the first thing for him to do is to get out. In addition to the natural desire to get out as quickly as possible, there is the consideration that the longer he is in, the greater is the chance that he will be recognized for another rap. The difficulty in getting out of the can is that they will not let you telephone to a lawyer or anyone else. But generally some member of the mob is not picked up, and he immediately starts action. And there are generally some friendly coppers around the station who will send out word for you. To some extent the cannons and other professionals have a regular system of phone calls to certain lawyers or to some of their women at agreed-upon hours, and, if these calls do not come in, action for a writ is started.

If a thief is taken to the can on a pickup, the usual method of getting out is on threat of habeas corpus proceedings. Any attorney hanging around headquarters can be used for this purely legitimate and mechanical service. The charge is sometimes $25, usually $10.

On dead-right pinches the thief most frequently gets out of the can on bond. Some thieves have friends or relatives who sign their bonds, and some have their own property which they turn over to a solid indemnity company so that they have bonds good any place in the country. Once the thief is out of the can, he may try to handle the case himself, or with the assistance of other grifters, by working directly on the victim or in other ways. The following method was used in New York City by friends of a three-handed cannon mob which had beaten a man for $55. An outsider saw the touch come off and caught the tool while the money was still on him. A pinch was made, and the case was to be heard in the night court. The partners who were not pinched dug up a friend, described the appearance of the complaining witness, and instructed him what to do. As the complaining witness entered the building, the thief's friend stepped up to him and asked, "Are you Mr. Brown, the complainant in the Smith case?" When he received an affirmative reply, he stated, "I am Kelly of the police department, and you were advised in error to appear in this court. The case is being heard at the Jefferson Market Court and I will be glad to take you there in my car."

The victim, knowing nothing of police or court methods, accompanied him. After stalling around the Jefferson Market Court for some time, the thief's friend stepped away from the victim and spoke to the court clerk about something foreign to the case and returned to the victim with the explanation, "The defendant has been released on bail, and it is not known when the case will be heard. Here is your $55 and $10 for your taxi. You go home and we will notify you when to appear again." In the meantime the case was called in the other court, and, because the complaining witness failed to appear, the case was dismissed in conformance with the court rules and the demands of a vociferous lawyer. The arresting officers could not understand why the complainant failed to appear, and the following day, when they looked him up and learned what had happened, they all, to put it mildly, were vexed. This occurred at a time when it was almost impossible to fix a case in New York City.

These and other methods of fixing cases by their own efforts are generally confined to local thieves or to mobs which have very little money. The professional thief generally depends upon a fixer to take care of his cases for him. Every police station and court in all parts of the country has many persons bouncing around, soliciting business with the claim that they can fix cases. They get many cases from amateurs, but the professional thieves do not use these phony fixers, for they are not reliable and generally do nothing except take your money. There is in every large city a regular fixer for professional thieves.[6] He has no agents and does not solicit and seldom takes any case except that of a professional thief, just as they seldom go to anyone except him.[7] This centralized and monopolistic system of fixing for professional thieves

[6] Billy Skidmore, originally a West Side saloonkeeper who graduated into politics and municipal contracts, had the reputation of being the fixer for professional thieves in Chicago for many years. The *Chicago Tribune* wrote regarding him in May 6, 1933, "Skidmore is said to be a fixer of such long experience and discretion that both gangsters and crooked politicians trust him implicitly." He has retained his influence and his contracts with the city in spite of changes of administrations and even of parties in control. During the last decade he has devoted his time to the gambling syndicate and is said to have transferred the thieves to a former assistant. A New Jersey pickpocket stated in conversation: "I knew Skidmore before he became wealthy, and he fixed all my Chicago cases for me. I served five months in Jackson, Michigan, and was pardoned for the rest of the five-year sentence. The pardon cost me plenty, too. Beauchamp did my work there for me."

[7] A professional bank robber commented on this: "Perhaps the author means by this that the fixer with whom he is acquainted works only on crimes not involving violence. It is true that there are specialists even in the fix line, and a man who has an in [advantageous position] to fix con cases might not be able to fix robbery cases. But if the author means that the fix does not exist in armed robbery, he is badly mistaken. It is merely a matter of knowing the right party to go to."

is found in practically all of the large cities and many of the small ones.

The fixer acquires his position with professional thieves by service. He tries to maintain a batting average of one thousand. Not all of them can do this, but their record is so good that the thief feels secure if a regular fixer is on the case.[8]

The regular fixer refuses to handle a case "second-hand," that is, after someone else has dealings with it. The first question he asks if approached on a case which is several days old is, "Has anyone else been in on this?" If he took a secondhand case, he would have to unfix all that the first fixer had done, and this might cause complications; also the division of the fee might be open to argument.

Whenever an out-of-town troupe arrives in a particular city, the first thing done is to inquire about the fixer. They must have assurance that the fixer is in a position to do things and will go for them. Fixing cases in a community is not like opening a shoestore: the service is not open to all and sundry. The fixer does not offer his services to any stranger until that stranger has been guar-

[8] Blonger, the Denver fixer for confidence men, had the reputation of not having one man sent to prison in twenty years while under his protection (Philip S. Van Cise, *Fighting the Underworld* [Boston, 1936], p. 135). Not all persons in the underworld have so great confidence in the fixer. An ex-burglar stated his opinion thus: "The criminal can seldom depend entirely on the fixer because the fixer is compelled to aid the police and prosecutor as well as the thieves. He takes his money for a specific service, but he may do him dirt the next day on something else. Most of the fixers are double-crossers. They trade cases, as do many of the criminal lawyers." Another underworld character who never engaged in professional theft complained: "Nothing is less likely than an honest fix. The fix is in with the law, but he must do the law favors for the favors he receives. Never trust a fix. Pay him well and hope for the best."

anteed by a reliable thief who had known him previously, or until the fixer has other satisfactory evidence that the newcomer is reliable. The out-of-town thief generally gets in touch with some local professional thief and asks if everything is O.K., that is, "Can a case be taken care of if he should have the misfortune to have a pinch?" In the event of a pinch this local professional is then notified, and he in turn notifies the fixer that a reliable thief is in trouble and, if necessary, he guarantees the fixer's fee. Another method on arriving in a strange city would be to go to the hangout of the fixer, tell him who you are, and whom you know that he knows. The fixer, after inquiry, would then tell you that the town is too hot at the moment and you had better not work, or else that everything was O.K. and to go to work. Once a fixer has taken a thief on, he will go for him after that.

The methods used by the fixer are not all open and plain even to the thief. The thief has personal knowledge only of the parts of it which he comes in contact with. The only thing the thief knows is that he pays his money to a fixer and that everything then is all right. It is none of his business what the fixer does or how he does it; he never inquires about this, and the fixer does not volunteer information. He does know the methods which might be used, but he does not know what methods are actually used in a particular case or how frequently one method is used in comparison with other methods.

In most cases the fixers use the coppers. The copper knows that, if he does not take the money, someone else will and that he himself gets no money but he gets in bad. The copper can be influenced to do two things: first, to hold up or be uncertain about his own testimony; second, to advise the complainant that the case will probably take a long time and cause him many inconveniences and that he would be wise, if he gets a chance, to get his money back and forget about the prosecution. Coppers can do more to straighten out the average complainant than anyone because, as a rule, the victim is unacquainted with the police and with court procedures and will therefore follow the advice of the police. In addition, the victim is likely to ask the policeman questions right along this line, and the policeman does not have to do anything that will look at all shady. The policeman does not himself give the money back to the victim but simply builds up a way for a favorable reception when others approach him.

If the victim cannot be bought off directly, circuitous methods may be found. A representative of a furniture-manufacturing house was beaten on a Pullman for $795 out of his drawing-room. The thief was identified and arrested. The arrest took place in a city where no sure-fire fix was operating and where the thieves were not acquainted. The fixers, such as they were, could only offer a jail sentence, for the victim wanted to prosecute, and getting his money back was a secondary consideration. The other members of the troupe learned that this complainant was en route to Chicago when he was beaten and that he was a regular guest of one of the large hotels and often gave parties in which the laws against adultery and liquor were flagrantly violated. One of the house detectives was a former city copper, and his services were enlisted for a stipend. Mr. Copper waited his opportunity and then walked into the victim's room at a time when every law except the law of gravitation was being violated. The copper, after convincing the furniture man that he had an open-and-shut case on him, said he would go into conference with him next day and in the meantime would let the party go on. The next day, after making the offense look pretty serious, the copper told the complainant that the defendant in the case of the theft on the train was his sister-in-law's boy and that the family would make good the $795 plus expenses if the furniture man would fail to appear in court when the case was called. The victim realized the pressure on him, agreed, failed to appear in court, and received his $795 out of the thousand dollars which were given to the copper.

If the case goes to court, the important thing is to have it dismissed in the lower court and not let it get into the criminal court, where fixing is more difficult. You can tell by the way the case is handled in court when the fix is in. When the copper is not very certain he has the right man, or the testimony of the copper and the complainant does not agree, or the prosecutor goes easy on the defendant, or the judge is arrogant in his decisions, you can always be sure that someone has got the work in. This does not happen in many cases of theft, for there is one case of a professional to twenty-five or thirty amateurs who know nothing about the fix. These amateurs get the hard end of the deal every time. The coppers bawl out about the thieves, no one holds up his testimony, the judge delivers an oration, and all of them get credit for stopping a crime wave. When the professional hears the case immediately preceding his own, he will think, "He should have got ninety years. It's the damn amateurs who cause all the heat in the stores." Or else he thinks, "Isn't it a damn shame for that copper to send that kid away for a pair of hose, and in a few minutes he will agree to a small fine for me for stealing a fur coat?" But if the coppers did not send the amateurs away to strengthen their records of convictions, they could not sandwich in the professionals whom they turn loose.

Regardless of what is being said or done in court, the defendant must never speak if he is represented by the fixer's lawyer. All the talking is done by someone else. The defense or alibi heard by the thief in his own defense may sound completely new to him, but it is none of his business. He will finally be turned loose when enough meaningless verbiage, hooey, and subterfuge have been spent to pacify the complaining witness and the crime commission.

If the testimony of the witness and the coppers cannot be fixed so as to justify dismissal, the prosecuting attorney may need to twist the testimony or else the judge may need to find an out (a way out of the difficulty). There are fewer cases taken care of by direct contact with the judge than by any other method. Unless the police and prosecutors are also fixed, they will yell their heads off, and this puts the judge on the spot. He must always be able to save his face and have an out for his decisions.

A case where the court was in a tough spot and received an out through a natural break occurred recently. Two heels were nailed dead-right with a quantity of merchandise belonging to Smith, Brown, and Company. The fix went in direct to the court, with an understanding that a fine of $200 would be assessed on each thief. This was thought sufficient to cool off the prosecutor and the copper. But when the judge announced that penalty, the prosecutor and copper, who had not been fixed, started to screech together, "Your Honor! This is not a case for a fine. Both defendants have long police records. They will pay these fines and be right back robbing the merchants before this court adjourns. They had over one thousand dollars worth of merchandise on them when arrested. They should be sent to the penitentiary, or at least receive the maximum workhouse sentence."

The court answered, "If I send them to the workhouse they will appeal and make bond at once. If I hold them to the grand jury, they will make bond as well. If I fine them, the city will at least benefit to the extent of $400."

Then Mr. Store Copper spoke up, strictly out of line, "It is all right with me, Your Honor, but what will Smith, Brown, and Company say?"

This remark made it easy for the court, and the judge remarked with great show of heat, "You run right over to Smith, Brown, and Company, and tell them that I, and not Smith, Brown, and Company, am running this court and that I shall not consult or consider them when disposing of cases. $200 and costs for each defendant. Next case." All the prosecutor and copper can do in a case of that kind is to smile, realizing that more power than they can counteract is operating.

The strength of the fix and the way it works in emergencies are shown in the following incident. A citizen was riding on the streetcar, felt a hand in his pocket, turned in time to see who held the pocketbook, and grabbed the cannon. The thief was arrested and provided his own bond. The case was called in court the following morning before things could be arranged with the fix.

The defendant demanded a continuance, but, as he was not "properly" represented, the court ordered the testimony to be taken. The complaining witness told the exact truth and in reply to questions several times gave positive identification of the thief. The defendant, feeling that he was due for the worst of it, started to raise hell, yelling that he had not signed a jury waiver and that he demanded a jury trial or else a continuance. The court, realizing that the defendant knew what he was talking about and that he might be someone, finally granted a twenty-four hour continuance. In the meantime the fix went in. Through an oversight the court was not made acquainted with this fact. When the case was called, the court asked the complaining witness again if he were positive of the identity of the defendant. To the court's surprise, the victim replied that he was not sure, that he was much excited on the streetcar and grabbed the person nearest him, and that after thinking it over another day he had become uncertain. The court realized that the victim had been reached (fixed) and started to blast him: "You came into this court yesterday and positively identified this defendant. Today you are not sure. I know what caused your change of mind and exactly what happened. Someone has got to you to change your story. Now, I demand to know who talked to you and unless you tell me I shall hold you in contempt."

Something had to be done and done immediately, for there was danger that the complainant would tell what actually happened between the two sessions of court and that the newspapers would have a story on it. So the fixer's lawyer, who was a stranger to the judge as well as to the thief, stepped to the end of the bench and whispered to the court. The court ended the harangue abruptly and with a decided change of tone and manner said to the complainant, "Well, if you are not sure of the identity of the defendant, I shall have to discharge him."

If the case is open-and-shut and no convenient out can be found, there are several possibilities. The first is that the court may impose a fine which will be small enough so that it can be paid, or else a bit which is short enough so that it can be served without difficulty. Another method is to impose a workhouse sentence and then vacate the order after court adjourns, and thus release the prisoner. Vacate orders are used as seldom as possible because no court wants such entries in the journal if it can be avoided. Sometimes when the judge will not issue a vacate order, a clerk or bailiff may be induced to forge one and thus release the prisoner from the sentence.[9] Also, there is always an opportunity of an appeal bond when no other avenue of escape is open. Sometimes it is necessary to lam (leave the jurisdiction) and forfeit the bond. In most states the surety must find and return the fugitive, but, if arrangements are made to reimburse him for his loss, he would not have a fugitive returned even if he knew where the fugitive was. The thief would forfeit

[9] A former superintendent of the House of Correction in Chicago made this comment on vacate orders: "There used to be a lot of vacate orders come out here to us from the judges. At one time they came so fast that we began to look around to see what was happening. We found that a clerk had secured a whole book of these orders, had signed them with a judge's name, and was peddling them around the city. About one hundred prisoners got out on these orders before we learned what was going on, and by that time the book of orders had been used up. Then they changed the regulation so that every vacate order now has to be signed by the chief justice, and very few of them are now sent to us."

the bond, however, only as a last resort because he forfeits as well his privilege of living or grifting in the city from which he lammed.[10]

Once the thief is in the penitentiary, the fixer for the professional thieves has no more to do with it. The prisoner may succeed in getting an early parole, extra food, a choice job, and other privileges, but this is arranged through friendships and politics rather than through the professional fixer.[11]

These different methods by which the professional thief escapes from all or a large part of the punishments

[10] A former member of the central detail of a police department read this manuscript. He made no objection to the description of the methods by which thieves fix their cases but declared that he knew a better instance of the fix than any described in the manuscript and that he himself had been involved in it as one of the detectives. A member of a confidence mob had been arrested in Akron and was wanted on another charge in California. Though his case could be fixed in California, the mob did not want to lose his services for the time required, and he did not want to suffer the inconvenience and expense of the trip. The mob met in a hotel in Cleveland with two detectives and a lawyer and decided to have a charge brought against the thief in Cleveland, where his case could easily be fixed. California had offered a reward of $100 for the delivery of this thief, and it was therefore necessary to pay the Akron police the same amount to have the thief sent to Cleveland. When the thief reached Cleveland, he was released on bond in the regular manner. One month later, when the case was called in court in Cleveland, the detective announced that the complainant in the case had died, and he presented as evidence a clipping from a newspaper. The mob had arranged in their earlier conference to have this announcement of a fictitious death available as evidence. The case was therefore dismissed, and the thief did not go to California.

[11] Eddie Jackson, a Chicago pickpocket, gives the following account of how he secured an easy berth in the State Penitentiary of Illinois: "I was assigned for work to the shipping room in the broom shop, and celled in the west cell block. Two days after this assignment I was transferred to the hospital through the influence of Dean McCarthy and Senator Horton. Here I was made head night nurse of the surgical ward. I was put

depend principally on the victims, next on the coppers, and then on the prosecutor and judge and their assistants. The judge generally knows what is going on, and the honest judge gets angry but can't do much about it. Even his anger sometimes provides a lucky break for the thief. Two cannons were pinched after beating a man on a streetcar for $158. The fixer was not used in this case as the cannons owed him money, and he would not perform for them until they paid their debt. The victim was induced to accept $200 as payment for his loss and for "laying off." When the case was ready for trial, the prosecutor informed the court that he had just learned that the complainant had accepted the amount of money he had lost and did not want to prosecute. The judge asked how much the man had lost and was informed that the amount was $158. The judge then asked how much he received as payment and was informed that the amount repaid was $200. When the judge asked what the extra $42 was for, he was informed that it was for lost time and expenses. The judge was infuriated and addressed the defendants: "You are both professional thieves with long records and should be in the penitentiary, but we cannot get you there if complainants make it a business to accept profits on their losses and

---

in there over the protest of Dr. Watson, who has lately been made postmaster of Joliet. The arrangement for my assignment to the hospital had been made three days previous to my commitment." The doctor in charge of the surgical ward, however, told Jackson that he could not use him and transferred him to the broom shop. When Senator Horton was informed of this transfer, he said "emphatically that the doctor was not running that hospital. Twenty minutes after the senator left me in the visiting room I was transferred from the broom shop to the hospital and I stayed in the hospital" (Landesco, *op. cit.*, p. 356).

refuse to prosecute. Take a good look at this complainant and rob him any time you see him and, if you come into my court for it, I shall discharge you." There was no fix involved in this so far as the court and prosecutor were concerned, for this judge is held in the highest esteem by everyone for his honesty and independence. But he is somewhat radical and does not shun publicity.

Fixing is a mixture of finance and politics. It is primarily a financial transaction, bought and paid for by everyone concerned. But it is made possible by politics and often involves political favors as well. There was more politics about it twenty or thirty years ago than there is now.

For the thief, fixing is almost always a financial transaction. The migratory thief never expects or receives favors because of his political connections, and the local thief only occasionally does so. If the local thief is really a professional, he will have so many cases that it would be ridiculous for him to depend upon any alderman or other office-holder. Even in the few cases where he does use the office-holder, he generally pays money to the office-holder. It is a sort of racket for this office-holder to tell the thief, "Of course, you realize I don't want anything for myself but we will have to give Smith five hundred dollars, for he is in a position where he can gum up the whole works." This Smith is generally an attaché of the court or of the prosecutor's office. It is doubtful whether Smith ever gets the money. So the local thief and the migratory thief pay their money to the regular fixer in most cases.

The migratory thief is not active in politics. He does not vote at all except as a political favor to some friend and then he votes only once, for by one vote he liquidates his obligations. He feels that he owes no favors to politicians or fixers because he pays for everything with money. The local thief is likely to be more active in politics, just as he is likely to appeal for aid to the politicians more frequently than the migratory thief does.[12]

Also, from the point of view of coppers, clerks, and bailiffs, fixing is primarily a financial transaction. They get paid for their services without quibbling. The prosecutor and judge are probably handled with more finesse. It is likely that they get presents at Christmas and other occasions and that they borrow money from the fixer and forget to repay it. For all these officers the financial motive is reinforced by political obligations. All judges, prosecutors, clerks, bailiffs, and coppers are politically sponsored, and they all have to do what their sponsors or the boss of their sponsors request. If a fixer who has an in with the political boss makes a request, these officers must grant it whether they take money for it or not, or else sacrifice their political futures. And, if they must participate in fixing the case anyhow, they might as well take the money. Besides, from both the financial and the political angles, they know that, if they do not do what is requested, the case will be fixed in some other way and they themselves will suffer the principal loss.

[12] The thief who wrote this document was migratory, paid no attention to politics, and depended for protection on a professional fixer whose power continued through changes of administrations and factions. Eddie Jackson, on the other hand, seldom left Chicago after the first years of stealing, and he depended primarily on local politicians, for whom he marshaled the repeaters in the elections but whose influence was completely destroyed in certain administrations. Two of his four prison commitments were due to factional fights among the politicians (*ibid.*, pp. 349 and 932).

From the point of view of the fixer, also, this is a financial transaction. One fixer said to a thief: "Everything I get is bought and paid for, just as you pay me. No one gets any political or other favors." The fixer can operate only if he has the consent and good will of those who are politically powerful. He may get a start on the basis of old friendship, but he can keep his position as fixer only if he kicks in. He must turn over to the political barons the larger part of what he gets from the thief, and his standing is determined by his reliability in dealing with them. His standing is *not* determined by his activity in a particular party or a particular administration. He has to be able to do things regardless of changes of administration. In most cases he is not active politically. He may contribute to campaign funds of both parties or of neither party, but he must pay in some form to those in political control.

There is in another way a correlation between fixing and politics. In a big city you have an efficient political machine, and the fixing is on a strictly business basis, bought and paid for. In the small town, where the political machine is not so well organized and the system of fixing is not organized at all, the thief must make his approach directly or indirectly to the political leader, whoever he may be, and he secures the release by political influence. But the thief pays his money just the same in the city and in the small town.

Three Chicago heels were grifting a midwestern city of considerable size, when one of them was picked up by a store detective who knew him. The copper agreed to give him a floater (out-of-state probation) for $50, but crossed him after the plea was entered, and the thief got a sentence of three years in the penitentiary. This took place in a city where the regular fixer could easily have been put in and everything could have been straightened out in the police court. But now it had become a second-hand case, and the fixer would not take it, and besides it is much more difficult to spring a man from stir (release a man from prison) than to fix a case in a police court. The fixer suggested that they see a certain young lawyer, who was a partner of the son of one of the high executives of the state. So they went to see him and told him their friend had been sentenced to the penitentiary for stealing a Spanish shawl from a department store, which they mentioned by name. He interrupted, "Oh! Did you happen to see there a pair of jade elephants?" They said they had not. He said, "They are beautiful, and I have wanted to get them for my girl, but they cost $1,700 and I can't afford them yet, since I started practice just a short time ago. I am going to get them if they still have them when I get some money coming in."

They told him they could perhaps get them cheaper by getting a wholesale price. They dropped the matter then and went on with their case. He said he would look up the law and suggested that they come back the next day. The next day he told them he thought there were some loopholes but that it would be rather expensive to get the evidence together. They asked him how much he thought it might cost and he replied, "Oh! Five or six or seven hundred dollars." Then they went on talking about the case some more. After a while he asked them if they had made any inquiries about the wholesale price of the jade elephants. They said they had looked them up but had not got down to a final figure. He asked about what they thought they could get them for, and they replied, "Oh! Five or six or seven hundred dollars."

He said he thought that would be all right, and after a while he said he would go ahead with the case. The thieves beat it over to the department store right away and in about half an hour returned and laid the jade elephants on his desk, and in about three days the third partner was released on some sort of appeal bond. No effort was made to catch him when he lammed.

The attitudes, importance, and financial conditions of the victim play a major part in determining whether a case can be straightened out and in the methods used. If the victim is poor, he is generally willing to drop the case if he gets his property back. If a small merchant catches a booster leaving his store with four dozen pairs of hose and causes his arrest, the stock of hose is four dozen pairs short until the case is disposed of, for the police hold the stolen goods as evidence. The several trips from his store to court together with the expense and the reduction in his stock are the motivating forces which cause the small merchant to take his property from the thief and turn him loose with a warning to stay away from his store in the future. If he could have the thief locked up today and finish the whole case tomorrow, he would probably cause an arrest in every case. If the victim is forced by the police or prosecutor to appear in court, a statement from him that he has his property back and does not want to prosecute is generally sufficient to have the case dropped.

In cases where the victim is a wealthy or important firm, an offer to return the property is generally useless.

In the larger stores the protective department can, if necessary, withhold a dozen mink coats for a year. Fortunately the store coppers will almost always listen to reason. It might be wondered, then, how they can make a showing to their employers. That is not difficult to explain. In a store averaging thirty arrests a week, only about two would be professionals and the rest amateurs. The amateurs would show convictions and punishment in 100 per cent, and even the professionals might show convictions of some sort, but with minor penalties. Consequently there might be twenty-eight convictions out of thirty cases, and that would not look bad.

Even when the store copper cannot be fixed, his main idea is to get all cases disposed of as rapidly as possible, and he is satisfied to have a thief sent to the workhouse at once for three months rather than go through the difficulties of a grand-jury indictment and drawn-out trial in the criminal courts. The thief does not like continuances any better than the victim does, and the workhouse-commitment order can be vacated.

Capper and Capper used to be the hardest-boiled of any firm in Chicago. If you got caught there, you were going to have trouble. When the case came up in court, representatives of the firm were right there, and, if any move was made to get in the fix, they made an awful howl. But they have slowed down, for, it is reported, someone went into their store with a bottle of acid and ruined a lot of goods. No professional thief would do a thing like that, for he is too busy making money where he can get it. But the Cappers thought it was retaliation for being so hard-boiled.

The railroads, banks, associations of jewelers, and

furriers are pretty tough. They have their own protective departments which can seldom be straightened out, like the city and store police can, and they can raise lots of hell if prosecutors or judges are lenient. These places are greatly feared by professional thieves.[13]

There are occasional cases of men of community importance and law-abiding type, irreproachable and unapproachable, who believe that laws are made to be enforced and that thieves should be locked up. Only at great intervals does such a victim appear. When he does, the thief is helpless. Every possible angle will be shot to bring the victim down. If he refuses to take his money back, an attempt will be made to reach him through friends, business associates, employers, fraternal affiliations, his bootlegger, etc. His private life will be looked over for some weakness whereby he can be handled. A famous case of this kind concerned an important official of the Illinois Central Railway in 1925. He lost his pocketbook containing $29, and the cannon who got it was apprehended on the spot. The fixer got to work at once; when the victim signed the complaint, an officer

[13] Hapgood's thief was committed to prison as a result of the pressure of the street-railway company of New York City. This company had complained to the superintendent of police, who decided to investigate and took a ride on the Third Avenue carline in citizen's clothes. When he had completed his ride, he found that he had lost his watch and two hundred and fifty dollars in money. The thief who did this was caught and sent to prison. Also, about this time Hapgood's thief was caught and his fixer was notified to keep hands off; so the thief went to prison (Hutchins Hapgood, *Autobiography of a Thief* [New York, 1903], pp. 69, 130, 224–26). A New Jersey pickpocket maintains that it is not only the cases against big corporations which are difficult to fix but that sometimes a workingman will fight as hard as a bank president, and the case cannot be straightened out in any way.

104

tried to get him to state that the amount in his pocketbook was less than $15, which would make it petty larceny. The officer told him that this would save everyone time and inconvenience, for it could be disposed of summarily. The victim would not agree, saying that he wanted the thief sent to the penitentiary where all thieves should be. The fixer was able to have the case continued fifteen times in the police court but even this did not wear the victim out. Finally it was announced that the case was continued until the tenth of the month, and the victim was so advised. However, the record showed that the case was on call for the ninth. The case was called on the ninth, and, because the complaining witness was not present in court, the case was dismissed for lack of prosecution. The victim appeared on the tenth and was informed that the case had been disposed of the day before, and the records were shown to him to prove that it was his error. The railroad man went to the district-attorney and asked that the defendant be indicted. This was done, and after a year of demurrers, continuances, and other motions, the thief was finally tried and convicted. No angle of approach was overlooked in trying to handle the victim except a threat of violence, and that would not have had an effect on this man anyhow. Another year and a half were taken up with proceedings in the Supreme Court, which resulted in an affirmation. Petitions for review consumed more time. The victim was again approached with the argument that since conviction had been obtained he should be satisfied with banishment (probation out of the state). He would have no part in this. He wanted the man in the penitentiary and made himself very clear in saying so. The thief finally wound up in the penitentiary, where he stayed about a year on a one-to-ten sentence. The complaining witness made attempts to prevent parole, but his efforts were not as aggressive as before conviction, perhaps because he realized that attempts to influence the parole board were extralegal and not a part of his duty as a citizen. Perhaps his energy before conviction was not expended primarily as a citizen but had an ulterior motive, for he had lost his pocketbook on his own railroad's property and many travelers had lost theirs as well.

This thief spent about ten thousand dollars trying to beat the case. He could, of course, have lammed, but he would have been free only until his next pinch somewhere else, for the victim was so earnest and aggressive that he would have had him returned for trial from anywhere he might be arrested. This case developed so much heat that no copper, prosecutor, or court officer would have anything to do with it in a manner the least bit off color. Cases of this type are so rare that, although they are the subject of much discussion among thieves, they do not have any effect on stopping thieves from grifting. No thief ever expects to have the bad luck to run into a case that cannot be fixed in some manner. This conclusion is not formed because of the thief's conceit but because of his knowledge of the weaknesses and limitations of the average citizen and public official.[14]

[14] The following statement by William B. Austin, the victim in the case described, gives confirmation of the story: "He took fourteen continuances, jumped his bond four times, took four changes of venue. . . . . I was approached upon numerous occasions during the thirty months when his case was pending by members of the State Senate, the House of Representatives, President of a well-known political club, numerous clerks of courts, including one chief deputy clerk of the appellate court, to release

It is sometimes believed that the fixer is the general boss of the thieves. This is an error. The function of the fixer is to get thieves out of trouble, not to control them. He often gives some advice to out-of-town professionals, after agreeing to take care of them. He might suggest that it would be wise to lay off certain spots, that certain railroad sheds, race tracks, theaters, etc., have incorruptible protection, and that, if certain coppers get you, he could do nothing. He is not interested in what they do other than, if possible, to prevent them from getting in a spot too tough for him to extricate them. Occasionally a copper will confide to the fixer his dislike for a certain thief, together with a threat to lock him up every time he sees him. The fixer will always pass this informa-

---

this man. . . . . I said 'I have shown him to be an ex-convict and he confessed to me that he had been a thief all his life, and why should I release him?' The President of the Club said, 'He is one of the best workers in the Republican party. . . . . The last attorney in the courts of this county who defended this man was a member of the House of Representatives. His chief champion was a member of the State Senate several years. He was also backed by several judges and the whole pickpocket trust. . . . . The lawyer in the final trial of the case before Judge Gemmill and one of the most noted criminal lawyers of this city received a fee of $1,000 per day for services. The culprit was finally sentenced by the court to from one to ten years" (Landesco, *op. cit.*, pp. 938–40; see also *David Stark* v. *People of the State of Illinois*, 324 Ill. 289–292).

Eddie Jackson had a somewhat similar experience when he picked the pocket of the cashier of the Chicago & Northwestern Railway. Landesco states regarding this case: "The efforts made by Jackson to obtain release reveal the interlocking organization of criminals, bondsmen, court officials, and politicians. In this particular instance the system failed to work. The attempts at release included twelve continuances of the case, the efforts of the clerk of the court to secure a lesser plea carrying a jail rather than a prison sentence, attempts to influence the jury, jumping bond, attempt to secure a suspended sentence, and an appeal to the Supreme Court." The persons who were seen in this case and who were prob-

tion along in the form of a suggestion to keep away from a certain spot or a certain copper. The fixer will also mention the transfer of certain coppers to certain details or stores, or the fact that a certain copper is on a leave of absence or any like information which could affect any of his clients. When this information is given to a particular thief by the fixer, it is passed along to the whole profession. These things always come in the tone of a suggestion rather than an order. In some cities the fixer would not even make these suggestions but would feel that, if you do not know your business, you should not be grifting there. In any case the fixer is not a boss of thieves, and he does not control them in any true sense of the word.

---

ably more effective in other cases than in this one included: the policeman who made the arrest, the attorney in the case, the justice of the peace, the judge of the criminal court, the jury, the clerk of the criminal court, various other clerks and bailiffs, precinct captains, saloon-keepers, and politicians. There were a hundred ways of escape that would have been available in ordinary cases, but everyone was afraid in this instance because of the great pressure of the prosecution. Even so, Eddie Jackson was on bail eleven months before conviction, had three months to perfect his appeal, and six months before the Supreme Court rendered a decision, a total of twenty months after arrest before final decision (Landesco, *op. cit.*, p. 352).

Norfleet conducted a determined pursuit of the confidence gang which swindled him, spending $75,000 in the attempt. This pursuit resulted in the imprisonment of four members of the gang, the suicide of another member, and the imprisonment of about seventy-five members of associated confidence gangs. Though the gang got $45,000 from Norfleet, they paid out more than $82,000 in protection to peace officers, or lawyers, and as cash bail which they forfeited, and were all imprisoned or dead after all. They stated that they had not had a moment's peace after Norfleet started his pursuit. This account is probably essentially correct, although somewhat glorified (J. Frank Norfleet, *Norfleet: The Actual Experiences of a Texas Rancher's 30,000-Mile Transcontinental Chase after Five Confidence Men* [Fort Worth, 1924]; see also Van Cise, *op. cit.*).

The system of fix which has been described applies in principle all over the country.[15] It is more difficult in some places than in others, and it is less organized in some places than in others, but the principle is the same. Kansas City is the easiest place in the country in which to straighten out a case. They have a system there by which you can practically take your choice of three judges in three different courts, and it is always possible to have one of the three who can be depended upon.[16] Milwaukee

[15] A professional thief who had specialized in rackets connected with carnivals wrote regarding this statement: "What the author has to say about the fix is Gospel-truth and is the common knowledge of every thief in the racket. The fix exists in every city, village, hamlet, and township in the country." Norfleet's account of his pursuit of the confidence mob which had swindled him indicates that he was hampered by the sheriffs and police in Fort Worth (*op. cit.*, pp. 50 and 201), Clearwater, Florida (pp. 62–64), St. Augustine, Florida (pp. 70–75), Tampa (p. 76), Key West (pp. 116–19), Los Angeles (pp. 154–56), San Francisco (pp. 132–33, 200–201), Jacksonville, Florida, (pp. 164–67), New Orleans (pp. 208–11), Kansas City (pp. 243–44, 252–59), and especially in Glendale, California, where two policemen captured the leader of the confidence mob and then permitted him to escape on payment of $20,000 (pp. 130–31, 199, 214–34). When a big raid was to be made against the confidence men of Denver, the district-attorney did not dare give information about his intentions or plans to the city police, because many of them had been in collusion with the confidence men, but handled the entire raid through the state rangers and used the basement of an outlying church rather than the police stations as temporary lockups (Van Cise, *op. cit.*).

Professional thieves are somewhat immune from punishment in European countries, also. Heindl states that of five hundred cases of picking pockets, scarcely one results in punishment. He cites the case of Mimi Lepreuil, known as the Golden Hand, because of his proficiency as a pickpocket, who had an annual income at his death of three hundred thousand francs from the estate built up by picking pockets, and he was never convicted in his life (Robert Heindl, *Der Berufsverbrecher* [5th ed.; Berlin, 1927], pp. 232 and 249).

[16] Josiah Flynt Willard in 1900 stated that Chicago had the reputation of being the best place in the United States for thieves, with New York

is one of the not-hard places, too. It is only the newspapers that tell you there is no grifting in Milwaukee. It differs from no other city of its size so far as professional thieves are concerned.

While the newspapers tell the professional thief to stay away from Milwaukee, the thieves tell one another to stay away from Connecticut. No state is shunned more consistently by professionals.[17] The city coppers are no smarter than in any other place, but few thieves are able to straighten out their cases there. If a complaining witness gets his money back and fails to appear to prosecute, the coppers do not drop the case but go right out and bring him in. The law-enforcement officers as a whole are not interested in whether the victim gets his money back; they are interested only in taking thieves out of circulation and keeping them out. The larger cities of the state are grifted regularly, but only when they can be grifted airtight.

There are fewer places for grift in the South than in the North, and consequently there are fewer cases of fixing. But, when persons in positions to profit get a chance to make some money from professional thieves, they take advantage of it as quickly as anyone else. In Florida, as

City slightly more difficult. He quotes an ex-thief to the effect that conditions had not changed in any of the large cities during the preceding twenty or thirty years (*The World of Graft* [New York, 1901], pp. 10 and 105).

[17] A New Jersey pickpocket, interviewed in 1933, made the following statement regarding Connecticut: "It is just as easy to fix a case there as anywhere else, but, if you don't get it fixed, Connecticut is a tough place, principally because of a hard district-attorney and a tough prison." Hapgood's thief described Connecticut as a particularly easy place in 1890 (*op. cit.*, p. 80).

well as in other places where there is a large transient population, there is generally a complete system of privilege, license and fix, organized and functioning perfectly. In these resort towns an ex-thief is often the fixer.

There is generally considerable difficulty in smaller towns in straightening out a case. The natives are more or less bloodthirsty and believe that, if someone is caught stealing, he should be deprived of his liberty. The police and prosecutor would have to explain to their personal friends why a thief was permitted to angle out of any pinch. In such places it is generally necessary to do some studying to find the surest and quickest way by which to get a man out of the can. Sometimes immediate payment of cash is helpful, and some mobs when en route on a trip carry fall-dough so that they can handle the business immediately.[18] Generally it is necessary to go to some politician. This may be done by others in the mob who were not pinched or by a wife or friend who is sent for immediately, if the members of the mob are too hot.[19] The politician is generally a lawyer or a judge; there may be a dozen persons in the town capable of accomplishing the result desired.

[18] Hapgood's thief, writing of conditions as they existed forty years ago, gave essentially the same statement regarding fall-dough, concluding, "I know that I can stay out of prison as long as I save my fall-money. When I blow that in, I ought to go to prison" (*ibid.*, p. 243; see also pp. 38–42). Thieves who have been interviewed more recently state that thieves no longer carry fall-dough because the police demand more money if they find large sums on the thieves and because it is not needed if they have the proper connections. They say, however, that it is customary to keep fall-money on tap with a pal, a sweetheart, a wife, or a mother.

[19] The New Jersey pickpocket stated that if a thief is arrested in a small town it is generally necessary to work through people in the cities, generally those who have political connections.

The way the fix is worked in these smaller towns was illustrated in a case a few years ago. One Saturday night five or six thieves were in a Chicago hotel on the North Side. They had in their room about ten thousand dollars' worth of property they had stolen that week, and they were smoking the pipe (opium). The telephone rang and two broads (women) who lived with a couple of thieves were calling. One of them said, "Say, we want you to get us out of here." When asked where she was, she said, "In the police station in Peoria," and she added, "The police were good to us and let us use their phone." The thief slammed up the phone with a curse; they packed their stuff, ordered a couple of taxicabs, and all beat it for the other side of town, leaving one person to keep watch to see what would happen. As expected, a squad car drove up within five minutes, and the thieves just missed spending some time in the can themselves because the broads had been foolish enough to call them from a police station where the call could be traced. The next day the fixer in the city told them he could not straighten out a case in Peoria but suggested that they see a certain member of one of the state commissions. That man gave them a letter to a man in Peoria who would fix the case. When this man was seen, his apologetic manner was amusing. He asked, "Are those two women married?" "What do their husbands do?" "These women are not professional thieves are they?" "They were just trying to get a dress they could not afford to buy, weren't they?" When these foolish questions were answered in a way to ease his conscience, he said he would see what could be done about it. So they left $400 with him and went away. The two broads got out of the can right away, but they were so dumb they did not know why; they thought they were released because the can got too full. The police told them they had been treated mighty well, for they might have been sent to Joliet, so they ought to tell where the other stolen things were. The girls agreed to do this and led the police around to the hiding-places. When anyone gets anything from a store in a small town, he wraps it up and leaves it in a drug store or restaurant, saying he will call for it later.[20] This is safer than taking it to a hotel room, where the maids are likely to find it and where the stuff is on you if a pinch is made. So these two fools led the police around to seven or eight places and picked up dresses and other bundles they had left. In a Greek restaurant the waitress had read in the paper about the arrest of two women and decided from their description that they were the women who left a package with her. So she opened it and found that it was a nice dress and was good enough for her. When the two broads came with the police for this package, the waitress said she had never seen the broads before and had received no package. They jawed about it until the police got tired and took the broads back to the can, for they now had some more evidence on them. So the friends from out of town had to come through again, this time with $600. This time they saw that the girls got out of town as soon as they were released. They had been kept by a couple of thieves and decided to have a little spree of their own but did not have enough sense to get themselves out of trouble.

Sometimes the vice boss in the smaller communities

[20] Another thief stated that a better method was to wrap up each article and mail it to a friend in the home city.

can be enlisted for aid in straightening out a case for a thief. There is no connection between thievery and protected vice or booze, but an administration that permits the latter is not unresponsive to the argument and money of the former. Three thieves were driving home from a week's work in southern Indiana, and their car was filled with merchandise. They had to stop overnight in a small town in the northern part of the state, and there two of them were pinched with the car. The one who was not arrested tried every available angle to straighten the thing out but could do no good. Then he called on the vice and booze boss. He did not tell this boss that his partners were in trouble as he himself was wanted in the case, and vice bosses are notorious for helping the police if the case is not in their own fields. He told the boss that he was in the vice industry in Chicago and just stopped on the way through. His purpose in this meeting was to learn who, if anybody, the vice boss knew in Chicago. It developed that the vice boss had been tried previously for murder and that he had imported a Chicago lawyer, who defended him successfully. The thief knew this lawyer well and phoned him at once regarding the local situation and asked him to phone the vice boss and put in the O.K. When this was done, the thief returned to the vice boss and told him of the case on his partners and enlisted his aid to straighten out the local chief of police. This was a simple matter. Upon payment of $100 the chief turned the two boys loose, gave them their car and its contents, and advised them not to come back.

There is comparatively little fixing of federal agents in the old-line branches of work. A thief once tried to straighten out a case with a federal officer with the proposition, "I will pay you this," holding out a bunch of ten brand-new, beautiful hundred-dollar bills, "if you will keep one of forty people who were brought up to identify me from coming into this room, and you do not know which one of the forty it will be or whether the one I pick will have anything on me." He just smiled and said, "I am working for the government now. If I took this money, I would be working for you, and I would have to keep on working for you. I believe I would rather continue to work for the government." But this same man later had a case against a big company on an interstate-commerce charge and was sure to make a lot of trouble for this company. He was getting $4,400 a year from the government. This company asked him if he did not want a job with them for $10,000. He took the job, and the company officials congratulated him on his wisdom and added, "When you come you might bring the files in our case with you so that we may look them over and profit by our mistakes." So they were able to fix their case because they could continue to give him a regular salary.

Also, there is not much fixing in the federal courts. The politics there are not quite so rotten as in the municipal and criminal courts. There are occasional cases of fixing, but the more usual method is to use tricks and to appeal to professional courtesy. In general, there is no arrest in federal cases until the case is made, and when it is made, there is no escape. You may as well plead guilty and start for the federal stir. It differs, however, in different departments. The post-office inspectors are thought to be most straight and efficient, and they do not frame

115

cases. The narcotic-drug and prohibition officers are a very different lot.[21]

The cost of fixing cases, whether federal, state, or municipal, is not standardized. Some cases are more serious than others. In some cases many angles have to be taken care of, such as the reinstating of an old case, a period of newspaper hysteria, the effrontery to the crime commission, and the addition of related charges, such as vagrancy or habitual criminal. The cost of fixing cases varies, also, in different parts of the country. It is less in Chicago than in many other organized cities, but is much less in the southern states and in the small towns everywhere than in the cities. Also, the regular fixer generally charges less than do some of the near-fixers and phony fixers.

The fixer takes some cases on credit, but the thief has to pay his debts to the fixer or lose this assistance. The fixer will not handle another case for a thief who does not pay his debts as soon as he has made sufficient money. If the thief then does a bit because the fixer did not go for him, and if he then pays the fixer for the previous

[21] Professional thieves, as defined in this document, seldom appear in federal courts except on narcotic-drug charges. While there is unquestionably less fixing of cases in federal courts than in municipal courts, the judges and the entire personnel of the federal court owe their appointments to the political leaders who control state and municipal politics, and these leaders can, when they desire, bring the same pressures to bear on federal officials as on state or municipal officials. A notorious case occurred in Chicago a few years ago in which hijackers in interstate commerce, who had been engaged for years in that crime, were placed on probation at the request of a politician without an investigation by the probation officer, though the regulations required the judge to ask the probation officer to make an investigation before granting probation. The judge had a reputation for integrity, but he had political debts and obligations, also.

116

cases, the fixer will act for him again, but never on credit. The fixer would refuse to act, also, for the thief who squawked, if there were such a professional thief.

A special form of fixing is known as "right grift." This refers to a situation where absolute immunity is guaranteed in so far as the police detailed to a particular spot are concerned. No immunity is guaranteed from police of another detail, but there is little chance of interference when spots are grifted right.

The period of time that the right grift lasts varies from one day to eternity. Some spots are handled by the same mob the year round, other spots are good only during fair week, football games, racing seasons, etc. A cannon who makes his home in a certain city may receive a phone call to bring his mob there for Saturday and Sunday. This mob grifts rip-and-tear for the time specified by the police. Other mobs keep away because they are not protected, and when the complaints come in, they will get all the raps.

The condition of grifting right exists in both public and private spots. In general, the private police are harder to deal with than city police because they are afraid of losing their jobs. On the other hand, most of the spots which are grifted right have private protection rather than city-police protection. Ocean liners used to be the best place for permanent right grift, but this has been done away with generally except on some of the coast-wise ships. In general, right grift is not nearly so prevalent now as it used to be.[22]

[22] Hapgood's thief had a right grift at the Polo Grounds in New York City in 1890 (*op. cit.*, pp. 125–27). Eddie Jackson had a right grift at certain entrances to the World's Fair in Chicago and at certain downtown

Payments for right grift are made direct to the protecting officer or left in a designated place. The coppers generally get one full end of the money between them; this is, if the mob is three-handed, the money is cut four ways, with the coppers splitting their end if there be two coppers protecting the spot. Sometimes a stated sum is paid daily, weekly, or monthly.

------

street corners in 1892 (Landesco, *op. cit.*, pp. 344–45). Pete Shea had a right grift on the Forty-third Street car line in Chicago for many years. A ring of confidence men operated in Chicago during 1911–13 with a special police detail assigned for their protection and for the discouragement of competition; the chief of detectives was convicted of bribery in connection with this protection, as were also other police officers (see *Illinois* v. *Halpin*, 114 N.E. 932; *Illinois* v. *O'Brien*, 115 N.E. 123; V. O. Key, "Police Graft," *American Journal of Sociology*, XL [March, 1935], 630). Denver had similar protection for the confidence ring which had headquarters there, and later Reno. The Chicago City Council Committee on Crime reported that it employed two investigators who posed as pickpockets and formed a partnership with two detective-sergeants of the police department who informed them of the most desirable places to work and occasionally accompanied them to protect them from other police officers or from victims (*Report of the City Council Committee on Crime* [Chicago, 1915], p. 185). The leaders of the confidence ring which swindled Norfleet explained that they had been promised protection by a police officer in Fort Worth and that this officer insisted that they beat Norfleet the second time (Norfleet, *op. cit.*, pp. 201–2). The circus management in earlier years made advance arrangements for gambling and crooked games; this included fixing the newspapers by taking out unnecessary advertisements or by straight payment of money (Josiah Flynt Willard, *Notes of an Itinerant Policeman* [Boston, 1900], pp. 77 ff.; Will Irwin, *Confessions of a Con Man* [New York, 1909], pp. 51–53, 87–88, 122–23).

CHAPTER 5
THE THIEF AND THE LAW

The term "the law" is used here to designate in general what are called the "agencies of justice," such as the coppers, the lawyers, the courts, and the prisons. The thief has plenty of opportunity to get acquainted with these agencies but not to discover any justice. The thief believes that these agencies do not operate to produce justice but to produce records for themselves unless they are prevented by superior pressure. Coppers keep up their quota of arrests by picking up professional thieves against whom they have no evidence of crime. Prosecutors seek convictions, and thieves seek acquittals—neither seeks justice. The professional thief can apply pressure to counteract the desire of the prosecutor, and therefore the prosecutor has to make his record by convicting amateur and occasional thieves. When a professional thief is pinched on a wrong rap, he does not depend on the fact that he is innocent but goes right ahead with the fix as though they had a good case against him. He would have to have a very beautiful imagination to believe he could get justice in a court where at other times he has his cases fixed and where perhaps at the moment the other side has the fix in.[1]

---

[1] A confidence man wrote: "Unquestionably a real thief would rather have an arrest on a good rap than on a bum one. When the rap is right, he knows what to do and how to go about it. He knows whom he must square. But in a bum rap he is entirely at sea. He didn't do anything and

The court may discharge a professional thief on a technical argument. The thief does not believe that the court does this in a spirit of justice but because it knows that the thief is well represented and because it knows it will be reversed by a higher court if the decision is not technically correct. The thief who is broke or not properly represented does not secure a discharge on any such technicalities.

No professional thief ever wants justice in a general way, although he might wish it in isolated instances. But the word "justice" does not enter into his complaints. The thief does not even complain if he is picked up when he is grifting or on his way to grift; that is just part of the racket. He may complain if he is picked up at other times; however, he only objects, and he does not speak of "injustice." A thief was picked up one evening as he was going to see a doctor after a period of sickness which

has no idea whom it will be necessary to fix or what it will be necessary to do. A right rap he does the framing to square; on a wrong rap he, himself, is being framed."

Eddie Jackson maintains throughout the account of his life that he was innocent of the charge which resulted in his first commitment to Joliet in 1909. He stated that he was not arrested until eight weeks after the crime and that he had a perfect alibi. Against the advice of a detective who was handling the case he refused to give the victim the amount which had been stolen. Landesco explains that there were some difficulties which Eddie underestimated. "The police captain involved had been appointed to his present assignment through the influence of the *Chicago American*, and the victim was a Hearst man, a friend of the editor. . . . . Through the newspaper, the victim was enabled to put pressure upon the captain to force the case to an issue. The usual method of evasion followed by Jackson failed to be effective against a law-enforcing organization determined upon prosecution" (John Landesco, "The Criminal Underworld of Chicago in the Eighties and Nineties," *Journal of Criminal Law and Criminology*, XXV [September, 1934], 353–57).

had kept him confined at home for six weeks. He was held in the can twenty-four hours before he could secure a release. During this time in the can he raved about what a dirty bastard the copper was, but the term "injustice" was not used.

It is not only in his own cases that the thief sees no evidence of justice. A mob in a jewelry store went to the floor with (dropped on the floor) a diamond they had just stolen when they thought they had been tumbled and wanted to get rid of incriminating evidence. A legitimate visitor in the store saw them drop the diamond, picked it up, and started after the mob to return it to them. The store detective believed this man was a member of the mob and locked him up. He was unemployed at the time, did not have an unimpeachable record, and had no important friends to vouch for him. After lying in jail for more than a month, he was given a year's probation. In another instance, a man who had just been beaten by a con mob in Jacksonville, Florida, was given the blowoff and was carrying out the instructions of the inside man so enthusiastically that he actually ran toward the railway station. The police saw him running, searched him, and found on him some diamonds which he had acquired in a legitimate manner. They laughed at his story and held him in jail for about a month. The thieves believe that in an important murder case in Chicago several years ago it was necessary for the police and the prosecution to get someone and that they cooked up a lot of evidence for that purpose. It is reported in the underworld that one of the witnesses for the prosecution was in the state prison of Wisconsin at the time of the shooting in Chicago and that another witness for the prosecution was not even near the scene of the shooting but was put in as a substitute for another witness who had been given some money by the prosecution and shipped out of the state because a part of his evidence would conflict with the rest of the story and he would not agree to conceal it.

If any system could be called an agency of justice, it would be in England. In England there is no such institution as the pickup. When they lock you up over there, they either have a dead-right case or else turn you loose at once. If they have you dead-right, you are going to get a bit right away, and you will do every day of your bit. There is no fix. But the sentences are short.

The professional thief in the United States is frequently arrested, occasionally convicted, and very rarely compelled to do a bit. In general, the cannon is arrested most frequently, and then in order come the booster, the heel, and the con. The cannon is arrested most frequently because the victim is in a position to catch the cannon and to make complaint. Cases are known where cannon mobs have had two or more pinches in the same day, and other mobs two or more in the same week. But also cases are known where cannons have gone six months, boosters and heels a year, and con men three years without suffering a pinch.

A large proportion of these arrests are pickups, or arrests on suspicion. A few coppers will pick up any cannon if with other members of his mob, regardless of whether they are grifting. Boosters and heels, if seen in a store by a store detective, will be picked up regardless and will be convicted unless the fix is put in. Store detectives have been known to walk up to thieves who were actually making legitimate purchases and order them out of the store. This attitude is not considered unreasonable by the thief, and he will rarely go into a store where he is known, except for the purpose of stealing. Three or four out of every five pinches suffered by the con mob are pickups on suspicion, for the sucker is not in a position to make a complaint. The thieves who grift short con around hot spots, such as railway stations, suffer more pickups than any other type of con men. These frequent arrests in the different rackets do not deter the thief, for he feels that nothing serious can happen to him.

Because of his frequent arrests, the thief is better acquainted with the coppers than with any other part of the system of "justice." But he comes in contact at present with few coppers except those in the central, specialized detail. These specialized details have made the business of stealing tougher than it used to be. The copper on specialized details learns lots more about the rackets than the copper on general duty could. He becomes acquainted with the spots where rackets are worked, with the thieves who work at the racket, and with the methods they use. It is almost uncanny the way some of these officers can pick out a thief who is lugging a sucker.

Thieves divide the coppers with whom they have contact into square coppers and burglar coppers. There are probably many honest coppers, but if so most of them are out in the sticks, and the professional thief never sees them. Almost all members of the special details in large cities are burglar coppers, and these are the ones the professional thieves see. They simply do not want to catch thieves except to get some money from them.

If a mob is grifting and a burglar copper is seen, one

of the thieves will say, "Go give that bastard a ten-dollar note and get him out of the way." If a square copper is seen, the thief will say, "That will be all for today, boys. Here comes the bad man, and we are all going to the can." There is not so much difference in this respect, however, as formerly. The burglar coppers used to be straightened out before they made arrests, but now they make their arrests and are straightened out afterward. In this manner they keep up their record of efficiency, while the thief can still keep from doing a bit, and all concerned are satisfied except, perhaps, the public; in view of its inertia, perhaps the public is satisfied also.

Whenever a big convention, exposition, or other meeting is to be held in a city, the newspapers print a lot of hooey about the coppers who are being imported from other cities to keep the exposition free from crooks from these other cities. This does not scare the professional thief at all, for he knows that the specialized details in the other cities are all right and that they can be straightened out in the exposition city as well as at home. This is part of the front the exposition city puts up to impress visitors, but it does not fool the thieves or the coppers. The people who go to conventions and expositions expect to get robbed anyway, and it does not make much difference to them whether the thieves or the concessions and merchants get their money.

Coppers are regarded by professional thieves in about the same light as a rainy day—something you can't get rid of, so why complain? The thief does not like to be pinched by any copper, and especially not by a copper who will not stand to be straightened out. But he does not have a general attitude of hatred toward either the burglar copper or the square copper. The burglar copper is not regarded as a traitor to the public or as a friend but as a sensible person who is playing the game intelligently. He is regarded as a part of the racket; most of the thieves would have to try to find jobs if the burglar coppers were eliminated. The thieves cannot exist without these coppers, and the coppers cannot exist without the thieves, so they both compromise a little, and everybody gets along. No copper of this kind ever seeks to crucify the thief anymore than he would kill the goose of golden-egg fame.[2]

The thief fears the square copper rather than hates him. But the saving grace is that the copper who will not take your money will not lie about you in court. If he picks you up just standing around, that is exactly what he will tell the court. His attitudes and earnestness never vary regardless of whether the defendant is a first-timer or has a record as long as the *Arabian Nights*. On the other hand, the burglar copper's attitude and earnestness depend on whether the fix is in. If a thief were in a spot where he had to stand a pinch with no possible fix, he

[2] A similar philosophical attitude is expressed by a professional bank burglar: "Thieves do not hate the coppers. As a matter of fact, this business of hating is ridiculous. What is the use of hating an individual? Let any man do what he pleases. If the thief has any dislike or hatred, it is not for the individual but for what the individual stands for." This philosophical attitude was not maintained by two pickpockets who were arrested on an elevated train by two policewomen in New York City in 1934; it was reported that these thieves felt bitter hatred toward the women who arrested them. Also, a policeman who had formerly been a bank burglar expressed hatred toward the dishonest policeman: "When I was a known gun, robbin' banks and bein' photographed an' shut up all over the world, in my own mind I was an angel in Paradise compared to what I think I am now. You see, I learned to know the kind o' copper't I am when I was a reg'lar gun, and, God, how I hated him" (Josiah Flynt Willard, *The World of Graft* [New York, 1901], p. 116).

would rather be pinched by the square copper. But since he has the fix, he makes every effort to duck the square coppers. There are so few of these square coppers that no special arrangements need be made.

Most coppers are more or less fair in their dealings with thieves simply because it pays them to be so. They will extend favors even after a pinch which they would not extend to nonprofessionals whom they lock up. They realize that it is safe to do this and that higher officials will not be informed as might be the case if favors were extended to amateurs. In many cities the thief is held incommunicado for three or four days after arrest to prevent him from making a bond. Certain coppers, in violation of regulations, will advise the thief's friends as soon as he is locked up or will enlist the services of one of the cheap lawyers who hang around police stations, and the lawyer will sue for a writ of habeas corpus. Many coppers are fair in their business dealings, also. A copper who had a thief dead-right was given $100 for a discharge. Just before the case was called, the copper took the thief aside and handed the $100 back, saying, "I can't do you any good because, if I have you discharged on my case, Kelly [another copper] is going to grab you on another case." The copper was given $50 because he helped all he could, and the Kelly case was taken care of later.

Thieves will not cheat a copper or take unfair advantage of him in a business transaction. Should a thief owe a copper money, he will pay him because it is the economically sound thing to do. He does not expect to die or to quit the racket right away, and he knows that the services of the copper will be needed again. Coppers have

126

always been safe in loaning money to thieves. A mob of loft burglars needed some capital in order to realize on some merchandise which they had secured in New York City. A thief explained the situation to a police official, and he loaned the thief the needed money. Within a week he had his money back with a profit of about $3,000. The police official would have had no legal redress if the money had not been returned, but legal redress is the weakest of the copper's weapons. The possibility of illegal redress is what convinces the thief that it is not safe to cheat a copper. On the other hand, the copper is generally a poor risk when a loan is made to him by a thief.

Most of the coppers are dumb and ignorant. Dozens of times policemen have been heard to ask, "How do you spell larcen*cy*?" Or, "How do you spell *in*dentification?" It is believed by thieves that one reason the police use the numbers of sections of statutes or ordinances, when making charges, is the trouble they have with spelling. The copper has a superiority complex, to begin with. Thinking he knows everything there is to know about thieves and practically everything else, he does not try to learn. However, almost every seasoned thief can relate instances when they have been outsmarted by policemen. Such incidents are rather rare and do not alter the general feeling the thief has about the intelligence of the policemen.

When a thief is arrested in a city where he is known, he makes no pretense of being anything except a thief. The police ask him no questions but enter his occupation on the arrest slip as pickpocket, con man, or thief. The thief is glad to have his real occupation recorded, for that decreases his chance of being identified in the showup for a heavy job (crime of violence). But if a mob is following a circus, carnival, or presidential candidate about the country and has a pinch in a strange city, they generally report to the police that they are employed in the circus (having arranged in advance to have this report substantiated), or that they have come to the city for the particular event and have a legitimate occupation.

Private police generally cause more trouble for the professional thief than the city police do. When the Eye (Pinkertons) are brought in to protect a race track or an exposition, that is bad. They don't think of anything except catching thieves. They only get $140 a month, but they want honor more than money. They would throw a thousand dollars on the floor and take you to the can. Some of the other well-known detective agencies, however, are all right; one of the best known would give you a license to steal anywhere in the United States for a proper consideration.[3]

The framework of the protective service of the larger stores consists of a staff of store detectives hired directly by the store or furnished by a private-detective agency, a head store detective, and city coppers assigned to the store. The store detectives will cause a thief to be locked up every time it is possible, but the case in court is gen-

[3] Private detectives in smaller agencies have frequently been found to be in collusion with thieves. One of the methods used by the thief in disposing of stolen jewelry is to trade it to the private detective in exchange for a part of the reward; the detective thus acts as a fence for the thief. If the work of the detective does not show adequate results, he sometimes develops a fake theft in order that he may be certain of recovering the stolen property. See the Noel C. Scaffa case in Miami Beach (Associated Press reports of June 31, 1935, and July 8, 1935) and the Meyer Bogue case in Chicago in 1936.

erally in charge of the city copper. Since most of the cases of professional thieves in the stores are taken care of by Mr. Fix, it is evident that the store detectives must get an end. Sometimes the store detectives will do business directly with the thief, but generally it has to go through the fixer. The result is the same in the end, but it costs more to have it done through the fixer. The same policy is generally used by the private protective agencies in railway stations, banks, and other places where grifting is done.

One trouble the professional thief has with store detectives is slugging. Many of the store detectives have not learned the difference between professional and amateur thieves and think they can slug a professional the same as an amateur. The professional thief generally gets back at the store detective and teaches him a lesson. In one of the cheaper Chicago stores, in which there is nothing worth stealing anyhow, the man in charge of the policing is a bruiser. You can get any case fixed in court, but first you get hell beat out of you in the basement. If professionals found this store worth stealing from, they would soon cure him of that as they did in another store, where a girl had been slugged by a broad detective (woman detective). This thief bought a flaming red dress in the store, talking about it enough so that the clerks would remember her. Then she went into a waiting-room, partially unwrapped the dress, removed the bill of sale, and placed the parcel under her coat in such a manner that the dress would be plainly visible. Then she went to the basement where the broad generally stayed, and she had to parade up and down that basement nearly an hour before the broad finally spotted her and went for her.

The detective made a raw speech, slapped the thief, and was about to slug her. The thief acted like a perfect lady, high-hatting the detective but making no explanation. The detective took the girl to the office and made the charge against her. The girl, in turn, made a charge that the detective had slapped her. The detective felt so confident that she not only admitted the slapping but threatened to start in again right there. After that admission, the thief stated that she had made a legitimate purchase and asked that the clerk be called to verify her purchase. This was done, and the clerk identified the girl as a legitimate customer. The girl then threatened suit, and the store had to pay her $1,500 and fire the detective. The thief could not have secured anything in court, but there would have been a lot of newspaper publicity about it, and this would not have done the store any good.

The stool pigeon is very rare in professional thiefdom. He is a person who makes regular reports to a law-enforcement officer regarding persons engaged in illegal operations; he secures this information because he is generally engaged in illegal occupations himself. Stool pigeons are used with considerable frequency and success by the narcotic agents. But a stool pigeon cannot give much information regarding the professional thief. The copper already knows who the professional thieves are and where they are likely to be working, and he does not want to arrest the thief too often or it will drive away his own income. Sometimes a stool pigeon may give an enforcement body information regarding a particular case about which he happens to know. The copper is more likely to advise the professional thief that the stool pigeon is giving information about him than he is to seek or use information from the stool pigeon. The word of a copper is never taken as conclusive proof that a person is a stool, for coppers will always lie about anyone they dislike. The thief tests the suspected stool pigeon by giving him false information; if this information comes back from an enforcement officer, it is taken as conclusive proof that the man is wrong.

The usual treatment for stool pigeons is to ignore them or kill them, with the less dangerous method as the rule except in the narcotic and liquor business. Even in the liquor business the number of stool pigeons killed is exaggerated. The newspapers, when in need of a motive, are very free to call the dead person a stool pigeon, and this is usually wrong. On the other hand, many stool pigeons do commit suicide, as the only relief from mental torture and anguish. Their suffering becomes unbearable when their treachery becomes known. They are persons who cannot bear much suffering, otherwise they would not have weakened and become stools.

The prosecutors and judges are not so well known to the professional thief as are the coppers, for there are few personal contacts with them. They are not regarded as enemies as are certain of the coppers because they do not institute proceedings against him. They are regarded, in most instances, as a part of the fixtures, just like the pillars and benches in the courtroom. They can't make any difference in his life, for the thief knows before he goes into the courtroom in most cases that everything is going to come out all right. If the prosecutor or judge cannot be handled, it comes out the same way, anyhow.

When the judge who had not been fixed realizes that the fix is in in his court, he may sit quiet, because he knows that he is helpless, or he may raise a lot of hell. If a judge or a prosecutor makes a vitriolic denunciation of a professional thief in court, the thief knows that it does not mean anything. Most of the open-court blastings are made for the benefit of the spectators, newspapers, and crime commissions and are as likely to be made when the fix is in with the judge as when it is in with the coppers. The thief generally knows in advance from the fixers whether he is going to have to take a blasting. If he should receive a blasting without warning, it still means nothing because it is only another blasting, and blastings do not hurt anyone who doesn't listen to them, especially if he has been receiving them all his life.

It is a very rare occurrence when a professional thief has to stand trial by jury, for he exhausts every possible means of handling the case first. If a jury trial is necessary, he tries to get either a rough-neck jury or a blue-ribbon jury. The first is composed of "slaves," such as hard-working laborers, artisans, or truck drivers, who have been battered around by so many laws and officers that they have, if not a disregard for law, at least a feeling of disfavor. The blue-ribbon jury is the opposite, composed of the highest possible type of intelligence. In the first type of case, no finely drawn points are presented, the jurymen lacking the intelligence to see them, but with the blue-ribbon jury finely drawn points are brought in whenever possible. The members of the blue-ribbon jury have never had contact with the police or with criminal practices, and, the whole thing being foreign to them, they are depended upon for their intelligence alone. A jury of this nature will see that the prosecutor is neglecting fine distinctions and is trying to secure a conviction regardless of justice, in contrast with the apparent great battle for justice being waged by the defendant's counsel.

Any jury selected between these two types is dangerous. Small storekeepers, foremen, and minor officials believe that all enforcement officers and prosecuting attorneys are honest and that everyone arrested must be guilty, or he wouldn't have been arrested. They are just about as shrewd as the prosecutor, and they respond to their own type of intelligence. When a decision or instruction unfavorable to the defense is made by the court, the slave jury doesn't understand it and therefore ignores it; the blue-ribbon jury looks for the justice in it and has sufficient intelligence to discern favoritism or prejudice; while the in-between jury takes the remarks of the court as law and never questions them and also generally assays the remarks of the prosecution as pure and truthful. These in-betweens are the type who raise their hats to the prosecutor should they meet him on the street during a recess.

The federal juries are different. In federal courts all jurymen are handpicked and instructed before they are admitted to jury service. An assistant United States attorney is assigned to weed out from the prospective jurors those who may be swayed or impressed by the defense. This is the reason the number of verdicts of acquittals is so small. It has been known in federal courts that when a jury returned a verdict favorable to the defense, the entire jury was excused for the balance of the court term, thus causing them to lose their jobs. They are instructed that they are a part of the government machinery and must carry out the wishes of the government as expressed by the prosecutor. Only rarely do they jeopardize their jobs by turning the defendant loose.

The new law which permits defendants to waive the jury and stand trial before a judge is approved by thieves. It is much harder to straighten out twelve men than one. Even aside from fixing cases, the judge is better acquainted with the police and the prosecutor than the jury is and, consequently, has less confidence in their testimony and oratory.

The professional thief is in favor of probation for young fellows and for old ones, too, but not for himself, as it prevents him from grifting in that state. He is willing to accept probation under certain conditions and then lam, but a case can generally be straightened out without resorting to probation.

The habitual offenders' acts are getting pretty thick, and some thieves say that it will soon be necessary to confine their activities to the federal government, which has no habitual act. When cons get convinced that these habitual laws really mean anything, they will change their tactics. They will get desperate and kill if necessary in order to keep out of prison. If they are sent to prison, they are going to put on a lot of riots, for the prisoner will feel that he is going to die in prison, so why not die trying to get out.

A sentence to a state or federal prison is tough, for it is very difficult and expensive to overcome. If the bit must be served, the important thing is to keep calm and take it easy. No one has trouble in prison if he settles down to do his time and does not make a fuss about it. The trouble is that first-timers are frightened and can't keep calm. After they have been there once or twice, they get philosophical about it.

The stories the cons tell to the psychiatrists, psychologists, and social workers who are supposed to help them adjust to the prison life would make you cry. The first-timers and softies tell long stories with the general theme that everyone else and everything else in the world except themselves were to blame for the crime. The old-timers generally won't talk. The social workers and psychiatrists in one prison tried to get the cons to tell how many sisters were born before they were and how many afterward and the same for brothers. That question about the order of birth burned up the cons. Every time the psychiatrist came around one of the cons would say to another: "Shame on you! A first-born child! How could you expect to be honest?" They did so much kidding about that question that no one would take it seriously. Then, they have so many questions that the con just shuts up and says that, with all due respect, he does not have to take this punishment of answering questions in addition to the two years for which he was sentenced. One of the psychiatrists went to the warden and tried to get an order to compel the cons to answer. The warden said, "You can't make a man talk if he doesn't want to."

The prisoners get in trouble in two ways: one is to get high-hat with the guards and try to fight back; the other is to snitch on other prisoners. It is generally possible to get privileges, like jobs and special food, that help to make prison life tolerable. This can be arranged through friendship, politics, and occasionally for money.[4] But there is little coddling in prison, though we read much

[4] For illustrations of such special privileges see Landesco, "Politics and Administration in the Practice of Penology," *Journal of Criminal Law and Criminology*, XXVI (July, 1935), 239; Hutchins Hapgood, *The Autobiography of a Thief* (New York, 1903), pp. 171–72.

of it in the newspapers. Probably a lot of the stories about coddling start like one which appeared recently. An ex-prisoner from Sing Sing started to blast a friend of his who was a writer and who had just spun a yarn regarding the coddling of prisoners. The reporter replied, "There is no use running off at the chin that way. I wrote that article because I had to." The ex-prisoner said, "You would not write an article like that if you did not believe it, would you?" The reporter replied, "That is my job. I will write anything they tell me to write in whatever way they tell me to write it. If they don't tell me how to write it, I will try to guess from the policy of the paper or the tone of voice of the editor who gives me the assignment. That is the way I find out what to put in an article."

The professional thief, on general principles, is not in favor of capital punishment. But it would be a good thing if some of the nuts who are sent to prison should happen to be hit by an automobile and killed. There is no chance to do anything for them, and death would be the best solution.

The professional thief seldom gets a parole. Because of his long record of arrests, he is held to the full sentence.[5] Consequently he is not personally interested in parole. Otherwise, parole is entirely a matter of politics. The members of the parole board do not often get any money for themselves, but the political go-between who asks for

[5] Eddie Jackson, though a professional thief, secured a parole as soon as he was eligible for it. During his parole period he continued to steal and was, in addition, operating a saloon. When he was caught during this parole period, he straightened out the complaint at a cost of $3,500 (Landesco, "Politics and Administration in the Practice of Penology," *loc. cit.*, p. 244).

favorable consideration in certain cases does get money. This does not apply to federal institutions, where paroles are granted only on the merits of the case unless there are extraordinarily powerful connections.

If a thief should happen to be placed on parole, it would be regarded as good policy to refrain from stealing during the period of parole. The thief does not have a ready method of fixing cases with the parole board as he does with the police and the courts.

In the various relations to the agencies of justice, the thief regards lawyers as necessary.[6] Lawyers come into the life of the thief either on his own choice or by order of the fixer. The thief may by his own choice engage a lawyer to take care of writs of habeas corpus for him and also may engage a lawyer to represent him in criminal cases. For the latter purpose he is generally represented by one of a half-dozen lawyers identified more or less exclusively with criminal defense. Many other lawyers

[6] David Haggart, a Scotch pickpocket in the first quarter of the nineteenth century, stated that pickpockets did not employ lawyers: they either accepted their punishment or else escaped from jail (*The Life of David Haggart* [Edinburgh, 1821], pp. 76, 80, 135–38). Hapgood's thief reported that a lawyer was the fixer for professional criminals in New York City about 1890 (*op. cit.*, p. 87). Ernest Booth quotes the following statement made by a lawyer who had used illegal methods in securing the release of Booth: "Never be broke when you're pinched, kid. We can do nothing for you if you are. You better be careful—but if you stay in town to 'work' and do happen to need me—well, here's my card" (*Stealing through Life* [New York: Alfred A. Knopf, 1929], p. 150 [by permission]). Later Booth attempted to induce a Milwaukee lawyer to take an extradition case on credit and the lawyer replied: "In this game you must pay as you go along. Now as long as you're fighting cases in this State, I would carry you up to several thousand. But an extradition fight is different. If you lose—well, how should I get my money?" So Booth made an arrangement to turn over some of the cars he had stolen as an attorney's fee (*ibid.*, pp. 215–16).

solicit his business, but the professional thief confines his choice to the small number who know exactly how to handle these cases wherein the merits of the case are only the sixteenth consideration.

When the fix is in, legal ability is not necessary. The fixer designates any lawyer of no great reputation; any bright young lawyer just admitted to the bar will do. The lawyer is known by the police, the prosecutor, and the court to be representing the fixer and so things move along smoothly. This lawyer is likely to be changed frequently, for it would look bad on the record to have discharges every time he appeared, in case an investigation should be made. The newspaper reporters know that cases are fixed, but nobody cares particularly what the newspapers say. The important thing is to get in the fix in the lower court, for nobody pays any attention to what happens there. And any lawyer for the fixer can take care of it.

If the case goes to the criminal court, it is customary to use a man with a big reputation as a criminal lawyer. It is reported that years ago Cantwell and Erbstein had a practical monopoly of law business for thieves in Chicago. Erbstein read law and got his training in Cantwell's office, and they carried on together for a time until they quarreled. Half a dozen other lawyers since that time have been known in Chicago as thieves' lawyers, and the same thing is true in the other large cities. A man who was in his younger years a lawyer for the fixer is now a judge. He recently made a confidential statement that he was awfully sorry he had ever been mixed up in that mess, for it might come back at him at any time, but that the only difference is that now he has a dozen bosses in the politicians whereas before he had only one boss in the fixer. He has always been a good lawyer and is a good judge now. If a case of a professional thief comes before him now, he will ask the thief, "Did I ever act as attorney for you?" If the thief answers in the affirmative, the judge will insist that the case be transferred to another judge.

The big lawyer is not used now so much as formerly because more cases are straightened out lower down. But the principle is the same, namely, "Have all arrangements made." Then they had to have a lawyer, while now it is unnecessary except in cases where the fix is not in.

Though the professional thief uses lawyers in these ways and tries to get the most capable lawyers available when he needs one, he believes that few lawyers in any city are honest and that most of them win their cases by using crooked methods. Probably not more than one or two firms in a city would refuse to take a case if a person told them, "I was nudged a little by a streetcar, not enough to hurt any, but I want to sue them anyhow." The firm would take the case, regardless of what they thought of the merits of the case, if they could make some money from either the complainant or the defendant. The more important firms would not take it on a contingent basis, but they would take it if the retainer were large enough. They prefer to take cases which they can win, but more than that they prefer money.

CHAPTER 6
STEALING AS A BUSINESS

Professional stealing as a business is much like any other business. The conversation among thieves in a police station, prison, or hangout is concerned principally with their business, and it is no different in that respect from the conversation of monument salesmen in their meetings. Business possibilities, conditions, and returns are the foremost subjects of conversation, and just as the salesman learns of fertile territory, new methods, new laws which affect the business, so does the thief.

It involves as much hard work as any other business. There is little thrill about it. While a job is being pulled off, there is a tense and emotional situation, and the work cannot be routine. From the start of the actual mechanics of taking off a score until it is completed, the thief is under a strain caused by suspicion, fear of a tumble (not an arrest), saying the right thing at the right time, thought of whether his partners will perform properly, retention of composure, appearance of nonchalance, hard thinking and other things. These are parts of a series of actions which culminate in a touch being taken off or blowed. It is no more thrilling than the work of the factory slave; in both there may be a feeling of work well done when it is over, but this is different from the thrill of a horse race.

It is sometimes said that many thieves, especially women, love to steal. Some thieves who have been exhibitionists and have written their life-histories describe stealing as though it were all very thrilling. They do this to make the story dramatic enough to sell to a publisher. What the hell could anyone find to like about stealing, working hard all the time, always being likely to land in the can, paying over to the coppers and the fixer everything he gets? Writers of detective stories who have never stolen a quarter and have never been deprived of their liberty for an hour are the only ones who can perceive any glamor or pleasure in grifting. The eyesight of the professional thief has not been developed sufficiently to see any pleasure in it. A better description of the professional thief is that he seeks money, not thrills.[1]

[1] This is a point on which there seems to be little agreement. Josiah Flynt Willard quoted a professional thief as follows: "You ask me whether there is any fascination, as you call it, about stealin'. Not a bit. I've never been happy till the job I was doin' was over an' the swag or the dough planted. It's all rot about there bein' any fun in crooked work" (*The World of Graft* [New York, 1901], p. 102). A professional con man in prison at the time he read this manuscript stated: "There is no thrill in stealing. It is a business pure and simple, and the thief after a day's work could qualify as a tired business man. I consider this paragraph the best statement of fact in his entire work." A professional bank robber, also in prison, commented: "It is only the writers for the *Detective Story Magazine* who think the professional thief seeks thrills. Once I was asked what the cause of crime was and answered: Shortage of bucks. It is certainly the money and not the thrills that causes most crime."

On the other hand, the following statements are somewhat opposed: "There is also a fascination about crime which appeals to him [the young fellow from the slums]. Men describe it differently, but they all agree that it has a great deal to do in making criminals. My own idea is that it lies in the excitement of trying to elude justice" (Josiah Flynt Willard, *Notes of an Itinerant Policeman*, p. 38). A confidence man who had followed carnivals for thirty years, after two years of legitimate life, wrote: "Sometimes I see a stranger who looks like easy money. Sometimes a fellow with good-thing printed all over him, struts into my hotel. Then the old feeling rises up under my vest and makes me itch to get at him. Perhaps I can make

141

Every professional thief would pack in the racket tomorrow if he could get a legitimate job sufficiently remunerative to meet what he believed to be his necessary living costs. The thieves who get four or five thousand dollars in a winter's work generally do no grifting until the following winter, although there are plenty of lucrative spots and rackets available. They have enough to live on decently, and they stop grifting.

There is no way to compute the earnings of any thief. He does not keep books and does not remember his income, and no thief tells another how much money he is making. The earnings are very irregular. A cannon mob which had averaged $15 or $20 each daily made a touch of $2,800 one morning, but during the next month the top score was $110. Some mobs make it a rule to pack in each day as soon as they have knocked up $25, $35, or

it clear to you in this way: You like hunting? You know your sensation when a buck steps out of cover and you lift your gun to cover him? Well, it's like that, only a hundred times stronger. There's no hunting in the world like hunting men" (Will Irwin, *Confessions of a Con Man* [New York: Viking Press, 1909], p. 182 [by permission]). Eddie Jackson, the pickpocket, wrote: "I liked this racket for the fascination and freedom. I could lay off any time—my boys never kicked if I wanted to lay off. I would stick to my business even though I knew that if I stayed I would have more 'falls.' " Jackson's wife attempted to induce him to quit the racket and go into legitimate business, and he had money enough to permit him to do this. His reaction was: "I liked the excitement of the racket, the politics, and the fixing—the successes and the failures. . . . . You see there was a good deal of excitement and interest and some skill involved in the racket—and it was not an easy thing to separate from it for the sake of Miss Blank" (John Landesco, "The Woman and the Underworld," *Journal of Criminal Law and Criminology*, XXVI [March,1936], 895–96). A confidence man who followed carnivals wrote: "I get an awful wallop out of seeing someone clipped, and the humorous side of the thing appeals to me. I like to beat a sucker." See, also, the quotation from Norfleet, below, p. 184, n. 9.

$50, the amount varying with different mobs. But the annual earnings cannot be computed from this, for on some days they fail to realize the amount set, and on other days they may exceed the amount.

Likewise it is impossible to estimate how much he will have at the end of the year. He is likely to have $4 on New Year's Day one year, and $1,000 the next, be $1,000 in debt the next, and have forty cents the next. Most thieves are broke two or three times during a year, though there are a few who continue to add to their savings each year. One thief got $5,500 ahead and furnished an apartment, but within a month he had to sacrifice it for $2,500 to straighten out a very bad case. Another thief got $6,000 for his end of a touch, bought a car for $4,500 and within two months had to give the car to a bondsman. Another bought a home for $15,000, and in about a year had to mortgage it to straighten out a case, and in less than another year had to sacrifice his equity in the house to keep out of the can in another case.[2]

Likewise it is impossible to determine the average

[2] Eddie Jackson reported that it was a poor week when he got less than $1,500 for his own personal income from picking pockets (Landesco, "The Criminal Underworld of Chicago in the Eighties and Nineties," *Journal of Criminal Law and Criminology*, XXV [September, 1934], 345). The newspapers reported that a pickpocket mob in New York City in 1934 secured $1,100 from one victim and in Chicago $4,750. In September, 1933, the police estimated that pickpockets in the Chicago Fair had secured at least $20,000 in Railway Express money orders alone and that the total in all kinds of valuables would run into many hundreds of thousands of dollars. The confidence game yields larger returns per victim on the average. The con mob which beat Norfleet boasted that it took ten million dollars from American victims each year and almost as much more from the English (*Norfleet: The Actual Experiences of a Texas Rancher's 30,000-Mile Transcontinental Chase after Five Confidence Men* [Sugar Land, Tex., 1927], p. 381). Jackie French had a famous week in Florida in February, 1922, when he

amount required to fix a case. The simplest kind of pick-up will cost $50 to fix. If it is a three-handed mob, and all three are picked up, $150 must be knocked up before there is any money to pay the hotel bill. A $35 touch may cost $3,500 to square. Naturally the fixer gets the first call on any money knocked up if they are indebted to him.[3]

It is believed that the majority of thieves would gladly swap incomes and business expenses with the union carpenter who is working steadily. They have a bank balance sufficient to meet an ordinary emergency, while the thief lives in a hotel with all his worldly possessions in his trunk. If an emergency arises, he grifts so hard and so recklessly that another emergency is born of the first.

---

took $345,000 from three victims (Philip S. Van Cise, *Fighting the Underworld* [New York, 1936], p. 109). The state's attorney of Cook County, Illinois, in December, 1924, stated that Kid Weil and his troupe had taken more than a million dollars within six months in the Middle West and that he had a list of twenty persons who had been swindled for as much as one hundred thousand dollars each. The sums taken by confidence men in the Chicago Fair were probably smaller on the average, but they included $34,000 from Malone and Carter, of Sheboygan, $8,000 from Angerstrom, of East Rockaway, New York, $37,000 from Wilson, of Des Moines, $500 from John Allan, the house detective of the Dearborn Plaza Hotel. One of the men involved in these offenses was Harry Lewiston, who had a record for con games dating back to 1900, including $25,000 from Johnson, a St. Louis confectioner in 1922. William Elmer Mead, professional confidence man, known as the Christ Kid, beat Harrison, of Jefferson City, out of $50,000 in 1933, Barker, of Beverly, Massachusetts, of $59,000 in 1932, and Martin, of Jacksonville, Florida, of $11,360 in 1934. The federal authorities plan to accuse him of income-tax shortage of $60,000 for eight years, 1921–28, and have filed a lien against Chicago real estate which he holds.

[3] Josiah Flynt Willard reached the conclusion from questioning thieves that thieves pay fully half and perhaps two-thirds of their income for protection to the policemen, the prosecutors, their attorneys, and others (*op. cit.*, p. 158).

A depression is as hard on a thief as anyone else. Pocketbooks which used to show $40, $50, or $100 show only $3, $5, or $10. Merchandise declines in value, so that the booster cannot steal enough to live on, or find purchasers for what he steals. But the costs of the coppers, fixers, and lawyers do not decrease, and fines remain as heavy as in boom years. A con man who got a job as driver for a bus company during a depression had a wage of $35 per week, and the thieves who met him invariably told him that he was better off than they were.[4]

In some of the rackets the thieves get money, and in others they get merchandise. They get money on the cannon, the con, and the shake, and merchandise on the boost, heel, pennyweight, and hotel prowl.[5] Thieves who

[4] A confidence man who followed carnivals wrote: "I do not agree that the average thief would gladly swap incomes with a steadily employed carpenter. This is not true of any thief I ever met. The only time a man is apt to make comparisons is when he gets in prison or gets in a jam, and then the feeling is only temporary. Unless the author were stealing more than $50 a week, which is what a carpenter would get from steady work, he is by no means a professional thief. I get letters in here frequently from fellows on the racket. They all agree that things are awfully tough and they frequently change from one racket to another. But none of them are going to work. Once a fellow has had a taste of high life it is darn hard for them to get used to just plain living again. When thieves do go to work it is with the idea that they will 'cop the edge' or apply some method of larceny in the job."

[5] The method of dividing the proceeds of a theft in Kid Weil's mob of confidence men is described as follows: "They meet in a prearranged place and wait until all are present. With all of us gathered around the table the bag is opened and the money is dumped carelessly in a pile in the center. Expenses come off the top. . . . . By expenses I mean the money spent by the several mobsmen out of their own pockets for their parts in the play. If I, for instance, have been working two weeks, living at different hotels, traveling, engaging motor cars, I figure the total cost up and announce the total as we all sit around the table. . . . . I say, for example, two hundred dollars. He peels two hundred dollars off the

steal clothing, jewelry, and such articles dispose of them in various ways. They sell much of it to so-called fences, for these persons maintain a market at all times and always have money to pay for goods. Each outfit may have its own spot for disposal of its articles.[6] Also, thieves generally sell many articles to other thieves or to semilegitimate friends, and to coppers, prosecutors, and others in public positions.[7]

A few heels or boosters steal to exact order—perhaps not more than six in the United States and none at all in Europe.[8] The customer will ask the booster to get a small-size mink coat, or a size sixteen dress, or a specific kind of

---

top and tosses it to me. He looks at the next man and that one names a figure. It is handed him without a word. . . . . We trust each other. No lengthy itemized expense accounts. Some of the boys couldn't add one up if they had to. No quibbling over taxi bills and tips to bellboys. . . . . In all my life I never heard of a racket man padding an expense account. We're honest. . . . . After the 'top money' has been paid out, we cut the rest according to an agreed-upon plan. The Yellow Kid and Buckmeister naturally took larger shares than the rest of us" (Mort King, "The Secrets of Yellow Kid Weil," *Real Detective Tales*, January, 1931, p. 45).

[6] See David Haggart, *The Life of David Haggart* (Edinburgh, 1821), pp. 38, 67, 69, 79; *Report of* [Chicago] *City Council Committee on Crime* (Chicago, 1915), pp. 166–70.

[7] A high-class confidence man wrote: "A number of boost mobs have a kind of clientele or trade. After they obtain a certain amount of goods, they make the rounds and call on their customers like legitimate salesmen and show them their stock. These customers are often thieves in other rackets, kept ladies, former members of the profession who are now on the legit; strange as it may seem, there are no small number of strictly legitimate people on the list of customers."

[8] The testimony of others does not agree in regard to the extent of stealing to order. A con man who worked around carnivals wrote: "The statement that there are perhaps not more than six heels or boosters in the United States who steal to order is certainly wrong. I have come into contact with hundreds myself who would take your order and then go

luggage, or anything else. The thief tells the customer to examine the article in the store, get the stock number and price, and report to him. When the customer returns with this information, the thief will quote a price and, if agreeable, will attempt to get the article. If he is unable to get it in a day or two, he will send the customer to another store for the necessary information there and try to get it in that store.

Stealing to order is more dangerous than ordinary stealing because it may take the thief a longer time to determine the location of the article, and it may require two trips, which increase the danger of identification. It is probably because of this danger that so few thieves undertake this type of stealing. But it yields better returns than to steal something first and then try to find someone who wants to buy it.

The most successful heels never cut any price agreed upon and never lie about the articles they have stolen. If his reputation is such as it should be, there is no ground for controversy or sparring—it is either a sale or it is not. But some customers try to beat the thief down in his

---

out and procure the article. Over a period of at least six years every suit I owned was procured from a boost mob, and I would specify color, size, and manufacture." Another confidence man who specialized in high finance wrote: "Stealing to order by boosters is quite frequent. There are a few mobs which steal only to order, but they are the exception. These mobs are probably the highest type of boost mobs there are. In addition there is hardly any boost mob working which will not take an order and do its level best to fill it." A professional bank burglar wrote: "In all my experience I have heard of only one case of 'stealing to order.' This does not mean that there may not have been much of it going on, for I was always careful to stay away from boost mobs. As a matter of fact I have never in my life worn a piece of stolen clothing. This is not a matter of morals but of common sense."

price, as in the case of a customer who asked a thief to get her a black foxskin, priced at $695 in the store. The thief agreed to get it for her for $300 and returned with it in half an hour. The customer, feeling that the thief was making $300 too easily, started to find reasons why it did not suit her and wailed about it not being worth $300. Finally the thief, tired and disgusted, threw the skin to his wife, saying "Here, take this and wrap it around your neck when you go to the grocery store." The customer left, very angry, but later sent her husband back with $300 to get the skin. The thief refused to sell it, explaining that the customer had tried to make a sucker out of him and that she could go to the store and buy a black fox fur if she still wanted one. This is unusual because the customer is getting the exact article wanted at a greatly reduced price and generally takes it eagerly.

The thief who does stealing to order does not drum up orders. When it becomes known that he specializes in this particular field, the customer will look him up, approaching him through someone else if they are not personally acquainted with him. Those who steal articles to order are generally interested in some other racket and steal to order only as a side line or between touches in their other racket.

A great many articles are sold to the public by jobbers who buy direct from the thief. A thief may steal four dozen pairs of women's silk hose of a standard brand and sell them to someone else who goes at the lunch hour to an office building where many girls work and offers them for sale at a price far below the standard price, generally explaining that the price is low because the stockings were stolen. Before the war, people would have called the police if any stolen articles were offered for sale, but no one complains now.

The fixer has no connection with the disposal of the stolen property. On rare occasion he may ask a heel or booster to get some particular article which he wants as a gift to someone. But he never has anything in his house or office or on his person which he did not purchase legitimately.

In a large city there is no standard or restricted area where a mob would grift. There are many spots where the grift is lucrative, but the same mob would not work there continuously because of the danger that a victim of yesterday might recognize them today. The shopping districts are the spots where moll-buzzers do their best work. Railroad stations, steamship docks, and similar points where transients congregate are the best spots for mobs on the short con, and hotel lobbies for mobs on the major con rackets. The boosters concentrate on the better stores in the central business district but sometimes get forced out of this district because it is burned out for them. They have been spotted in all the stores, are known as professional thieves, and have to get out of that territory. Some of them work the outlying stores, such as those on Sixty-third Street or Milwaukee Avenue in Chicago, or in the suburbs, such as Evanston, Oak Park, or Aurora. Aurora is the town they hit hardest, for it is near by, there is good transportation, and it is a good-sized city. For cannon mobs every streetcar crossing is a potential field, but most of the transfer points are not lucrative, and consequently the ones which are found to be fruitful get a strong play. The get-ons outside large factories or business centers get a strong play, too. There,

is no cannon mob which grifts continuously in the central business district. Most of the local mobs sneak into this district at intervals and grift for a few hours and then get out because the coppers know them and it is too hot for extended grift. Out-of-town cannon mobs, however, may grift the central business district for a week at a time.[9]

When a mob has exceptionally good luck at some spot, the other thieves go there too, thinking they may be as lucky as the first mob. But frequently, when a big touch comes off, it heats up the spot, and other mobs learn that and keep away from there. Every thief picked up there for the next month will be accused of getting the big score.

No good racket ever gets worn out in a particular city. It may be necessary to change the details of the racket so that it will not be so readily recognized and in order to keep ahead of the information about it. But every one of the principal rackets is being worked by professional thieves constantly in every city.

There are a few thieves in every racket who for years

[9] The places at which arrest of pickpockets are reported by the police include all kinds of places in which crowds congregate, such as the automobile races, state fairs, church conventions, football games, political rallies and conventions, on subway and elevated trains, and around theater entrances. A pickpocket mob followed Governor Talmadge on his campaign speeches in Georgia, but also a mob was busy in Rockford, Illinois, during the Lutheran convention. While the crowd awaited the announcement of the Hauptmann verdict in New Jersey, a pickpocket mob was collecting pocketbooks. In earlier days it was a part of the technique to attract a crowd so that pickpockets could operate. In Chicago one of the Schultz brothers was called "Pin-Cushion Mike" because he would stand at a busy intersection and stick needles through his arms, cheeks, and other parts of his body in order to attract a crowd, while his brother relieved the members of the crowd of everything of value.

at a time never leave their home towns. But most mobs become too well known to the police to remain permanently in their home town. Consequently they establish headquarters there and work in and out of that city. They arrange an itinerary, follow it for perhaps two months, and then go home and loaf until ready for another trip. This itinerary is never followed exactly. They may plan to work a week in a town but take off a hot one the first day and for safety's sake leave at once. They may leave at once, also, because warned by a private protective agency which they know to be incorruptible; it is rare that this order is not obeyed. In some cases an outfit will have bad luck in the city, making only enough money for the coppers, fixers, and lawyers, and will move to another city on that account. If a new or right administration is installed in a particular city, thieves will jump to that city and abandon their itinerary.[10]

Cannon mobs are more likely to grift one city for a longer time than any other mob is because they are not so much limited to a few spots or stores as are heels, boosters, and con men. But many mobs grift on the road the greater part of the time. Mobs grifting out of Chicago cover the entire Middle West, those out of New York cover the East and the South, while St. Paul mobs

[10] A con man writes: "There have been from time to time various cities which were positively known to be strictly one hundred per cent right. These cities were made the headquarters of quite a few big-time mobs, con mobs, pete mobs, and also petty racketeers, bank heists, etc. They paid for protection and received it. At no time, however, and this was an agreement, did they ever work in the city in which they resided, and from those cities it was practically impossible to take them at any time. If they were telegraphed for, the report would go back that they were not in that city. If out-of-town dicks came they would be arrested first by the local dicks, let out on bond, and given the chance to lam."

cover the American and Canadian Northwest. These mobs are likely to leave their usual territory at any time to make a trip into new territory. Most professional thieves have worked in every city in the country. If one member of a mob is a bad lamster there, a city might be closed to a mob. If that city is a very good spot, the mob would fill in another man for the stay in that city, and the member would be picked up later.

The higher-class boosting mobs plan similar itineraries, confining themselves somewhat more to the larger cities and also working in sections somewhat as the cannon mobs do. The type of merchandise most lucrative for boosters is not found in smaller cities, and also it is more difficult to make a getaway in smaller cities.

In Boston there is an organization of roving store detectives, who are continually in and out of the business places of their members. Some Fifth Avenue merchants in New York have the same kind of protection. In Chicago and most other cities each store has its own detectives. The roving detectives make stealing tough, for the thief does not know when an apparent customer may prove to be a store detective. Also, with that system a detective may follow a suspect from one store to another, whereas the individually protected store has no interest in a suspect once he has left the store.

In the event a mob were going to grift the winter in Florida, some mobs would grift all the larger cities en route, while others would not stop until they reached their destination. No mob would grift on the road if it were going to some spot in Florida to grift right because they might have the misfortune to get a bad pinch which would interfere with grifting under ideal conditions. This applies as well to a mob going to some big doings where it is expected that plenty of money will be made, such as a political convention. As a rule, the mob arrives in the city the day the doings start because earlier the imported coppers are moping around the stations and streets to catch thieves who may come in. These coppers flock to the doings as soon as the session begins, leaving the city wide open in order to hear the political spellbinders. No one tries to steal anything on the floor of the convention hall, but the hotels where the important men with important money remain are good spots at this time.

Certain types of theft or certain spots in which lucrative stealing may be done are sometimes suggested by persons who are not specialists in the particular racket. This is known as a putup, and the person who suggests the spot gets 10 per cent of the proceeds but may get more if the spot is unusually easy. In earlier days bellboys and porters in hotels entered into collusion with professional thieves in this way, but this is now generally out, principally because the bellboys do all the stealing themselves.

CHAPTER 7

THE SOCIAL AND PERSONAL LIFE OF THE THIEF

The personal life of the professional thief is somewhat distinct from his professional life. Thieves may be personally unfriendly and still work together in perfect cooperation. Similarly the fixer may feel unfriendly toward a thief but still go for him. This shows that these professional relations are commercial and not based on sentiment or friendship.

The professional thief has a wife, or else lives for a long time with the same woman if either of them has an undissolved previous marriage which prevents them from remarrying. He does not bring a strange woman to his room because of the danger involved in having strangers around. But the unattached thief, while in a hotel, may chase any woman he sees, just as does the traveling salesman, or the doctor who is attending a convention, or the rancher who is attending a stock show in the city.[1]

[1] Hapgood's thief said he generally had a girl living with him and that there was a "long succession" of such girls (Hutchins Hapgood, *Autobiography of a Thief* [New York, 1903], p. 125). Furey, one of the confidence mob which swindled Norfleet, had two homes; one home was in a very good residential district in Los Angeles, where he had a fine son and a wife who was opposed to stealing; in the other home was a wife who apparently had some connection with the rackets (J. Frank Norfleet, *Norfleet: The Actual Experiences of a Texas Rancher's 30,000-Mile Transcontinental Chase after Five Confidence Men* [Fort Worth, 1924], pp. 128–30, 147–48, 175, 199, 203, 219–21). Eddie Jackson, the Chicago pickpocket, had five wives: (a) a

154

The standard of proper treatment of the wife of a thief is the same as for a legitimate person—just as well as he can and just as well as she will let him. But if he does not observe that standard, no other thief interferes, for it is regarded as a personal and private matter. If a thief kicked his wife around (which he doesn't) or cheated on his wife (which he does), the other thieves would do nothing about it, though they might say, "Isn't it a damn shame the way he treats her? Why in hell doesn't she quit him?" But the wives are generally able to take care of themselves, for in some cases they have been thieves or prostitutes previously and in any case are fully capable of making a living. Realizing their independence, thieves do not as a rule give their wives much the worst of it if they wish to keep them.

These wives do not work while they are living with professional thieves. They lead a strictly social life and have no income except from their own men.

Thieves who grift winter resorts generally take their wives or girls with them and establish a home there for the winter. But if they are on the road, just working a few days in a city, they practically never take their wives.

---

brothel madam who mothered him during his early life; (*b*) a conventional woman who had nothing to do with his mob and who bore him a child; (*c*) a companionate wife whom he could not marry because his former wife would not grant him a divorce, but for whom he felt a real affection; she knew that he was a thief and she liked his companions but she attempted to change him to a life on a legal plane; (*d*) a rich but degenerate wife whom he married while drunk and who meant nothing to him; (*e*) a wife whom he really loved in his later years when he was rich and engaged in the liquor business as well as stealing (John Landesco, "The Woman and the Underworld," *Journal of Criminal Law and Criminology*, XXVI [March, 1936], 891–902).

Rather they establish a home for them somewhere and work in and from that city.

The thief depends on his wife for assistance in his business in certain respects. If one of the members of a mob gets a pinch while on the road, and the town is too hot for the other members to arrange matters, they may send for one of the wives. She would be met in a near-by town and instructed what to do.

If a thief has to do a bit, his wife is expected to keep him informed of any developments, of changes in political parties or enforcement officials, or of contacts which might be taken advantage of to shorten her man's bit. If money will help her spring her man, she informs other mobs, and they get her the money. She handles the situation in all its other angles.

While he is in the can, she either goes to work legitimately, rejoins her family, or is cared for by other thieves. Since a great many thieves have her needs in mind, it is not long until something is found for her whereby she can make a living. She will rarely turn to stealing because there is the possibility that she will get a bit, too, and then be unable to assist her man. The home of any thief is always open to her so long as she deports herself properly, and she generally does deport herself properly. It is not meant that all wives and girls are Penelopes, but there is an economic soundness in a woman being on the square with her man while he is in the can because any looseness on her part soon becomes generally known, and she sacrifices all assistance, which is considerable, that she might receive from thieves and mobs.

Thieves determine their places of residence in accordance with their tastes.[2] Every mode of home is used—loop hotels, hotels near the loop, hotels in residence areas, furnished apartments, unfurnished apartments, and suburban homes. Probably a majority live in or near the central business district. They practically never live in the hotels known as right hotels, which are protected by the police. No professional thief would depend on that protection, for the major income of the hotel is from prostitutes who are hustling the streets, and no hotel will jeopardize its major income from prostitutes by protecting a thief who may, at most, be paying $28 for a room each week. The only right hotel for a professional thief is the most legitimate one he can find. If he minds his own business, keeps his mouth shut, and conducts himself properly in the hotel, he will never be bothered, no matter how respectable and exclusive the hotel may be.

In the past when grifting resorts, the thieves lived in the smaller isolated hotels. The other thieves still do this, but the con men for business reasons now make early reservations at the larger hotels and arrive with golf bags and plus fours. They mix a great deal more than they used to do with the regular guests, which gives them

[2] Heindl in his study of the professional criminal reports that a study of professional criminals in France in 1869 and another study of the same group in 1894 agreed in the conclusion that the places of residence of professional criminals were in the slums immediately adjacent to the central business district of Paris, where the streets are narrow and unlighted, the buildings old and unsightly, and where prostitutes were easily accessible; moreover, he contends that the reports of the police departments of the large European cities show that the same condition is found in all of them and has been so for fifty years. He is not speaking exclusively of professional criminals in the sense here defined but of a larger group which includes burglars, robbers, and all other criminals except the occasional criminal (Robert Heindl, *Der Berufsverbrecher* [5th ed.; Berlin, 1927], pp. 221–22).

157

an opportunity to put the story into more people. Also, whereas in the past the women in these resorts were never prospects for con games, many women are played for now.

When thieves finish the day's work, they generally congregate in hangouts. There they are thieves together regardless of their rackets, with one common love—money—and one common enemy—the law. In the old days the hangouts were almost always saloons. In Chicago, Andy Craig's saloon on South State Street was one of the principal places for thieves, for Andy himself was reputed to have been a cannon in his earlier days and was known by all thieves. Other saloons on the edge of the Loop were used by the professional thieves in general, while the thieves who were home boys used saloons a little farther out.[3] At present the speakeasies, restaurants,

[3] The relation between the hangout, the fixer, and politics is shown in the following quotation from Landesco's life of Eddie Jackson, the Chicago pickpocket: "In 1886 Al Connolly, first ward committeeman, was the fix for the pickpockets and was at the same time the maker of councilmen who are still in the city council. He had a saloon near Harrison and State Streets and fixed at the Central Station and other places. . . . . " Bob Duncan had been a pickpocket for a time, robbed his brother-in-law, was committed to prison and paroled, and then later "he became an important figure due to the fact that his saloon became a central hang-out for crooks of all kinds. Later Bob Duncan had two saloons, one near 500 South State Street, and the other near 400 South State Street. Both of them were hangouts for safe blowers who hung around dressed in overalls and black shirts like bums. They would lay 'it' [the loot] all down at one saloon and would stay there for days and drink until the bartender would tell them they were broke. At one of these saloons Bob Duncan had a resort for crooks. It was a music hall. All the girls were soliciting. There were rooms upstairs and music, dancing and drinking in the basement. There was gambling, craps, faro, two or three poker games, draw and stud poker. About 1900 Bob Duncan's saloon became the center for pickpockets. At this time Bob Duncan must have had ten different pickpocket

cigar stores and such places are used, but they are not used as permanently and generally as headquarters for thieves as the old saloons were. Practically every mob has its own hangout now and, in the majority of cases, in a place of legitimate business. Members of a mob who are grifting in town may drop into a cigar store a couple of evenings a week and stand around chewing the fat for a while, naturally meeting other thieves who frequent that spot. Hundreds of other thieves never go near that spot, having a place somewhere else where they hang out. It is rare when more than two or three outfits make it a practice to hang out in the one spot continually. Moreover, thieves do not hang out there constantly, and

---

mobs hanging around his place. Councilman O'Leary and King were his friends. There was not so much cold cash. Favors were paid by spending over the bar. There was 'peter' men and crooks of all types hanging around Duncan's. Nine times out of ten he didn't want anyone in until 2 P.M. The girls were not hustling until two in the afternoon. This was before the one o'clock closing law [1 A.M.]. When the public 'suckers' began coming in, we of the mobs would all go downstairs to the gambling which opened at 8 P.M.

"Another resort in the 90's and in the early part of the century was William Rourke's on the North Side near Kinzie Street and Clark Street. Rourke's was a big gambling house and he was known as boss of the North Side as a Democratic politician under Thomas McCarthy. He was a bondsman and fixer; he did his fixing as political favors. 'None of us paid, but all of us gambled and drank in his saloon.' On the West Side Jimmy Calhoun's gambling house and saloon was the fix and the crook's hangout. The same friendly relation, spending over his bar and helping him at election time existed. . . . . " A little later "Busse was the mayor and was a good fellow among all classes, the bankers downtown as well as the thieves at William Rourke's house. 'When Mayor Busse came into Casey's at Taylor and Clark, tables were drawn together, and if fifteen people were around the table twelve of them were thieves, with Busse buying for everybody!" (Landesco, "The Criminal Underworld of Chicago in the Eighties and Nineties," *Journal of Criminal Law and Criminology*, XXV [September, 1934], 341–58).

there is nothing significant in a place to identify it as a hangout for thieves.[4]

If a well-known thief for any reason finds it necessary to see some other thief, he can easily find out where he hangs out and can go there and find out where he may be at the time and what he is doing. Should a stranger go in and ask for the same thief, even though the thief may be standing within hearing distance, the stranger will be told that the person for whom he inquires was never heard of but that the stranger may leave his name and the message will be delivered if the person comes in. The place of residence of a thief is generally known to his intimate friends, except in dope circles. The dope-fiend thief guards his address most carefully as he cannot stand to have coppers come to his room because he has dope there most of the time.

In addition to these hangouts, there are restaurants which are on the border line. These are regular restaurants during the daytime, patronized by legitimate customers, but at night they are patronized principally by thieves. The proprietors are generally not thieves and get no share, but they want to sell their food and selling it to thieves is better than not selling it at all. In the same way every other large city has its hangouts for thieves and its borderline restaurants. In New York they are generally found near Broadway and Forty-seventh Street, near the hotel and theater district.

[4] For descriptions and discussions of the social life and hangouts of thieves see David Haggart, *The Life of David Haggart* (Edinburgh, 1821), p. 50; J. G. W. Colburn, *The Life of Sile Doty* (Toledo, 1880); George M. White, *From Boniface to Bank Burglar* (New York, 1907); Hapgood, *op. cit.*, p. 75; *Report of the* [Chicago] *City Council Committee on Crime* (Chicago, 1915), pp. 162–63.

When the hangouts were in the saloons, the thieves who had been stealing all day spent the proceeds drinking all night. That type is rare now, and thieves seem to have more business acumen than they did then. Some of the money now secured from stealing goes into gambling, and it ought to be understood that the patrons of gambling houses are confined almost entirely to the underworld. If you go into any gambling house in any city, you will find the crowd made up of bootleggers, pimps, whores, and thieves. There is hardly a respectable person in the ordinary gambling place, unless you call the politicians respectable, for many of them go there too. But there is not much sense in the statement that gambling places are kept open because respectable people demand such places. This is not true of the horse poolrooms, where 95 per cent of the play is by legitimate persons.

Aside from the unusual expenditures for drinking in the old days and for gambling both then and now, and aside from the business expenses (for most of the thief's income goes to the coppers, lawyers, and fixers), the thieves spend their money in much the same way as does the average citizen. The thief's recreations are perhaps milder than those of the average citizen—movies, theaters, and an occasional night of cabareting which is more for business reasons than anything else, since he hopes to see and be seen by politicians, fixers, and similar people who operate and patronize places of this sort. Most thieves manage to spend a few weeks at the lakes in the summer and at the springs late in the winter, but these are purely recreational trips with no thought of grifting.

Some thieves spend their money on junk (narcotic

drugs). When they do this, they start secretly, not wanting anyone to know of it. Some of them keep up the deception for some time. They are ashamed to let this be known because thieves believe that a dope fiend is not as reliable or capable as one who is not a user. Many outfits will not permit a user to work with them.

Surplus funds seldom bother the thief. A few buy real estate if they happen to get a surplus; they seldom invest in securities. Many of them who have as much as one thousand dollars knocked up keep it sewed up in their clothes so it will be ready in case of an emergency. Others maintain safety-deposit boxes in banks which will permit the keys to be left in the office, and others have savings accounts and leave the book in the bank. No thief wants to have a box key or a bankbook on him when arrested, as it would cause the coppers to believe he had plenty of money, and they would put the sting on stronger than usual. Checking accounts are rarely used, first, because too many questions are asked when an account is opened and, second, because a check is of value to a thief only among his friends. There are, however, banks in the larger cities which cater to the accounts of thieves, knowing them to be such, and accept their deposits without the regular routine. There is another type of thief who sends his surplus funds to some legitimate person for safe keeping, feeling that his money would be more accessible there than in a bank and safer than on his person. The main consideration in any method used is ready accessibility. If the money is not immediately available, the opportunity for a quick and cheap straightening out of the case may be lost.

Thieves generally pay their legitimate bills. When a

thief rents an apartment or house, he is usually asked for a reference. This is taken care of by a connection with an office-holder or a friend in a legitimate occupation who will vouch for him. The person in a legitimate occupation knows that no trouble will come from this, for the thief does not want to let down a friend who has involved himself on his behalf and also because he knows it would be economically unsound. A case is recalled where a judge sublet his apartment to a thief who had been a defendant in his court several times, with full knowledge that the thief would occupy it. The judge knew that the thief would pay his rent and would bring no heat to the judge or to the apartment. In this case the judge, of course, did not have any direct contact with the thief in subleasing the apartment.

When a thief beats a hotel bill in a place where he is known, it is thought to be very poor judgment by the other thieves. It is rarely necessary to do this, where one is known as a thief, because he can always go to the manager, tell him he is broke and wants to go on the road for a while and will pay his bill upon his return. The manager will always agree to this because he knows that the thief will beat him anyway if he objects.

Thieves will beat every hotel when making a trip. This is the rule rather than the exception. In this way they have the best place to live in every city and no expense. This is rarely done by broke guys because, if they got a tumble, they would be unable to pay their bill, and it would mean another trip to the can. Sometimes the beating of a hotel bill is very expensive, for he may get a bit for beating the hotel and also get caught on other bills.

The thief generally has a few friends who are perfectly legitimate in their occupations and behavior. The thief prefers the companionship of his own kind, but some of his legitimate friendships are kept alive for years, even though contacts are made infrequently. Persons who are not criminals are known and liked by thieves in exactly the same way that thieves are known and liked. There is no degree of ill feeling or contempt for these persons because they are not thieves. Anyone whom he considers as a friend is aware that he is a thief, for he never has any friendships that are not genuine. Not all of these friends condone his means of livelihood, but, since they are not affected by his business, there is no danger to them in these friendships.

The thief does not call upon these legitimate friends for assistance that is not perfectly legitimate. Sometimes a reference is needed when renting an apartment, opening a savings account, buying an automobile, or other transactions. The thief feels free to call upon his friends in the legitimate world for this purpose and will never do anything to jeopardize this person.

These personal acquaintances of the thief are scattered in various occupations, but are rarely among preachers, social workers, or other reformers. Also they are very rarely in the radical group of communists or anarchists. They are generally in business.

The professional thief also has semilegitimate acquaintances among lawyers, fences, fixers, bondsmen, and politicians. These are persons who are making money from the thief but are supposed to be members of legitimate society. He may call upon them, also, for assistance for the less legitimate purposes, such as a statement that the thief is employed by them.

164

The thief is somewhat suspicious of all individuals in legitimate society other than those mentioned. He believes that whoever is not with him is against him. Any noncriminal individual not personally known to the thief is a possible danger and, as an individual, is somewhat disliked on that account. This feeling is reinforced by occasional trouble which results from perfectly proper acquaintances. A certain thief, while making a coast-to-coast trip, became acquainted with a Greek who could not talk English very plainly. A very casual acquaintance was formed on this trip. On the return trip the thief found the same Greek on the train, and the acquaintance developed a little further, merely as a means of passing the time. When the train reached Pittsburgh, where the Greek wanted to locate some friends but did not know just how to do it, the thief volunteered to go into the station with him and phone to the friends. As soon as the thief appeared in the station with this Greek, a private detective working for the railways, who was himself an ex-thief, saw and recognized him and started to make a pinch. The thief tried to explain, the Greek became excited, and it looked like a sure-enough pinch. The Greek disappeared and soon returned with a couple of Greeks from a restaurant across the street who could interpret for the excited Greek. They informed the copper that the thief was merely trying to be benevolent in an honest way and that no story had been put in and no designs were had against the Greek. This illustrates the danger that the thief may run into if he tries to make legitimate contacts with strangers.

Because of this, the professional thief lives largely in a world of his own and is rather completely isolated from

165

general society. The majority of them do not care to contact society except professionally. They do not occupy conspicuous seats in theaters or restaurants because they may be recognized by victims of the past. They have favorite restaurants and avoid the larger and louder showplaces. In spite of precautions, they are sometimes recognized, and this may cost them considerable money to straighten out. This does not, of course, stop anyone from stealing any more than it stops them from eating in a restaurant. It is just another one of those things in the life of the thief.[5]

The thief will generally avoid others in public places. When he makes a railroad jump and is not grifting the

[5] A professional thief who had read the manuscript wrote regarding these paragraphs: "I believe that the average thief acts just like any other person in the same economic class. If he has $60 in his pocket and nothing to worry about, he'll do the same things any other person would in the same circumstances. The author states that the professional thief does not occupy conspicuous seats in theaters and restaurants, fearful that he might be recognized by some victim of the past. Considering that the guy is stealing over a period of years, where in the Hell is he going to eat? I believe that they act just like anybody else would. In my experience, after the scores are made and there was no rumble about the taking of the score, I immediately forget all about it. The only time I might ever think of it again was if I happened to pass the place where the score was taken, which I have done a number of times. This is especially true in any large city. Of course in a smaller town extra precautions must be taken because there are probably only two eating places in the town, but even then the only chance of your attracting attention is that you are a stranger. Even then anyone in the racket need not hide or stay out of the limelight. For over a period of five years I was connected with carnivals, going from town to town, staying only a week at a time in each town. During the week we agents clipped many and many a sucker. Nevertheless at the end of the day's work we walked about the town, entered any restaurant that appealed to us, went to shows, dances, and parties, and never again gave the matter of meeting one of our victims a second thought. And during all that time we didn't have a rumble."

train, he will keep to himself. This is caused partly by his inability to find interest in the conversation of legitimate persons, and partly by his difficulty in holding up his end of a conversation on topics in which he is not interested, and partly by a realization that if he gets to talking it may start inquiries about who he is. The thief would have an answer all ready if inquiries should be made about him, but it is better to give no opportunity for such questions. The thief's motto is to keep out of sight, out of danger, attract no attention, and keep quiet, unless he is working a grift. He does not mix with people and does not talk for amusement unless he is among friends.

The thief tries to avoid crowds except for professional visits. A thief was being given a psychiatric test in prison and was asked what he would do if he should see a woman and her daughter thrown out of a car and injured in an automobile accident. The thief asked, "Where does this accident occur?" The psychiatrist answered, "On the street." The thief asked again, "What street and where?" The psychiatrist answered, "Oh, any street, anywhere. That does not make any difference." The thief replied, "For me it depends almost entirely on where the street is. If it were a street in Chicago, where I am known, I would walk right on past and not even look around. If it were a street in some city where I was not known, I might stop and watch or even go to help them. But even there I would be slow about it, for as sure as I tried to help an injured person a crowd would gather. Pretty soon along would come a policeman, find me in the crowd, and accuse me of trying to steal the earrings off the injured woman. The only safe thing for a thief is to

keep out of crowds of all kinds except for business purposes. Someone else will be along right away to take
care of the injured woman unless it is on an unfrequented
street, and there it would perhaps be safe for the thief
to offer to help."

Though the thief shuns these contacts, he does not feel
uncomfortable when he is in a restaurant or theater or
ballpark merely because he is in public. He may be
keenly observant and suspicious of everyone, but this does
not make him uncomfortable. Of course, if a bad copper
or a former victim came into the place, the thief would
be uneasy until it became evident whether he would be
pinched. In addition, the thief's philosophy is that, if he
is due for a pinch, he will get it regardless of where he is.
Still he makes no effort to invite it but tries rather to
avoid it.

Also, the thief does not like to see his name in the paper
because publicity is the thing he doesn't crave. The newspaper account of the theft is never correct because the
victim, especially in a con touch, does not tell that he
was beaten while trying to beat someone else. The newspaper account is not very dangerous, but there is some
danger in it, for the prospect may have read about the
racket. The number of prospects who do know the racket
is always very small.

It is evident that one of the personal characteristics of
the thief is extreme suspicion. This may be accounted for
by the fact that he exists in a suspicious world. While
grifting, every move he makes and every word he utters
are carefully guarded to avert suspicion. The first thing
in his mind in every touch is whether he is under suspicion, and, if he is capable, he has learned to determine

this by a glance. He must decide whether there is an ulterior motive in any word or act of a prospect. He must often be courteous, kindly, and solicitous, and, because he has to play this role, he is naturally very sensitive to these characteristics in anyone else. Therefore, if someone would do or offer to do something for him which is unusually kindly, he immediately becomes suspicious. If someone offers to make a sacrifice for him, he feels that there is something phony about it. On a train on which a thief could not get a lower berth a passenger offered to share a drawing-room for no charge; the thief suspected many ridiculous motives that the other passenger might have and refused to accept it. The thief feels that no one should be doing him any favors and that, if such favors are offered, there is an ulterior motive.

It is generally believed that the thieves are full of ego, and it must be so since they have the conceit to align themselves against all law-detection and law-enforcement bodies, even if the conflict between them is only nominal. But there are differences among thieves, some being boastful and some not. Since success in stealing is the principal distinction that thieves have, many of the successful ones let their accomplishments be known. A cannon mob had been grifting a spot with very little success and was about to quit when one member, seeing a street cleaner at work, said, "Lets put him on." The idea was ridiculous and was suggested more as a joke than anything else. But they pushed the old man around and beat him for $420. Every one of the mob was dumbfounded, even the one who suggested it, but his ego prompted him, and he said later, "You guys listen to me, I know where the good stings lie. I haven' been in the racket all my life for nothing." To this day he uses that instance to prove what a brilliant fellow he is, but he probably uses that instance because he has had little success in picking other good ones since that time. Another case of a once-in-a-life time score occurred when one of the boys suggested playing for a painter at nine o'clock one morning, the painter being in full working uniform, overalls and all. His pocketbook showed four one-thousand-dollar bills, and the entire mob could have used smelling-salts to advantage. It was learned later that he had withdrawn the money from his bank the day before, when he was afraid of a run, and was on his way to deposit it in another bank when he was beat. When a score like this occurs, it is talked about for a long time, especially by the one who suggests it and who claims the credit for picking it.

Whenever one mob succeeds at something another mob has failed to do, there is a good deal of razzing and boasting by one mob and explaining and talking about lucky breaks by the other mob. A high-class boosting mob had been trying for a platinum wrist watch on a special order and had been in stores at least forty times for it and got every other kind of watch but could not get the kind wanted. One afternoon about 4:30 they were talking it over in their hotel room in the presence of two snatch-and-grab boosters who knew nothing of local spots and conditions. These two walked out and in half an hour came back with the watch which was desired. The expert boosters were greatly surprised and asked, "How the hell did you get it?" The others answered facetiously, "There was nothing to it. We just walked in and took it. The only thing needed was a little skill and larceny sense. The trouble with you guys is that you do not know how

170

to steal. Some day we will take time to show you a little about it." That mob was happy because they were able to make suckers out of a couple of expert boosters, and these two were burned up about it. Later they learned of a lucky break the snatch-and-grab boosters had by which they were able to get the watch.

Many thieves realize that much depends on a lucky break and do not boast very much, even when they feel elation. A mob may come in from some spot and relate how much money they made at a spot where another mob had bad luck. One mob may grift a spot all day without a score, and another mob come right in behind them and take off a good one. There is not much difference in capabilities; it is principally the slant which they get which makes the difference. This is especially clear in the cannon grift, because no thief can tell whether an unseen wallet is going to show one, ten, one hundred, or one thousand dollars. But it is true that the thief has a great deal of confidence in his ability and will never admit that there is a situation he could not handle successfully.

The thief, like other people, is always making excuses when he does not succeed. Sometimes he does this seriously, sometimes facetiously, but he always blames someone or something. If a thief gets a pinch, he will say, "If it had been raining today, I would have stayed home and then I would not have been pinched." He can always find something to blame it on. He may lay it on another thief, just in the same spirit he lays it on the rain or lack of rain. But the thief is seldom willing to give the copper credit for out-smarting him or to admit that he himself overlooked anything or made an error.

CHAPTER 8

THE THIEF AND SOCIETY

The professional thief does not regard society in general as an enemy or perpetrate crimes against society because of hatred toward society. The thief's idea is to make money, and he must necessarily make it from society. The only persons who can make money off the antisocial group are the coppers, lawyers, fixers, and politicians. Rather than hate society, the professional thief rejoices in the welfare of the public. He would like to see society enjoy continuous prosperity, for then his own touches will naturally be greater.[1]

The thief does not hate those members of society who protect themselves against theft. Thieves appreciate smartness in anyone, and if a store, bank, or individual is sufficiently shrewd to overcome the possibility of theft, they would (unconsciously perhaps) admire rather than hate. Should two boosters be walking along the street

[1] Ernest Booth, a burglar rather than a thief in the sense defined here, had confined his crimes to petty affairs in early life; he was beaten by the police and developed a general hatred of the agencies of the law and of society in general. "Burglary provided an outlet for the spirit of revenge that rose within me—serious burglaries—not the curious visits to homes I had been making in California. . . . . I was a man with a mission. I knew some of the heretic ecstasy of a crusader. I had been grievously wronged—I was imposing a just retribution on the creatures who had persecuted me. . . . . I found that I was not only justified but performing an exalted work" (Ernest Booth, *Stealing through Life* [New York: Alfred A. Knopf, 1929], pp. 126–27 [by permission]).

and one suggest going into Smith's store for a score, the other might reply, "That joint is out, they're smart to every angle and cannot be beaten." Smith would not be an object of displeasure or vilification because of this but would rather be respected.

The thief does not feel contempt for the sucker or think of him as a helpless boob. The term "sucker" applies to everyone who is not a thief, not merely to the prospect or mark. Suckers are considered to be more or less shrewd. This attitude is caused by two things: first, all thieves consider the accumulation of wealth as a sign of shrewdness, be the possessor sucker or thief; and, second, a thief believes it is his superior smartness which causes him to be successful, and there would not be much personal gratification or glory in beating a boob. The thief feels that if a sucker is not sufficiently smart to protect himself, his rights are gone. This is illustrated by an unexpected touch of $3,500 on the cannon, when one of the troupe remarked, "If a guy doesn't protect $3,500 any better than that, he ought to lose it." It was a jug touch, and the sucker had simply slipped the package of money into his outside overcoat pocket, but the thief's reaction would have been the same if the sucker had put the money in his inside vest pocket.

The thief does not like to be beaten any better than anyone else, and it is just as easy to beat him. He will holler as loud as anyone if he loses some money. A thief whose pocket was picked on a train just as it was coming into Detroit yelled and raised hell as though he had lost a million dollars. This was not put on for any purpose either. It probably makes a thief more angry to be beaten than it does an ordinary citizen, for it is a reflection on a thief to be a sucker.[2]

In general, the professional thief does not have any attitude toward his victim. The victims are just means to an end, the possessors of wealth which the thief desires. He attempts to get the wealth without any consideration of the victim. The victims are thought of just like a fisherman thinks of a place to fish or a hunter of a place to hunt.

Thieves make some distinctions among suckers and also make some attempt to justify the distinctions. Persons who are personal or business associates are safe from thieves of all professional types. A heel touch of $16,400 was made in an eastern city, and the troupe returned to New York. It was a putup, and the money would not be cut until all were present. While awaiting the man who put up the touch, it was learned that the person who was beaten was the one whom the thieves used to get out of trouble in this particular city. Immediately one of the troupe was dispatched back to the victim with the entire proceeds, and the putup man was bawled out for not advising the troupe of the status of the victim. Recently the fix in one city was the victim of burglars, and thousands of dollars worth of family stones were taken. Every thief in the Middle West tried to find out who got the touch, but to no avail. If it had been learned who got the touch, the property would have been returned to the owner.

[2] Hapgood's thief wrote: "More than anybody else a thief hates to be 'touched,' for he despises the sucker on whom he lives" (Hutchins Hapgood, *Autobiography of a Thief* [New York, 1903], p. 78).

174

Cannons, as a rule, make no distinctions between the rich and the slaves (workers, laborers, factory hands). Affiliates of other rackets, as a rule, do not steal anything which distresses the owner by the loss thereof. They do not approve or have any part in slave grift, feeling that, if the money of a poor man is taken, his family will be distressed. They do not like the cannon grift because you may be robbing a poor man who really needs the money for his family. The cannons, who do not make this distinction between rich and poor, say, "To hell with them. They are the kind who sit on juries and send people away, aren't they?"

Though cannons do not make distinction between rich and poor, they do make other distinctions. Catholic cannons will rarely beat a Catholic priest. Jewish cannons will beat a Jewish rabbi whenever possible, as well as Catholic priests and Protestant ministers. Also Catholic cannons will beat rabbis and Protestant ministers. There is a generally accepted rule among cannons not to beat cripples. It is believed that this rule is due to a feeling that the cripples are less capable of getting money, and also there is a certain amount of superstition involved in it. Cannons generally do not beat coppers, for it would heat the coppers up against cannons, causing hardships on all cannons.

Heels and boosters confine their efforts mostly to the larger stores, principally because these are the only stores which contain the merchandise the thieves want. But if a thief were asked why he beats Marshall Fields or Maceys, he would answer, "They have plenty and can stand it," or "The cheap bastards are paying girls only $8 a week to be on their feet all day, and they ought to be beat." This is not just an excuse, but is actually the way the thief feels about it. He would probably pick out the bigger stores to beat even if they paid the girls $100 a week, but it eases his conscience a little to have this justification.

The con man has little difficulty in easing his conscience, for in the con the sucker is always beaten while he is trying to beat someone else. The sucker is generally gloating over his prospective gain and has no sympathy for the person he expects to victimize, so that the thief gets a feeling of sweet vengeance in beating him. A case in point occurred when a con mob beat an elder in a Methodist church. He fell for the story, went in the company of the steerer to his home town, where he drew his entire cash balance of $4,000, mortgaged a piece of property for $2,000, and withdrew from the Methodist church treasury, of which he was custodian, $5,000 more. The steerer had to sleep with the elder that night, and the elder knelt by his bed and prayed before retiring. The steerer asked the elder what he was going to do with the money he would win. The elder told the stereotyped story they all tell—he was going to return the money to the church, build a new house, send his wife and daughter for a trip to Europe, and establish an apartment for a blonde stenographer in whom he had a fatherly interest. The steerer asked if he were going to make a gift of a few hundred dollars to the church for the use of the money from their treasury, and the elder replied very emphatically, "No! They have plenty of money. I need it more than the church does." It might be added that after this man was beat for $11,000, he returned home to face criminal prosecution for embezzling $5,000 from the church, and that the church sent the elder to the penitentiary for three years, which was their method of teaching "Go forth and sin no more"—for three years. In this touch there were enough incidents to ease the conscience of a con mob for an entire season. It is admitted that this is a weakness on the part of the mob because a thief should never have genuine emotion, although made-to-order emotion is one of the most used articles in his stock in trade.[3]

There are other incidents in con touches that provide ease for the conscience. Many victims state that they plan to put their winnings in a private account so their wives will not know about it or have access to it. Again, the

[3] The courts in New York State decided in 1871 (*McCord v. People*, 46 N.Y. 470) that the law would not protect dishonest deals between rogues. On that basis, until 1905 when the law was changed, New York City was the headquarters for a large number of confidence gangs. Though the law was changed, the attitude of the court was shown to persist in the following statement by Judge Malone in 1915 at the time Fred Gondorf was charged with swindling O'Reilly and Curry and finally plead guilty to the swindle of Davis: "There is little, the court thinks, to choose between the complainant and the defendant in point of morals or social decency. To all intents, both might be denominated not unfairly 'plain common swindlers,' for the defendant and the complainant were assuredly conspiring together, embarked as it seems, in a general swindling project. In the contest of wits the rogues who lose in such case invariably become the complainants and the prosecution's witnesses, while the rogue who wins becomes the prisoner at the bar. Fortunately, no honest man is affected injuriously by the conduct or acts of either. Under the circumstances, ordinarily, it might be thought that both the complainant and the defendant should be allowed to stew in their own grease but our criminal machinery is not to be set in motion or employed by the individual alone, but for the great body of the People of the State" (*New York Times*, June 29, 1915, p. 8; see also, Will Irwin, *Confessions of a Con Man* [New York: Viking Press, 1909], pp. 14–15; Arthur Train, *True Stories of Crime* [New York, 1908], pp. 101–21).

steerer always asks, as a standard question, whether the sucker ever had any of his employees pinched or had ever been on a jury which convicted someone. An affirmative reply to either question is always a conscience palliative. Should the sucker start to moan, after he is beat, as he generally does, the thief consoles him on his way. The best consolation generally is a promise to give him an opportunity to recoup his losses at the expense of some other person. Thus the con mob generally has a good deal of contempt for their suckers. They believe that if a person is going to steal, let him steal from the same point of view that the thief does: do not profess honesty and steal at the same time. Thieves are tolerant of almost everything except hypocrisy. This is why defaulting bankers, embezzlers, etc., are despised strongly by the thief.

It is easy to find some sort of conscience easement, also, on the shake. There degenerates are beaten, and the repugnance toward the victim overcomes any thought of his rights. In other rackets at times considerable difficulty is experienced in finding palliatives, but one will finally be found, regardless of how farfetched or how weak it may be.

The thief does not try to justify his stealing in general but if he did he would refer to the fact that thieves are not the only dishonest people. The public does not hesitate to buy merchandise which it supposes has been stolen, provided the merchandise appears to be a bargain, and practically never informs the police. The slum hustler who accosts citizens with the story that he is a pickpocket and will sell at a ridiculously low price a watch which he has just stolen, sells hundreds of them.

The public is interested in bargains, not in law enforcement.[4]

Every day cannons when caught in the act drop or throw the pocketbook or roll of bills rather than have it found on them. Rarely are these turned over to the police.[5] Every instalment house, auto-finance company, milk company, and many other companies maintain a corps of tracers or detectives to catch up with customers who try to jump their bills. The public telephones are equipped for slugs, so that the public cannot cheat on its calls. Many persons bribe the tax assessor to place a false value on property. When the business man is dishonest, it is described as "good business."[6] Such things make it appear that every person is born a thief, and many others than professional thieves have never learned to act otherwise. Besides, every adult will steal if he gets hungry enough.

Many persons who are supposed to be legitimate are at least on the border line of illegal behavior. A cigar store is used as an arsenal for a gang, whose members

[4] The Chicago Council Committee on Crime, as a part of its investigation, opened a shop in which the customers were led to understand that the goods had been stolen; the shop had a large patronage (Charles E. Merriam, *Chicago* [New York, 1929], p. 65).

[5] The Chicago newspapers report that a thief had taken $50 from a cashier in change and small bills and that, as policemen were about to catch him, he threw the money in the street. Pedestrians made a dash for the money, motorists stopped their cars and shared in the scramble, a traffic snarl developed, but none of the money was turned over to the police. This occurred in July, 1935.

[6] Yellow Kid Weil, the confidence man, was making big returns in his confidence games, but he turned it over to a real estate man to invest and soon he was broke; he put as much confidence in the realtor as his suckers had put in him (Mort King, "The Inside Story of Yellow Kid Weil," *Real Detective Tales*, February, 1931, p. 70).

leave their automatics and machine guns there when they are not on a raid. The owner may get an end or he may not get a cent; he depends on them for trade, perhaps for gambling. Then there are many politicians who help their friends out when caught by the police. Many parents use the things their children steal, knowing or at least suspecting that the things have been stolen; probably they objected at first but put up with it rather than drive their children away from home. In the same way the parents often use the money which, in some mysterious way, the daughter "earns" without working. The hangouts of thieves are generally in legitimate business places, and the proprietors generally get nothing from the thieves except their legitimate patronage, but these places are an essential part of the business of stealing, and the thieves would be hampered if no such place were available.[7] Finally, there are many people who regularly do things which they know are socially harmful but are careful to do them in a manner that will not make them liable to criminal action.

Where can the line be drawn? Many things are criminal, many others are on the border of crime, many others are socially injurious—perhaps more injurious than out-and-out crimes—but are not specifically prohibited by laws. Then there are others who protect criminals, either for money or friendship, and others who condone crime. Maybe this general easy attitude toward law enforcement and law observance resulted from the poor Eight-

[7] A large confidence game must have the co-operation of a printing house to print the fake stock certificates, fake letterheads, and other literature; of a trucking concern that can be depended upon; and, generally, of a bank, as well as of the political agencies.

eenth Amendment, which is blamed for everything. The same is true of traffic laws. The sharp edge of emotional opposition to the violation of laws has been dulled, and the easy way in which people take the violation of laws by all sorts of people makes one wonder.

A thief who was in England for six years returned with the statement that he liked England. He gave his feelings about England as follows:

I would like nothing better than to live in England the rest of my life if I could get a legitimate job there. I like the climate in spite of all the howls you hear about it. I like the beauty of their lawns and houses and castles. I like the simple way in which they live. And most of all I like the honesty of the English people. It would be very easy for anyone like me to keep honest in England, because everyone else is honest. But it would not be so easy to stay honest here in the United States, because so few other people would keep me company in honesty.

Though the professional thief does not believe that the public is awfully honest, he doesn't relish being a thief himself. He realizes that his life is antisocial, and he wants to be a social being. Hundreds of thieves do not like any feature of their lives. Every thief has an ambition to get out of stealing and get into a legitimate occupation. This is a question which is not discussed by thieves even among themselves, except rarely by thieves who are very intimate friends. Every once in a while some thief will say, after he has had a lot of trouble: "I am through with this damn racket. I am going to get me a whore and be a pimp. They never get into trouble." They are generally kidding when they say this, for lots of pimps are in prison, and they generally say it only while they are in prison and are thinking about sex. They do not mean it, for they have a lot of contempt for pimps.

There is not much talk about reform even among intimate friends in thiefdom. If a thief were asked what he expects to be doing ten years from now, he would either make some joke about it or else answer: "That's none of your business. Get to hell out of here." No thief would ask another thief a question of that nature in a serious manner. If it were asked as a joke, the answer would be: "Robbing the public, same as now," or "Doing it all under the habitual," or "Living off the old woman and trying to keep my kids out from under my feet." The answer which would be given most frequently would be: "Get the big one and retire or go into some business." Every thief has the ambition of getting enough money so he will not need to continue stealing. The thief knows, however, that this is not a real possibility, although there are some cases in which it has been done. Recently two of the boys got a $60,000 score in Florida and immediately purchased farms in Michigan, where they are settled and are apparently happy. It is reported that if a thief should show up there he would be chased off with a shotgun. A jewelry store in Youngstown, Ohio, was opened with the proceeds of a touch, as was a clothing store in Dayton, and a chain of dress shops in Chicago. Many cigar stores and hotels are owned by ex-thieves.

This ambition to get the big one and retire is very vague. The average thief does not look ahead, for he has no possibilities of advancement in his line, as does the man who is working on a track gang. The surplus of the average thief does not increase, and many thieves who do make an occasional big score are soon broke.

The important thing is that the thief refuses to think seriously about his ultimate end. There is no serious discussion or consideration of the future.[8] Thieves cannot consider the future, for that would bring them back to reality. They must refuse to face many questions, especially the question regarding the future and the question regarding the effects of their stealing upon other people. They simply shut these questions out of their minds. When they talk about these things, they do it in the form of joking. They could not go ahead with stealing if they did face the questions. Consequently the thief would not ask another thief what he expects to be doing ten years from now because he knows how he himself would be affected by this question. Questions like that cause the thief to think and to return to reality, which condition is not welcomed by any thief. The answers to such questions would be strictly bravado because he knows he is wrong but will not admit it. He must assume this bravado attitude in the presence of thieves and friends, attempting to justify his mode of living but being aware that the attitude is assumed and knowing that it is unreal. He knows that his existence is unreal and

[8] Eddie Guerin, an international bandit in the last quarter of last century and first quarter of this century, wrote: "The average crook rarely thinks of the future or gives himself the time to cogitate on what will be the ultimate effects of spending the best years of his life sinning against society. He never stops to think that the time will come when the years will find him with fingers less nimble and brains no longer agile. If prison authorities would put in each cell a series of pictures, showing what crime does for a man at different stages of his life, ending up with the poorhouse or perhaps dying in jail, friendless and forlorn, it would do more to cure crime than all the savage sentences ever imposed. I know. It is when you are approaching the threescore years and ten alloted to man that you realize the fatuity of it all" (*I Was a Bandit* [Garden City, N. Y.: Doubleday, Doran & Co., 1929], p. 74 [by permission]).

counterfeit. The nearest to an ambition that he has, therefore, is to steal the big one. When a thief wants to go straight and get into a legitimate business, he must steal his capital, for no business house would offer him an opportunity to start in a lower position and work up to a higher position.[9]

Not many thieves pack in the racket. Those who do are generally middle-aged or are getting old. Almost never does a young thief pack in the racket for good. The young kid does not have sense enough to look ahead and does not have to block off the future the way the older thief does. He thinks he knows it all. One middle-aged professional thief said, "When I was twenty to twenty-five years old, I thought I was just the smartest thing

[9] Joe Furey, leader of the confidence gang which swindled Norfleet, when asked why he had not reformed, replied: "I don't know why I did not. It would have been far better if I had. Somehow, the excitement had become necessary to me. I had to keep on from one thrill to another to keep from remembering all the things I had done. Memory is a luxury that only those who go straight can afford. I believe that three months with no new thrills to quiet my memories would have driven me screaming 'bug house.' I had to go on" (J. Frank Norfleet, *Norfleet: The Actual Experiences of a Texas Rancher's 30,000-Mile Transcontinental Chase after Five Confidence Men* [Fort Worth, 1924], p. 203). Will Irwin's confidence man, who specialized in circus confidence games, largely three-card monte or poker, wrote: "An honest dollar is the only dollar that don't do stunts on your pillow at night. No matter how they stall about it, the grafters, big and little, are haunted men. For one thing, they're always afraid of the penitentiary. . . . . No matter how clever you are, you will make your slip. Guns are another horror to the profession—the percentage of mortality by violence is high. . . . . I had escaped penitentiaries and guns by some pretty narrow margins; and at forty-six I determined to lead such a life, from then on, that I would dare to look over my shoulder in the dark. That's all there is to my reformation. . . . . I never carried around any conviction of moral wrong" (Irwin, *op. cit.*, pp. 15–16 [by permission]).

there was on earth. You could not tell me anything. A little later I got along far enough so that I could say that I didn't know, and still many years later I advanced far enough to say that I was wrong."

It is generally necessary for the thief to suffer some shock or jolt before he will face the future seriously. This occurs most frequently in the form of a long prison sentence, sometimes complicated by additional shocks. The length of sentence to prison has a lot to do with the extent to which he faces the problem of the future. If he gets a couple of days, a week, a month, or even a year, the continuity of his regular existence is not broken, nor has he become dissociated from his outfit or its ideas. There is a chance to rest, get acquainted with the new system, go ahead with hard work, so that the time in prison soon passes, and he can slide through it without trouble. He does not sever his social and commercial connections. He is waiting to rejoin his mob when he is released, and his mob is waiting for him. Almost daily contacts are possible if the institution is in a city. With each visit from a friend or associate comes word which renews his desire to get back with his outfit. Everything and everyone keeps encouraging him on one particular line—grift. Nothing happens which would cause him to analyze the situation. Any thinking he may do will be along the line of choosing new spots, whether to grift with a particular mob, what racket to follow, etc.

In contrast with this, a long sentence is itself a shock. In one case a thief who had expected to get two years was given a five years' sentence. He described the effect of his sentence thus: "I never had such a shock in my life. Things simply turned black. I was punch drunk, just like a prize fighter. I could not say a word and I did not have a thought." When the thief, with a sentence like that, gets to the prison, he is discouraged. He feels that he has been given the worst of it. Contacts with friends are fewer and fewer, until they dwindle to an occasional visit. He does not receive money as he did when he was doing a short bit. Letters from outside tell how tough conditions are. He cannot keep from thinking about how much conditions will be changed when he gets out. He knows that his connections will be lost, a new bunch will be grifting, and he will not be able to build up gradually as things develop. He becomes absolutely dissociated from his outfit and its ideas. He learns of illnesses and perhaps want in his family. In all these things he has food for thought, and he has time to think under conditions more conducive to constructive thought than when he was with the mob, where he could not face the problems of reality. He will analyze and take an inventory of himself and will find himself in the red.

All this will cause a different outlook. He places new values on everything. For the first time some of the beauties of life come to his attention. It is believed that this effect of a comparatively long bit is because it is a period wherein healthy thought, away from the bravado of the underworld, is indulged in, and the unpleasantness of grifting is made plain. It does not work this way with the thief who retains a considerable amount of money, as this keeps him in the realm of unreal values. But the axiom among thieves is that no lawyer will let you go to stir until you are broke, and few prisoners have any money. Also the effect is quite different on the amateur first-timer, who does not like to be deprived of his liberty and who admits it freely. Unless his bit is so long that it wrecks his ambition or he is inveigled by the false glamor of professional thievery, it will take very little thinking on his part to straighten him out. This reference to the young amateur is not meant to include the hoodlums from the slums of the big city, who were delinquent for a long time before they were first arrested. The only thing that will straighten out that type is a big funeral at which they are the main attraction, leading the procession one way.

After the professional thief has had a shock and reached this point in his thinking where he admits that the whole thing is economically unsound and wrong, he may go on to either one of two conclusions. A great many thieves state that they would be glad to pack in the racket if there were a chance to get along otherwise, but they know there is no chance and consequently they leave stir with a feeling that they are compelled to return to grifting, which they hate. They shudder at the idea of returning to the old fight against society, but in a short time they are back with their old outfits. They have quit shuddering, for they have acquired the bravado way of thinking again and have blocked off the troublesome questions about the future and about the effects of thefts upon the suckers and are as happy as they were before they went to stir.

Other thieves leave the institution with the determination not to resume the racket. But as soon as they get out they meet trouble. They have ten dollars and a suit of clothes which spots them as just out of stir. Unless he has friends, he has to begin his career by stealing a suit of clothes. The job he has promised him if he has come out on parole, which seldom happens for professional thieves, is generally phony. No one wants to employ a professional thief, and he cannot get a job by his own efforts.[10] Someone must have confidence in him and get a job for him. A thief can go to a legitimate or semilegitimate person and borrow a thousand dollars to straighten out a case, but if he asked the same person to help him get a job, he would be laughed at. A certain thief stated about one month after he had been released from prison: "During the last month I have had at least forty invitations from thieves to go out stealing with them, but I have not had a single suggestion from a legitimate person about how I could make some money honestly." About the only persons who will have confidence in him are his old associates and persons engaged in semilegitimate work, like gambling, whorehouses, speakeasies, and politics. If he takes a job with a liquor or gambling syndicate, he is sure to get killed, if he has any ambition. Then, too, if these off-color and political concerns had any stealing they wanted done, they would pick on the professional thief to do it. He would not feel any better about himself at these semilegitimate jobs than at professional stealing; in fact, they are probably less honorable. He gets panicky about his ability to get a job; he keeps wondering how long he can last. At the same time he has the confidence

[10] Booth describes some of the other influences than lack of employment. He reports the following conversation in prison, after he had told a pal that he was going to reform: "You'll be just like the rest of us. Soon's you get out, you'll meet some of the guys from here . . . . and right away you'll be one of them again. Because you're in a spot here where you don't have to mix with anyone very much, you get those funny ideas of reforming. But a few drinks, a shot of junk, or a few hours with the bunch—aw, you know how it is" (*op. cit.*, p. 169 [by permission]).

188

in his ability to make plenty of money by stealing. He says to himself: "Why the hell should I starve to death when I can go out and steal all I want? Why live in this lousy place in dirty and patched clothes when I can by stealing get all the comforts of life?" His confidence in his ability is the big thing about his continuing in the racket. To steal a living is strictly an individual affair, in which he is not dependent upon anyone else except, perhaps, some partners. But he cannot be independent when he tries to quit stealing. So he, also, in many cases goes back to the racket, reluctantly and with shudders at first. But he, also, becomes detached from the reality of social life in a short time and grifts with his old vigor. This does not describe an isolated individual but a great many cases which are well known to many thieves. Thieves who have confided to their intimate friends in stir that they are going to pack it in and who are later found grifting are asked, "Were you trying to kid me when you said you were going to pack it in?" The answer would be: "I tried to pack it in, but they [society] wouldn't let me."

It is not to be understood that long prison sentences will always or even usually change the desire of professional thieves. More thieves leave stir with the same attitudes they had when they entered than leave it with an awakened social conscience and a conception of the rights of others. A long sentence will be more likely to make this change than a short sentence. But there are other angles to the long sentences, for crooks would use more violence to avoid them than they would to avoid short sentences.

Sometimes shocks of other kinds are combined with the shock of a long bit, or they may occur separately. The following are some cases of such shocks which were known personally. A cannon of long standing was doing a bit when his mother died and he could not attend the funeral unless he went under guard, which would disgrace his family. Under the circumstances he preferred not to go, but he swore that he would never be locked up when another member of his family died. Upon release he joined a brother in the clothing manufacturing business and has never stolen a dollar since. In a second case the wife killed herself when her husband, who was a con man, got a long bit. Her husband was strongly attached to her and felt morally responsible for her death. It changed his outlook on life, and when again at liberty he associated himself with her father in the candy business, where he is still working.

In a third case the wife of a cannon, while he was doing a bit, became ill and in want and finally dropped into prostitution as a way of making a living. He was so affected that when he was able to rejoin her he went to work in a gambling house and is now connected with an organization which supplies race returns in one of the large cities. In a fourth case a thief was driving home with his wife from downtown when they had an accident which caused the wife's death. The thief, while recovering from the injuries which he received, did considerable thinking, with the result that he never returned to grifting. With the insurance money which he received he purchased a legitimate business, which he still conducts. In a fifth case a thief while trying to avoid arrest by stranger coppers was shot and seriously wounded. While convalescing, he went to work in a small hotel, eventually becoming its owner. He never returned to grifting. In a sixth case the wife of a thief got a bit on a wrong rap, for she herself did not grift at all. The thief had some money knocked up, and he invested this in a semilegitimate business, fearing that if he should get a bit while she was away it would jeopardize her still more; he is still connected with this business and is not grifting. In a seventh case two con men had beaten a woman for a sum of money and were still in her house trying to beat her again. Because of a matter with which the thieves had nothing whatever to do, she killed herself in another room. The thieves were charged with the murder. The case looked very bad, and when at its worst one of the thieves declared that if he beat this case he would pack in the racket and go back to the small town from which he came and stay there. They finally beat the murder rap, and the thief made good his declaration. Similarly, some female boosters, after the shock of a difficult case, marry men engaged in legitimate occupations and pack the racket in.

No thief ever decided that he would not grift any more simply because he felt that he might get arrested. Arrests and a bit are always a possibility in the life of the professional thief. These are taken as a part of the hardships of life, and the thief learns to take them just as they come. It is just like the inconvenience of walking from your home to your office on bad days. You don't like it, and you are glad when it is over, but you take it as it comes and do nothing except cuss about it a little. When you have finished a walk to your office through the rain, you go ahead with your work as though the weather had been good. Of course, if you find that the walk in the rain is too inconvenient, you may move closer to the office so that the exposure to the bad weather will not last so long. In the same way if you have been grifting in the South and find that the chain gangs are pretty bad, you may decide to move North or West or some other place where they do not have chain gangs.

The thief is not likely to be affected by having some-one tell him he ought to pack the racket in. Statements of that nature by reformers mean nothing, and statements of that nature would not be made by old thieves, for they would have too much sense; if they should make them, they would do no good, either. If the proper inducements are present for the thief to quit the racket, not much talking is necessary, and if the inducements are not clear and substantial, all the asking from now on would not cause him to quit.

When the thief does pack in the racket, he does not deserve any credit for it. The chief of detectives in Boston used to say that the strange thing was not that some thieves go straight but that people who have been honest ever turn dishonest. Here are a hundred million people going along the highway and some fool makes a detour when he does not need to do so. It is not surprising that he comes back from the detour after while; the surprising thing is that he was such a fool as to get off the highway at all. Coming back is the natural thing for him to do.

Moreover, the attitude expressed by the thief in the following incident is believed to be general. He said:

I have lived a social life for the first time during the last six months, and strange as it may seem I like it better than an antisocial life. I like it because I feel better about myself. Someone said that fifty million Frenchmen can't be wrong; in the same way a hundred million Americans can't be wrong. Most Americans are not professional thieves, and I feel better being with the majority.

192

When a thief does quit the racket, the attitude of other thieves is one of continued friendliness and a great amount of envy. No thief ever takes exception to another person's bettering himself, and to be on the legit is recognized as bettering one's self.[11]

[11] Victor F. Nelson maintains that thieves do react unfavorably toward the reformed offender. "The only reputation, notoriety, or importance the criminal possessed he has achieved through his criminal activities. To show a desire for reformation, therefore, is to admit that he has failed, that he has been unable to finish the game he has chosen to play. It is to admit that the reputation he has won, spurred on by the need to make himself important in the eyes of his associates, is spurious. The reaction of the prison herd to an evinced desire for reformation is revealed by expressions of scorn and contempt directed at those who express a desire to 'go straight.' 'Losing your nerve, are you,' they say. Or, 'I always thought you was yellow,' or 'You must be getting religion or something.' It is distinctly unflattering and ruffling to the criminal's ego to have to admit failure where other men have been (or have seemed to be) successful. It is, therefore, only very rarely that the professional criminal has the moral courage to reveal any desire he may feel for reformation and in so doing lay himself open to the sneers and jibes of his fellow convicts" (Victor F. Nelson, *Prison Days and Nights* [Boston: Little, Brown & Co., 1933], p. 108 [by permission]).

PART 2

INTERPRETATION AND CONCLUSION

CHAPTER 9

INTERPRETATION

The essential characteristics of the profession of theft, as described by the professional thief in the preceding section of this book, are technical skill, status, consensus, differential association, and organization. Two significant conclusions may be derived from analysis of these characteristics. The first is that the characteristics of the profession of theft are similar to the characteristics of any other permanent group. The second is that certain elements run through these characteristics which differentiate the professional thieves sharply from other groups. The similarities and differences will be indicated in the following elaboration of these characteristics and of the implications which may be derived from them.

I. THE PROFESSION OF THEFT AS A COMPLEX OF TECHNIQUES

The professional thief has a complex of abilities and skills, just as do physicians, lawyers, or bricklayers. The abilities and skills of the professional thief are directed to the planning and execution of crimes, the disposal of stolen goods, the fixing of cases in which arrests occur, and the control of other situations which may arise in the course of the occupation. Manual dexterity and physical force are a minor element in these techniques. The principal elements in these techniques are wits, "front," and talking ability. The thieves who lack these general abilities or the specific skills which are based on the general abilities are regarded as amateurs, even though they may steal habitually.[1] Also, burglars, robbers, kidnapers, and others who engage in the "heavy rackets" are generally not regarded as professional thieves, for they depend primarily on manual dexterity or force. A few criminals in the "heavy rackets" use their wits, "front," and talking ability, and these are regarded by the professional thieves as belonging to the profession.

The division between professional and nonprofessional thieves in regard to this complex of techniques is relatively sharp. This is because these techniques are developed to a high point only by education, and the education can be secured only in association with professional thieves; thieves do not have formal educational institutions for the training of recruits.[2] Also, these techniques generally call for co-operation which can be secured only in association with professional thieves. Finally, this complex of techniques represents a unified preparation for all professional problems in the life of the thief. Certain individuals, as lone wolves, develop to a high point the technique of executing a specific act of theft—e.g., for-

[1] Several statistical studies of habitual thieves, defined in terms of repeated arrests, have been published. Some of these are excellent from the point of view of the problems with which they deal, but they throw little light on professional thieves because they do not differentiate professional thieves from other habitual thieves. See Roland Grassberger, *Gewerbs- und Berufsverbrechertum in den Vereinigten Staaten von Amerika* (Vienna, 1933); Fritz Beger, *Die rückfälligen Betrüger* (Leipzig, 1929); Alfred John, *Die Rückfallsdiebe* (Leipzig, 1929).

[2] Stories circulate at intervals regarding schools for pickpockets, confidence men, and other professional thieves. If formal schools of this nature have ever existed, they have probably been ephemeral.

gery—but are quite unprepared in plans, resources, and connections to deal with emergencies such as arrest.

Because some of the techniques are specific, professional thieves tend to specialize on a relatively small number of rackets that are related to one another. On the other hand, because of the contacts in the underworld with criminals of all kinds and because of the generality of some of the techniques of crime, professional thieves frequently transfer for longer or shorter periods from their specialty to some other racket. In some cases they like the new racket better than the old and remain in the new field. In many cases they dislike the new racket. Hapgood's thief was primarily a pickpocket; he participated occasionally in burglaries but never liked burglary and remained at heart a pickpocket; he wrote regarding burglary: "It is too dangerous, the come-back is too sure, you have to depend too much on the nerve of your pals, the 'bits' [prison sentences] are too long, and it is very difficult to 'square' it."[3]

The evidence is not adequate to determine whether specialization has increased or decreased. Cooper asserts that it has decreased and explains the decrease as due to the war, prohibition, and the depression. He asserts specifically that confidence men, who, a generation ago would have been ashamed to engage in any theft outside of their own specialty, are now engaging in banditry, kidnaping, and other crimes, and he gives a detailed description of a conference of confidence men held in Chicago in which they attempted to formulate a code which would prohibit their colleagues from excursions outside

[3] Hutchins Hapgood, *Autobiography of a Thief* (New York, 1903), p. 107.

their own field.[4] Byrnes showed in 1886 in his history of professional criminals in America that many thieves participated for longer or shorter times in crimes outside their own special field.[5]

II. THE PROFESSION OF THEFT AS STATUS

The professional thief, like any other professional man, has status. The status is based upon his technical skill, financial standing, connections, power, dress, manners, and wide knowledge acquired in his migratory life. His status is seen in the attitudes of other criminals, the police, the court officials, newspapers, and others. The term "thief" is regarded as honorific and is used regularly without qualifying adjectives to refer to the professional thief. It is so defined in a recent dictionary of criminal slang: "Thief, *n*. A member of the underworld who steals often and successfully. This term is applied with reserve and only to habitual criminals. It is considered a high compliment."[6]

Professional thieves are contemptuous of amateur thieves and have many epithets which they apply to the amateurs. These epithets include "snatch-and-grab

[4] Courtney R. Cooper, *Ten Thousand Public Enemies* (Boston, 1935), pp. 271–72; "Criminal America," *Saturday Evening Post*, CCVII (April 27, 1935), 6. A confidence man, when asked regarding this conference of confidence men in Chicago, said that Cooper's writings regarding it should have been entitled "Mythologies of 1935."

[5] Thomas Byrnes, *Professional Criminals of America* (New York, 1886). Grassberger (*op. cit.*) has several ingenious methods of measuring the extent of specialization, but the conclusions apply to habitual criminals in general rather than to professional thieves, and the habitual criminals in general probably have less tendency to specialize than do the professional thieves.

[6] Noel Ersine, *Underworld and Prison Slang* (Upland, Indiana, 1935).

thief," "boot-and-shoe thief," and "best-hold cannon." Professional thieves may use "raw-jaw" methods when operating under excellent protection, but they are ashamed of these methods and console themselves with the knowledge that they could do their work in more artistic manner if necessary. They will have no dealings with thieves who are unable to use the correct methods of stealing.

Professional thieves disagree as to the extent of gradations within the profession. Some thieves divide the profession into "big-time" and "small-time" thieves on the basis of the size of the stakes for which they play, on the preparations for a particular stake, and on connections. A confidence man who regarded himself as "big-time" wrote as follows regarding a shoplifter:

While he is undoubtedly a professional thief, I should a few years ago [before he was committed to prison] have been ashamed to be seen on the street with him. I say this not out of a spirit of snobbishness but simply because for business reasons I feel that my reputation would have suffered in the eyes of my friends to be seen in the company of a booster [shoplifter].

On the other hand, the thief who wrote this document insisted that there are no essential gradations within the profession:

I have never considered anyone a small-time thief. If he is a thief, he is a thief—small-time, big-time, middle-time, eastern standard, or Rocky Mountain, it is all the same. Neither have I considered anyone big-time. It all depends on the spot and how it is handled. I recall a heel touch [sneak theft] at ten one morning which showed $21 and three hours later the same troupe took off one for $6,500 in the same place. Were they small-time in the morning and big-time in the afternoon?

The confidence men who play against a store [using a fake gambling club or brokerage office] expect to get large amounts. But there is considerable interchange, some working for a time at short con and then at elaborate con rackets. Those who play against a store know those who engage in short con; if not, they have many mutual friends.

This difference in opinion is quite similar to the difference that would emerge if lawyers or doctors were discussing the gradations within their professions. In any case there is pride in one's own position in the group. This pride may be illustrated by the action of Roger Benton, a forger, who was given a signed blank check to fill out the amount of money he desired; Benton wrote a big "Void" across the face of the check and returned it to the grocer who gave it to him. He explains, "I suppose I had too much professional pride to use it—after all I was a forger who took smart money from smart banks, not a thief who robbed honest grocerymen."[7]

III. THE PROFESSION OF THEFT AS CONSENSUS

The profession of theft is a complex of common and shared feelings, sentiments, and overt acts. Pickpockets have similar reactions to prospective victims and to the particular situations in which victims are found. This similarity of reactions is due to the common background of experiences and the similarity of points of attention. These reactions are like the "clinical intuitions" which different physicians form of a patient or different lawyers form of a juryman on quick inspection. Thieves can work together without serious disagreements because they have these common and similar attitudes. This consensus ex-

[7] *Where Do I Go from Here?* (New York: Lee Furman, Inc., 1936 [by permission]), p. 62.

tends throughout the activities and lives of the thieves, culminating in similar and common reactions to the law, which is regarded as the common enemy. Out of this consensus, moreover, develop the codes, the attitudes of helpfulness, and the loyalties of the underworld.

The following explanation of the emphasis which thieves place on punctuality is an illustration of the way consensus has developed:

> It is a cardinal principle among partners in crime that appointments shall be kept promptly. When you "make a meet" you are there on the dot or you do not expect your partner to wait for you. The reason why is obvious. Always in danger of arrest, the danger to one man is increased by the arrest of the other; and arrest is the only legitimate excuse for failing to keep an appointment. Thus, if the appointment is not kept on time, the other may assume arrest and his best procedure is to get away as quickly as possible and save his own skin.[8]

One of the most heinous offenses that a thief can commit against another thief is to inform, "squeal," or "squawk." This principle is generally respected even when it is occasionally violated. Professional thieves probably violate the principle less frequently than other criminals for the reason that they are more completely immune from punishment, which is the pressure that compels an offender to inform on others. Many thieves will submit to severe punishment rather than inform. Two factors enter into this behavior. One is the injury which would result to himself in the form of loss of prestige, inability to find companions among thieves in the future, and reprisals if he should inform. The other is

[8] *Ibid.*, p. 269 (by permission).

203

loyalty and identification of self with other thieves. The spontaneous reactions of offenders who are in no way affected by the behavior of the squealer, as by putting him in coventry, are expressions of genuine disgust, fear, and hatred.[9] Consensus is the basis of both of these reactions, and the two together explain how the rule against informing grows out of the common experiences of the thieves.

Consensus means, also, that thieves have a system of values and an *esprit de corps* which support the individual thief in his criminal career. The distress of the solitary thief who is not a member of the underworld society of criminals is illustrated in the following statement by Roger Benton at the time when he was an habitual but not a professional forger:

I had no home, no place to which I could return for sanctuary, no friend in the world to whom I could talk freely. . . . . I was a lone man, my face set away from those of my fellows. But I didn't mind—at least I didn't think I minded. [A little later he became acquainted in St. Louis with Nero's place, which was a rendezvous for theatrical people.] I liked Nero. I liked the crowd that gathered in his place and I wanted my evening entertainment there to continue. And I found that I was hungrier for human companionship than I had known. Here I found it. . . . . It was a gay interlude and I enjoyed it thoroughly, and neglected my own work [forgery] while I played and enjoyed the simple, honest friendships of these children of the stage. [Still later.] I could not rid myself of the crying need for the sense of security which social recognition and contact with one's fellows and their approval furnishes.

[9] Philip S. Van Cise, *Fighting the Underworld* (Boston, 1936), p. 321; Josiah Flynt Willard, *Tramping with Tramps* (New York, 1899), pp. 23–24, and *My Life* (New York, 1908), pp. 331–40.

I was lonely and frightened and wanted to be where there was someone who knew me as I had been before I had become a social outcast.[10]

Among the criminal tribes of India the individual was immersed almost completely in a consistent culture and felt no distress in attacking an outsider because this did not make him an enemy in any group which had significance for him. Nowhere in America, probably, is a criminal so completely immersed in a group that he does not feel his position as an enemy of the larger society. Even after Roger Benton became a member of the underworld as a professional forger, he felt lonely and ill at ease: "I was sick of the whole furtive business, of the constant need to be a fugitive among my fellows, of the impossibility of settling down and making a home for myself, and of the fear of imprisonment."[11]

The professional thief in America feels that he is a social outcast. This is especially true of the professional thieves who originated in middle-class society, as many of them did. He feels that he is a renegade when he becomes a thief. Chic Conwell states that the thief is looking for arguments to ease his conscience and that he blocks off considerations about the effects of his crimes upon the victims and about the ultimate end of his career. When he is alone in prison, he cannot refrain from thought about such things, and then he shudders at the prospect of returning to his professional activities. Once he is back in his group, he assumes the "bravado" attitudes of the other thieves, his shuddering ceases, and everything seems to be all right. Under the circumstances he cannot

[10] *Op. cit.*, pp. 62, 66–67, 80–81 (by permission).
[11] *Ibid.*, p. 242 (by permission).

develop an integrated personality, but the distress is mitigated, his isolation reduced, and his professional life made possible because he has a group of his own in which he carries on a social existence as a thief, with a culture and values held in common by many thieves. In this sense, also, professional theft means consensus.[12]

IV. THE PROFESSION OF THEFT AS DIFFERENTIAL ASSOCIATION

Differential association is characteristic of the professional thieves, as of all other groups. The thief is a part of the underworld and in certain respects is segregated from the rest of society. His place of residence is frequently in the slums or in the "white-light" districts where commercial recreations flourish. Even when he lives in a residential hotel or in a suburban home, he must remain aloof from his neighbors more than is customary for city dwellers who need not keep their occupations secret.

The differential element in the association of thieves is primarily functional rather than geographical. Their personal association is limited by barriers which are main-

[12] The document in Part I provides internal evidence of the lack of integration of the professional thief. The tone of the first chapters is significantly different from the tone of the last chapter. In the first chapters the thief is idealized and described in a jaunty manner; in the last chapter the thief is frustrated and regards himself as the principal "sucker." This difference in tone is not due to changes which occurred in the thief during the course of his work on the document, for the materials were not organized in their present form until he had completed his work; some portions of the last chapter were written previous to much of the first chapters. The inconsistency in tone is related to the topics under consideration. The thief assumed one tone when discussing the techniques and the internal relations of the profession and a different tone when discussing the relation of the profession to the larger society.

tained principally by the thieves themselves. These barriers are based on their community of interests, including security or safety. These barriers may easily be penetrated from within; since other groups also set up barriers in their personal association, especially against known thieves, the thieves are, in fact, kept in confinement within the barriers of their own groups to a somewhat greater extent than is true of other groups. On the other hand, these barriers can be penetrated from the outside only with great difficulty. A stranger who enters a thieves' hangout is called a "weed in the garden." When he enters, conversation either ceases completely or is diverted to innocuous topics.

Many business and professional men engage in predatory activities that are logically similar to the activities of the professional thief. But the widow-and-orphan swindler does not regard himself as a professional thief and is not so regarded by professional thieves. Each regards the other with contempt. They have no occasion to meet and would have nothing to talk about if they did meet. They are not members of the same group.

The final definition of the professional thief is found within this differential association. The group defines its own membership. A person who is received in the group and recognized as a professional thief is a professional thief. One who is not so received and recognized is not a professional thief, regardless of his methods of making a living.

Though professional thieves are defined by their differential association, they are also a part of the general social order. It would be a decided mistake to think of professional thieves as absolutely segregated from the rest of society. They live in the midst of a social order to which they are intimately related and in many ways well adjusted. First, the thief must come into contact with persons in legitimate society in order to steal from them. While, as a pickpocket, he may merely make physical contact with the clothes and pocketbooks of victims, as a confidence man he must enter into intimate association with them. This intimacy is cold-blooded. The feelings are expressed as by an actor on a stage, with calculations of the results they will produce. He is like a salesman who attempts to understand a prospective customer only as a means of breaking down sales resistance and realizing his own objective of increased sales.

Second, he has some personal friends who are law-abiding in all respects. He is generally known to these friends as a thief. In his relations with these friends the reciprocity of services does not involve criminality on either side.

Third, he receives assistance from persons and agencies which are regarded as legitimate or even as the official protectors of legitimate society. In such persons and agencies he frequently finds attitudes of predatory control[13] which are similar to his own. The political machine which dominates the political life of many American cities and rural districts is generally devoted to predatory control. The professional thief and the politician, being sympathetic in this fundamental interest in predatory control, are able to co-operate to mutual advantage. This involves co-operation with the police and the courts to the extent that these agencies are under the control

[13] I am indebted for this term, "predatory control," to my colleague, Dr. A. B. Hollingshead. It seems to be a proper term to apply to the salesman, described above, to the thief, to many politicians, and to others.

of the political machine or have predatory interests independent of the machine. The thief is not segregated from that portion of society but is in close and intimate communication with it not only in his occupational life but in his search for sociability as well. He finds these sympathizers in the gambling places, cabarets, and houses of prostitution, where he and they spend their leisure time.

Fourth, the professional thief has the fundamental values of the social order in the midst of which he lives. The public patterns of behavior come to his attention as frequently as to the attention of others. He reads the newspapers, listens to the radio, attends the picture shows and ball games, and sees the new styles in store windows. He is affected just as are others by the advertisements of dentifrices, cigarettes, and automobiles. His interest in money and in the things that money will buy and his efforts to secure "easy money" fit nicely into the pattern of modern life. Though he has consensus within his own profession in regard to his professional activities, he also has consensus with the larger society in regard to many of the values of the larger society.

V. THE PROFESSION OF THEFT AS ORGANIZATION

Professional theft is organized crime. It is not organized in the journalistic sense, for no dictator or central office directs the work of the members of the profession. Rather it is organized in the sense that it is a system in which informal unity and reciprocity may be found. This is expressed in the *Report of the* [Chicago] *City Council Committee on Crime* as follows:

While this criminal group is not by any means completely organized, it has many of the characteristics of a system. It has its own language; it has its own laws; its own history; its traditions and customs; its own methods and techniques; its highly specialized machinery for attack upon persons and particularly upon property; its own highly specialized modes of defense. These professional criminals have interurban, interstate and sometimes international connections.[14]

The complex of techniques, status, consensus, and differential association which have been described previously may be regarded as organization. More specifically, the organization of professional thieves consists in part of the knowledge which becomes the common property of the profession. Every thief becomes an information bureau. For instance, each professional thief is known personally to a large proportion of the other thieves, as a result of their migratory habits and common hangouts. Any thief may be appraised by those who know him, in a terse phrase, such as "He is O.K.," "He is a no-good bastard," or "Never heard of him." The residue of such appraisals is available when a troupe wishes to add a new member, or when a thief asks for assistance in escaping from jail.

Similarly, the knowledge regarding methods and situations becomes common property of the profession. "Toledo is a good town," "The lunch hour is the best time to work that spot," "Look out for the red-haired saleslady—she is double-smart," "See Skid if you should get a tumble in Chicago," "Never grift on the way out," and similar mandates and injunctions are transmitted from thief to thief until everyone in the profession knows them. The discussions in the hangouts keep this knowledge adjusted to changing situations. The activities of the pro-

[14] P. 164.

fessional thieves are organized in terms of this common knowledge.

Informal social services are similarly organized. Any thief will assist any other thief in a dangerous situation. He does this both by positive actions, such as warning, and by refraining from behavior that would increase the danger, such as staring at a thief who is working. Also, collections are taken in the hangouts and elsewhere to assist a thief who may be in jail or the wife of a thief who may be in prison. In these services reciprocity is assumed, but there is no insistence on immediate or specific return to the one who performs the service.

The preceding description of the characteristics of the profession of theft suggests that a person can be a professional thief only if he is recognized and received as such by other professional thieves. Professional theft is a group-way of life. One can get into the group and remain in it only by the consent of those previously in the group. Recognition as a professional thief by other professional thieves is the absolutely necessary, universal, and definitive characteristic of the professional thief. This recognition is a combination of two of the characteristics previously described, namely, status and differential association. A professional thief is a person who has the status of a professional thief in the differential association of professional thieves.

Selection and tutelage are the two necessary elements in the process of acquiring recognition as a professional thief. These are the universal factors in an explanation of the genesis of the professional thief. A person cannot acquire recognition as a professional thief until he has had tutelage in professional theft, and tutelage is given only to a few persons selected from the total population.

Selection and tutelage are continuous processes. The person who is not a professional thief becomes a professional thief as a result of contact with professional thieves, reciprocal confidence and appreciation, a crisis situation, and tutelage. In the course of this process a person who is not a professional thief may become first a neophyte and then a recognized professional thief. A very small percentage of those who start on this process ever reach the stage of professional theft, and the process may be interrupted at any point by action of either party.

Selection is a reciprocal process, involving action by those who are professional thieves and by those who are not professional thieves. Contact is the first requisite, and selection doubtless lies back of the contacts. They may be pimps, amateur thieves, burglars, or they may be engaged in legitimate occupations as clerks in hotels or stores. Contacts may be made in jail or in the places where professional thieves are working or are spending their leisure time. If the other person is to become a professional thief, the contact must develop into appreciation of the professional thieves. This is not difficult, for professional thieves in general are very attractive. They have had wide experience, are interesting conversationalists, know human nature, spend money lavishly, and have great power. Since some persons are not attracted even by these characteristics, there is doubtless a selective process involved in this, also.

The selective action of the professional thieves is probably more significant than the selective action of the potential thief. An inclination to steal is not a sufficient

212

explanation of the genesis of the professional thief. Everyone has an inclination to steal and expresses this inclination with more or less frequency and with more or less finesse. The person must be appreciated by the professional thieves. He must be appraised as having an adequate equipment of wits, front, talking ability, honesty, reliability, nerve, and determination. The comparative importance of these several characteristics cannot be determined at present, but it is highly probable that no characteristic is valued more highly than honesty. It is probably regarded as more essential than mental ability. This, of course, means honesty in dealings within their own group.

An emergency or crisis is likely to be the occasion on which tutelage begins. A person may lose a job, get caught in amateur stealing, or may need additional money. If he has developed a friendly relationship with professional thieves, he may request or they may suggest that he be given a minor part in some act of theft. He would, if accepted, be given verbal instructions in regard to the theory of the racket and the specific part he is to play. In his first efforts in this minor capacity he may be assisted by the professional thieves, although such assistance would be regarded as an affront by one who was already a professional. If he performs these minor duties satisfactorily, he is promoted to more important duties. During this probationary period the neophyte is assimilating the general standards of morality, propriety, etiquette, and rights which characterize the profession, and he is acquiring "larceny sense." He is learning the general methods of disposing of stolen goods and of fixing cases. He is building up a personal acquaintance with other thieves, and with lawyers, policemen, court officials, and fixers. This more general knowledge is seldom transmitted to the neophyte as formal verbal instructions but is assimilated by him without being recognized as instruction. However, he is quite as likely to be dropped from participation in further professional activities for failure to assimilate and use this more general culture as for failure to acquire the specific details of the techniques of theft.

As a result of this tutelage during the probationary period, he acquires the techniques of theft and consensus with the thieves. He is gradually admitted into differential association with thieves and given tentative status as a professional thief. This tentative status under probation becomes fixed as a definite recognition as a professional thief. Thereby he enters into the systematic organization which constitutes professional theft.

A person who wished to become a professional thief might conceivably acquire some knowledge of the techniques and of the codes by reading the descriptions of theft in newspapers, journals, and books. Either alone or in the company of two or three others he might attempt to use these techniques and to become a self-made professional thief. Even this, of course, would be tutelage. Aside from the fact that hardly ever is the technique of a theft described in such manner that it can be applied without personal assistance, this part of the skill of the thief is only a part of the requirements for a successful career. This person would not have that indefinite body of appreciations which is called "larceny sense," nor would he have the personal acquaintances with and confidence of fences, fixers, and policemen which are necessary for security in professional theft. He would quickly land in prison, where he would have a somewhat better opportunity to learn how to steal.

A person who is a professional thief may cease to be one. This would generally result from a violation of the codes of the profession or else from inefficiency due to age, fear, narcotic drugs, or drink. Because of either failure he would no longer be able to find companions with whom to work, would not be trusted by the fixer or by the policemen, and therefore he would not be able to secure immunity from punishment. He is no longer recognized as a professional thief, and therefore he can no longer be a professional thief. On the other hand, if he drops out of active stealing of his own volition and retains his abilities, he would continue to receive recognition as a professional thief. He would be similar to a physician who would be recognized as a physician after he ceased active practice.

The professional thief who wrote the manuscript in the preceding part of this book did not make a comparative study of professions as a method of reaching a conclusion that stealing may be a profession. Rather he assumed that it was and merely applied the name "profession" in accordance with the traditional language of his group. It may be worth while to consider very briefly whether theft is really a profession.

Carr-Saunders and Wilson list the following as the characteristics of the learned professions: technical skill, formal association as in medical and legal societies, state regulation of the conditions of admission to the profession by examinations and licenses, a degree of monopoly growing out of the formal association and of the regulations by the state, and ethical standards which minimize the pecuniary motive and emphasize the social welfare motive.[15]

The profession of theft has most of these characteristics. It has technical skill, an exclusive group, immunity from punishment which almost amounts to a license from the state to steal, a degree of monopoly growing out of their exclusive group relationship and of their recognition by the agents of the state. Each of these is less formal than in the other professions. They do not have written constitutions for their groups or licenses which they may hang on their office walls. They do have the informal equivalents of constitutions and licenses.

The one characteristic listed by Carr-Saunders and Wilson which they lack is the ethical standards which minimize the pecuniary motive. When this point was mentioned to this professional thief, he admitted that his profession did not have this characteristic, but he added that the medical and legal professions would have very few members if that were used as a criterion of membership.

The learned professions do have a huge body of knowledge in written form, and a long period of formal training in sciences which are basic to their vocational activities. The profession of theft, also, has a body of knowledge, not nearly so large and not in written form, which has been accumulating over several centuries. It includes articulate formulation of the principles of the different rackets. This body of traditional knowledge is transmitted to the

[15] A. W. Carr-Saunders and P. A. Wilson, *The Professions* (Oxford, 1933).

student by apprenticeship methods rather than through a professional school. For this reason professional theft should not be regarded as a learned profession. It is probably more nearly on the level of professional athletics, so far as learning is concerned.

The profession of theft, with the characteristics which have been described, is organized around the effort to secure money with relative safety. In this respect, also, the profession of theft is similar to other professions and to other permanent groups. For money and safety are values inherent in Western civilization, and the methods which are used to realize these objectives are adjusted to the general culture.

The thief is relatively safe in his thefts for three reasons: First, he selects rackets in which the danger is at a minimum. The shakedown (extortion from homosexuals and certain other violators of law) is safe because the victims, being themselves violators of the law, cannot complain to the police. The confidence game is safe for the same reason, for the victims have entered into collusion with the thieves to defraud someone else and were themselves defrauded in the attempt. Stealing from stores is relatively safe because the stores are reluctant to make accusations of theft against persons who appear to be legitimate customers. Picking pockets is relatively safe because the legal rules of evidence make it almost impossible to convict a pickpocket. The professional thief scrupulously avoids the types of theft which are attended with great danger and especially those which involve much publicity. The theft of famous art treasures, for instance, is never attempted by professional thieves. It would probably not be especially difficult for them to steal the treasures, but it would be practically impossible, because of the publicity, for them to sell the treasures. It is significant that the two most famous thefts of art treasures in the last century—Gainsborough's "Duchess of Devonshire" and Da Vinci's "Mona Lisa"—were not motivated by the expectation of financial gain.

Second, by training and experience the professional thief develops ingenious methods and the ability to control situations. A thief is a specialist in manipulating people and achieves his results by being a good actor. Third, he works on the principle that he can "fix" practically every case in which he may be caught.

Because of the importance of "the fix" for a general interpretation of professional theft, it is elaborated at this point. Cases are fixed in two ways: first, by making restitution to the victim in return for an agreement not to prosecute; second, by securing the assistance of one or more public officials by payment of money or by political order or suggestion. These two methods are generally combined in a particular case.

The victim is almost always willing to accept restitution and drop the prosecution. This is true not only of the individual victim but also of the great insurance companies, which frequently offer rewards for the return of stolen property with an agreement not to prosecute and are thus the best fences for stolen property. The length of time required for the prosecution of a case is one of the reasons for the willingness of the victim to drop the prosecution. At any rate, the victim is more interested in the return of his stolen property than he is in maintaining a solid front of opposition against theft. He tries to get what he can, just as the thief tries to get what he can; neither has much interest in the general social welfare.

The violation of trust by the office-holders is also necessary for the success of the fix. The party machine is an agency for the organization of violation of trust by office-holders. The party machine is for the most part unofficial and exists primarily for its own welfare. It is engaged in predatory control in many places and in many respects. This is best seen in the patronage system, which is generally regarded as beneficial for the party but is certainly injurious to the country. It reaches out, partly by means of the patronage system, to control predaciously all aspects of political life. The muckrakers in the first decade of this century found predatory political organizations in practically all the large cities.[16] The Hofstadter and Seabury Commission in New York City, Merriam in Chicago, and others elsewhere have shown that the system has not changed appreciably since the first decade of the century.[17] Intimate details of the picture are brought out in the autobiographies of office-holders who have made some effort to work for the public interest,[18] and in the

[16] See, esp., Lincoln Steffens, *Autobiography* (New York, 1931).

[17] Samuel Seabury, *Final Report in the Matter of the Investigation of the Magistrates' Courts* (New York, 1932); W. B. Northrup and J. B. Northrup, *Insolence of Office: The Story of the Seabury Investigation* (New York, 1932); Charles E. Merriam, *Chicago* (New York, 1929), pp. 24–69.

[18] See, for instance, Carter H. Harrison, *Stormy Years: Autobiography of Carter H. Harrison* (Indianapolis: Bobbs-Merrill Co., 1935). Harrison states that in the decade of the nineties in Chicago "the control of public affairs was the exclusive appanage of a low-browed, dull-witted, base-minded gang of plug-uglies, with no outstanding characteristic beyond an unquenchable lust for money" (p. 72 [by permission]). Harrison made the charge in the Democratic National Convention in Baltimore in 1912 that a post of authority under the sergeant of arms in that convention was

biographies of persons who, while holding public office, act as the agents of special interests.[19] The attitudes of the common people are revealed in Caroline F. Ware's illuminating description of Greenwich Village in New York City.[20]

These are samples of the available descriptions of the predatory control in the enacting and blocking of legislation, in voting, in granting franchises, letting contracts, making purchases, depositing public funds in banks, and making appointments to offices. The "badness" is practically always in the form of collusion between those in public offices and others who are not in public offices, and in both groups appears to be a product of natural forces in the social order.

The fixing of criminal cases is a part of this general system of predatory control. And the fixing of cases by professional thieves is a part of the much more general system of fixing cases. A retired police detective made the statement: "Everyone is going to try to get out when arrested. The method that he uses depends on the people he is dealing with rather than on his own moral ideals."

The fixing of traffic tickets is especially prevalent. A judge in Chicago, in charge of the court which had jurisdiction over traffic offences, asserted that 90 per cent of the persons who received citations for traffic violations attempted to fix their cases. The Chicago newspapers in April, 1934, reported that only one-tenth of 1 per cent of the persons who had received such citations during the

being held by the proprietor of a Chicago saloon which was a hangout for pickpockets and which was owned by Roger Sullivan, the head of the rival faction of the party in Illinois.

[19] C. H. Woody, *The Case of Frank L. Smith* (Chicago, 1931).

[20] *Greenwich Village* (Boston, 1935), pp. 267–91.

preceding three months were punished in any way whatsoever. This condition in Chicago is probably typical of most large American cities.

The fixing of cases of violations of laws against gambling, prostitution, and alcohol is more organized than the fixing of traffic tickets. John C. Weston, deputy district-attorney in the Woman's Court in New York City, testified before the Hofstadter Commission in 1931 that he had received $20,000 in bribes from lawyers, policemen, bondsmen, and others for aiding in the discharge of six hundred cases of prostitution in that court, that a ring of twenty-one lawyers participated in this business, and that two police-detectives on the vice squad were included in the organization. This situation, also, could be duplicated in many other large cities and also in smaller cities.

The fixing of cases occurs, also, though probably less frequently, in more violent crimes. Sile Doty, horse thief and burglar in New York, Michigan, and Indiana from 1820 to 1850, stated, "In case I should get overtaken in any of my exploits I had the means to buy my liberty, which I could do of nearly all of the officials."[21] Langdon W. Moore, a professional bank burglar in the last half of the nineteenth century, reported that it was almost always possible for him to secure immunity from punishment for bank burglary by bribing public officials.[22] George M. White, another bank burglar in the same period, reported that members of the police department of New York City who co-operated with the bank burglars were known as the "bank ring," that they received

[21] J. G. W. Colburn, *The Life of Sile Doty* (Toledo, 1880), p. 137.
[22] Langdon W. Moore, *His Own Story of His Eventful Life* (Boston, 1893).

10 per cent of the proceeds of all bank burglaries committed by the protected burglars, and also gave the burglars information regarding banks that might easily be burglarized; two members of the "bank ring" subsequently became superintendents of police in New York City.[23] Pat Crowe, kidnaper and robber, explained that many of his serious crimes were fixed with the assistance of prominent lawyers, including two senators and a national committeeman for the state of Iowa.[24] The Associated Press reports of July 18, 1936, contained testimony that of the $100,000 ransom paid in the Hamm kidnaping, $25,000 went to Thomas Brown, formerly chief of police of St. Paul and at the time assigned to the kidnaping squad, in return for information regarding the police plans for the capture of the kidnapers.

It is in this situation that the professional thief finds ways of making money safely. The situation may be called, generically, "social disorganization." The society is not working harmoniously and smoothly for the suppression of theft. Enough of the office-holders are cooperating with the thief so that he can carry on his occupation with security. Also, the victim who agrees to drop the prosecution in return for the restitution of his stolen property is typical of the individual in modern society: his interests are immediate and personal, and the public welfare means little to him. Because the public welfare means little to the average citizen, we have

[23] George M. White, *From Boniface to Bank Burglar* (New York, 1907), pp. 278–380, 440–80.

[24] Patrick T. Crowe, *Spreading Evil: Autobiography, as Told to Thomas Regan* (New York, 1927).

thieves, corrupt political machines, and inefficient office-holders. The public is not united for its own welfare; that absence of unity is social disorganization.

The profession of theft, with the characteristics and relationships which have been described, apparently originated in the disintegration of the feudal order and in the mobility which resulted from that disintegration. The early history of the profession has been well described by Avé-Lallemant, with special reference to Germany,[25] and by Aydelotte, with special reference to England.[26] The substitution of wages and rent for feudal services gave the serf the right to move about in search of better wages, and the employer the right to dismiss the serf when his services were no longer needed. The serfs secured the initial advantage, especially in England, in the period immediately following the Black Death when the supply of labor became completely inadequate. Later, when the population had returned to its normal level and sheep-raising had been substituted for agriculture, the demand for labor was not sufficient to provide employment for all the serfs. Displaced from residences and employment, these serfs took to the road either as searchers for work or as beggars and thieves.

These homeless men and women came in contact with

[25] Friedrich Christian Benedict Avé-Lallemant, *Das deutsche Gaunertum in seiner sozial-politischen, literarischen, und linguistischen Ausbildung zu seinem heutigen Bestande* (Leipzig, 1858–61). For an excellent summary of Avé-Lallemant's thesis, see Alfred R. Lindesmith and Yale Levin, "The Lombrosian Myth in Criminology," *American Journal of Sociology*, XLII (March, 1937), 653–71.

[26] Frank Aydelotte, *Elizabethan Rogues and Vagabonds* (Oxford, 1913); see also A. V. Judges, *The Elizabethan Underworld* (London, 1930); Frank W. Chandler, *The Literature of Roguery* (Boston, 1907).

223

the pariah groups of that time—Jews, gipsies, gamblers, prostitutes, and liquor dealers. In the cities they secured segregated quarters where they could live in anonymity a social life of their own. The thieves developed a large number of specialties, which at the time were known as "laws" and at present as "rackets." The "conny-catchers" or "card sharps" were the nucleus of the entire profession of thieves and swindlers. The technique used in approaching a victim in the sixteenth century was very similar to the technique used today.[27] In the literature of the day it was claimed that the pickpockets had an association through which territory was allotted to its members, money for protection was collected and disbursed, and a school for recruits was operated. They hired assistants—ballad-singers, steeple-climbers, street salesmen, or any freak exhibitor—to attract a crowd in which the pickpockets could operate. Clever and bold procedures were developed, as in the case of the pickpocket who rushed up to a woman, pretending that she was a relative for whom he was looking, threw his arms around her, and kissed her while he was appropriating her pocketbook.

The beggars were repressed with some effectiveness by the poor laws, but the efforts to repress the thieves met with little success. The thieves were more clever than the beggars, frequently improved their techniques, and kept their activities hidden from the public. There was no organized police force, no fingerprint system or rogues' gallery. But, Aydelotte concludes, "the most important reason for the conny-catchers' immunity from legal interference was what we should call in modern American parlance 'graft.' They had influence in high places."[28]

[27] Aydelotte, *op. cit.*, pp. 86–87.   [28] *Ibid.*, pp. 103–4.

224

Among the influential friends, the gamblers were probably the most important, with the innkeepers and fences as secondary aids.

The profession of theft had its good years and its bad years thereafter, but remained relatively strong until the last part of the nineteenth century. The thieves' quarter in London is thus described in 1860:

As you penetrate further into the *arcanum* of the thieves' quarters, you gradually become acquainted with a complete organization and system of things of which the outside world knows nothing, and with which no stranger is allowed to meddle. They have public-houses, shops, tradesmen, lodging-houses, private regulations, an upper and lower class—in short an *imperium in imperio*, by means of which they are enabled to carry on their nefarious practices with greater secrecy, security, and success. In many instances they are kind to each other. A man coming out of prison is provided with a home, food, and boon companions. They help their sick, bury their dead, and do something for the bereaved children. . . . .

The thieves' organization helps to perpetuate crime. Men and women get so linked in and interlocked with the general colony, that it is almost impossible to escape to honest circles and industrial life. Mutual obligations, mutual crimes, and even the attachments of friendship arising out of companionship in danger, suffering, sensuality, and crime, render it very difficult for the confirmed thief to tear himself from the haunts and the society of criminal life. This "thieves' quarter" enables the thieves to escape for a time detection and arrest. All are so far pledged to one another, that they will do anything to facilitate the escape of one of their clan, and when the police are anxious to catch a thief, they have not only to contend with his ability to keep out of their hands, but they have also to struggle against an expert fraternity located in every important town in England. Every thief tries to escape detection, and almost every other thief in Britain will do his best to conceal and help him. Again, if a youth takes to thieving and is alone in his course, he soon finds company and a home in the thieves' quarters, where his lagging courage will be stimulated and the ignorance of his inexperience be corrected.[29]

Thus the profession of theft originated and has been perpetuated in social disorganization. Efforts to repress professional theft have given little consideration to this social disorganization and probably for that reason have had very little effect. These repressive efforts have been of three principal types. One consists in the development of protective facilities for trade groups, such as banks, hotels, or jewelers, generally by the employment of a private-detective agency or by the development of their own protective force. This method of protection often fails to solve the problem even for the establishment or trade association and generally makes little impression on the profession as such. Many of the detectives are no more honest than the thieves. The detective agency attempts to make a record in the protection of its clients and to that end may enter into collusion with thieves, in general, in ways which promote rather than retard professional theft. Van Cise makes the following statement regarding such collusion between the president of one of the largest detective agencies and Blonger, who was the fixer for professional thieves in Denver:

They corresponded regularly and met annually in Hot Springs, Arkansas, to talk over the criminal situation, the president to find out from Blonger and his friends the names of those who had attacked his clients, such as wholesale houses, hotels, or contractors; and Blonger, in turn, to get from the

[29] "Thieves and Thieving," *Cornhill*, II (1860), 327, 331.

226

detective whatever information the latter had gleaned about the activity of police departments or victims against Blonger and his gang in Denver and elsewhere. It was a *quid pro quo* of mutual profit to the great detective and the great crook.[30]

This collusion is further evidence of the social disorganization which promotes professional theft. At this point, as at other points, the interest of an individual is in conflict with the interest of the general society. Furthermore, even though the detective agency may be efficient in the identification of thieves, the thieves may remain relatively immune because the municipal police and the courts are not changed by the development of these protective agencies and, therefore, counteract more or less successfully the efforts to protect the trade groups.

A second repressive effort consists of brief and sometimes almost violent drives against thieves. The chief of police may make such a drive, or the prosecuting attorney; seldom do they co-operate in a drive, with the consequence that one group often counteracts the other. Van Cise as prosecuting attorney made such a drive in Denver and found that the municipal police were opposing him at every step. The principal effect of most of these drives is to increase the severity of penalties for amateur thieves, while the professional thieves continue to receive protection and to remain relatively immune. Even if the drive is a success in a particular community, the professional thieves merely make headquarters elsewhere. In a short time, they know, the drive will be ended, and then they may safely return. Van Cise concluded his description of his drive against confidence men

[30] *Op. cit.*, p. 97 (by permission).

in Denver with the announcement that the thieves were already returning to Denver to resume their operations.

A third repressive effort consists in the attempt to develop more efficient personnel in the police departments and the courts. This program includes training, selection, supervision, tenure, and morale. Civil service is an illustration of this program and, as is true of the program as a whole, is concerned with many problems other than the repression of professional thieves. While civil service has made some progress in the last seventy-five years, it still covers a relatively small part of all public offices and is frequently violated in principle in those areas in which it is formally in operation. The reason for the failure is that the political party needs the patronage system. It needs this system, first, as a means of rewarding those who have rendered services to the party; second, as a means of control (a recalcitrant member of the organization can be punished by being deprived of his patronage privileges); and, third, as a means of winning coming elections.

In general, these efforts at repression attempt to eliminate the professional thief and leave everything else just as it was. Even the effort to improve personnel is confined within restricted areas of government. Any modification in the social organization that will be worth while in the repression of professional thieves must be based on an interest in the general social welfare which will, at the same time, repress all other predacious interests.

CHAPTER 10
CONCLUSION

The document in Part I, which was prepared by a professional thief, together with the annotations gathered from other professional thieves and from other persons acquainted with professional thieves, should have at least five values. First, it should reveal to the person in middle-class society the details of a profession with which he has had little contact and which he has probably not even recognized as a profession. Second, it should reveal to the student of an individual professional thief the general setting of that thief. It is practically impossible to understand an individual professional thief without this more general knowledge of the group to which he belongs. Third, it should throw some light on our general culture and the working of our general social institutions. By showing how the culture of the underworld grows out of and is related to the general culture, and how the institution of professional theft is related to our general social institutions, this document should be a contribution to our general sociology. Fourth, this document should make it clear that adequate control of professional crime cannot be attained by proceeding against thieves one at a time either by punitive or by reformative policies. Control calls, in addition, for modifications in the general social order out of which professional theft grows. Fifth, this document should be useful for subsequent research in regard to the professional thief. In typewritten form the document has been an open sesame to professional thieves, detectives, and other agents of criminal justice. These persons are interested in what a professional thief has written about the profession and in commenting on the document. They can, if they wish, speak impersonally about this as an impersonal problem without incriminating themselves or anyone else. Also, it is possible to secure their comments upon topics dealt with in the document without asking them to read the entire document. By this method it should be possible to develop a more complete body of knowledge regarding the professional thief and his relations to the general society.

This study of the professional thief obviously raises more problems than it solves. Even the problems which are solved are solved only in tentative fashion. Additional studies should be made on all the topics which have been discussed. Of the problems which might be selected to advantage for additional work, a few stand out as especially significant.

Recognition and tutelage are presented hypothetically as the universal elements in the genesis and definition of the professional thief. This proposition should be verified and developed. It is desirable to know in greater detail the processes of recognition and tutelage by which a person becomes a professional thief. Also, it is desirable to study the selective process, for not every person is eligible for tutelage and recognition by professional thieves.

The institutional nature of professional theft should be studied from the point of view of the genesis and development of the argot, the techniques, and the co-operating agents. These elements in the profession have a long history, and any particular generation of thieves operates with the residues which have been left by previous generations.

The integration of the professional thief, on the one hand, and of the agents of criminal justice, on the other, is a problem of especial significance. The description given by Chic Conwell shows that the professional thief is torn by conflicting tendencies; he is preying on society and at the same time is not happy as an enemy of society. It is even more probable that the dishonest policeman, prosecutor, or judge is unhappy in his dishonesty and in his organized violation of the trust which he has assumed. In many cases he started as an honest person, anxious to serve society; he found himself enmeshed in the gears of politics and carried along in spite of his opposition and ambitions until he lost his integrity; he, like the professional thief, finds some consolation in the social life of his own group but must conceal his behavior from the larger society. If it be true that the thief and the dishonest official are not well integrated, it is highly important to have an interpretation that will go beyond the sketchy and rationalistic interpretation which is implied in the document itself.

GLOSSARY

GLOSSARY

AIRTIGHT, *adv.*—With every possible precaution; certain.

ANGLE, *n.*—An aspect or element of an act, a method of approach.

BADGER GAME, *n.*—A type of extortion in which a victim is lured into a room by a woman and is there discovered in a compromising situation by a man who represents himself as the husband.

BADMAN, *n.*—Policeman or other peace officer.

BANDHOUSE, *n.*—House of correction or workhouse.

BEAT A SPOT, *v.*—Steal from a certain place.

BIG MITT, *n.*—A confidence game involving fraud in a card game.

BIG ONE, *n.*—A large gain from theft.

BIG-TIME, *adj.*—Theft in which preparations are elaborate and prospective gains large.

BIT, *n.*—Prison sentence.

BLAST, *v.*—Berate, scold.

BLOW, *v.*—Feel the loss of a pocketbook.

BLOW A SCORE, *v.*—Fail in an attempted theft.

BLOWOFF, *n.*—The final act in the operation of a confidence game, resulting in the separation of the thieves from the victim.

BLUE-RIBBON, *adj.*—Characteristic of persons of education and high social standing.

BOOST, *n.*—The racket of shoplifting.

BOOSTER, *n.*—A shoplifter.

BOOT-AND-SHOE, *adj.*—Inefficient, financially incapable; refers to a person who is not able to buy a pair of shoes and who therefore picks up a shoe here and a boot there.

BREECH, *n.*—Front trouser pocket.

BROAD, *n.*—Female, woman.

BUILDUP, *n.*—Part of a confidence game designed to develop confidence in the victim.

BURN, *v.*—Hold out part of the proceeds of a theft from the partners in the theft.

BURNED OUT, *v.*—Exhausted, used up.

BUZZER—*See* Moll-Buzzer.

CAN, *n.*—Police lockup.

CANNON, *n.*—The pickpocket racket; a member of a mob engaged in the racket of picking pockets.

CASE, *v.*—Watch carefully.

CHILL, *v.*—Stare icily, refuse to recognize.

CLEAN, *v.*—Rid one's self of stolen property; take money out of a stolen pocketbook; take labels out of stolen clothing.

CLIP, *v.*—Steal from, beat.

CON, *n.*—Confidence game.

CONVINCER, *n.*—Money which a prospective victim of a confidence game is permitted to win, as a means of inducing him to continue further.

COOL OFF, *v.*—Assuage or comfort a victim after he has suffered a loss; leave a dangerous situation until the danger decreases.

COPPER, *n.*—Policeman.

COPPER-SHY, *adj.*—Afraid of policemen.

COP THE EDGE, *v.*—Take advantage of an opportunity, as by stealing from an employer.

COP A HEEL, *v.*—Sneak out of prison, as a trusty.

CRASH, *v.*—Break into a place for the purpose of stealing; make a forcible escape from prison.

CUT INTO, *v.*—Make contact with, interfere with.

CUT UP, *v.*—Distribute the proceeds of a theft.

DEAD-RIGHT, *adj.*—With definite proof, certain.

DOUGH, *n.*—Money.

DICK, *n.*—Detective.

DUKE, *n.*—A confidence game involving fraud at cards; the hand, in connection with picking pockets.

236

DUKEMAN, *n.*—A man engaged in cheating at cards.

END, *n.*—Share, portion.

EYE, *n.*—Pinkerton Detective Agency.

FALL, *v.*—Suffer an arrest; *n.:* an arrest.

FALL-DOUGH, *n.*—Money to be used in case of an arrest.

FENCE, *n.*—Receiver of stolen property.

FILL IN, *v.*—Add a member to a mob.

FIX, *v.*—Arrange immunity for a thief on a criminal charge; *n.:* the act of arranging immunity; one who arranges immunity.

FIXER, *n.*—One who arranges immunity for thieves.

FLOATER, *n.*—Probation or other release from punishment with a provision that the offender leave the jurisdiction of the court.

FOB, *n.*—The small pocket under the belt at the top of the trousers.

FOOT RACE, *n.*—A confidence game in which a runner enters into collusion to defraud a victim who bets on the race.

FRAME, *v.*—To use false evidence, to arrange anything.

FRONT, *n.*—Dress or appearance; *v.:* to use one's influence for another.

GAFFED, *v.*—Fixed mechanically so that losses can be controlled; refers to gambling, carnival, and bazaar games.

GETAWAY, *n.*—Departure from a place where theft has been committed.

GET-ON, *n.*—Place where many people enter a streetcar or other public conveyance.

GLIM-DROP, *n.*—A confidence game involving the use of an artificial eye.

GLIM-DROPPER, *n.*—One who plays the glim-drop.

GO BACK, *v.*—Repetition of a theft against a particular victim.

GOLDBRICK, *n.*—Confidence game in which a relatively worthless brick is sold as solid gold; frauds and confidence games in general.

GONNIF, *n.*—Thief, supposed to be derived from Yiddish.

G-RAP, *n.*—Charge made by the federal officers.

GRIFT, *v.*—To steal; *n.:* theft.

GUN, *n.*—A pickpocket; a professional criminal of any kind.

GUN-MOLL, *n.*—Female pickpocket.

HAND, *n.*—Member of a mob; used especially when designating the number of members in a mob, as "three-handed."

HANG A RAP, *v.*—Make a charge.

HANGOUT, *n.*—Meeting-place used somewhat regularly by a mob or other group.

HANG PAPER, *v.*—Write fraudulent checks.

HEAT, *n.*—Danger in general; an investigation; a policeman.

HEAVY, *adj.*—Involving force or violence.

HEEL, *n.*—The racket of stealing by sneaking; one who is a sneak thief; a discredited member of the profession.

HEIST, *v.*—To rob, especially with a gun; *n.:* robbery, especially with a gun. Also spelled "hoist."

HOOK, *n.*—A member of a pickpocket mob who extracts the pocketbook from the pocket of the victim; *see also* Instrument, Tool, Wire.

HORSE POOLROOM, *n.*—Poolroom in which bets are made on horse races.

HOT, *adj.*—Containing elements of danger; irritated.

HOTEL PROWL, *n.*—Theft from hotel rooms by a sneak thief; a sneak thief who steals from hotel rooms.

HUSTLE, *v.*—Operate a racket.

HYPE, *n.*—A confidence game involving short change.

IN, *n.*—An advantageous relationship.

INSIDE MAN, *n.*—A member of a confidence mob to whom a victim is brought.

INSIDER, *n.*—A pocket inside the coat.

INSTRUMENT, *n.*—The member of a pickpocket mob who takes the money from the pocket of the victim; same as "hook," "tool," and "wire."

238

JOINT, *n.*—A fake gambling establishment or brokerage office used in the more elaborate confidence games (same as "store"); any place, such as home, office, hangout.

JUG, *n.*—Bank; jail.

JUNK, *n.*—Narcotic drugs.

JUNKER, *n.*—Drug addict.

KISSER, *n.*—Face; photograph.

KNOCKOUT DROP, *n.*—Chemicals placed in intoxicating drinks or used otherwise to render one unconscious; same as "Mickey Finn."

KNOCK UP, *v.*—Accumulate, collect.

LAM, *v.*—Run away from the jurisdiction in which a crime was committed; *n.:* the act of running away.

LAMSTER, *n.*—One who runs away or is a fugitive from justice.

LAY PAPER, *v.*—Pass fraudulent securities, such as forged checks.

LEGIT, *n.*—Legitimate behavior.

LEMON, *n.*—A confidence game involving collusion in betting.

LONG-HAIR, *adj.*—Artistic.

LUG, *v.*—Conduct, lead.

MAKE, *v.*—Carry on successfully; succeed.

MARK, *n.*—Victim; same as "sucker."

MATCH, *n.*—Fraudulent racket in which coins are matched.

MEET, *n.*—A meeting at a prearranged time and place.

MOB, *n.*—A group of thieves who work together; same as "troupe" and "outfit."

MOCKEY, *adj.*—Jewish.

MOLL, *n.*—Female.

MOLL-BUZZ, *v.*—To steal from pockets of women.

MOLL-BUZZER, *n.*—One who steals from pockets of women.

MONEY MACHINE, *n.*—A confidence game involving a machine represented as capable of making money or of raising the value of money.

MOUSE, *n.*—Extortion in connection with homosexual attempts; a homosexual person.

239

MUG, n.—Same as "mouse."

MURDER GRIFT, n.—Stealing under conditions in which thieves are unhampered and unafraid.

MUZZLE, n.—Same as "mouse."

NAIL, v.—Arrest.

NIX, interj.—A word of warning.

NUT, n.—The sum total of expenses.

OFFICE, v.—To signal by a movement or word.

OPEN-AND-SHUT, adj.—Definite, positive, clear cut.

OUT, n.—A way out of a difficult situation.

OUTFIT, n.—A group of thieves who work together; same as "mob" or "troupe."

OUTSIDE MAN, n.—A member of a confidence mob with whom the victim makes contact on the basis of friendship.

PACK IN, v.—Cease, desist, abandon.

PAPER, n.—Checks, securities, marked cards.

PAY-OFF, n.—An elaborate confidence game, including the "wire" and the "stock market."

PENNYWEIGHT, n.—The racket of stealing by substituting spurious jewelry for good jewelry.

PENNYWEIGHTER, n.—One who steals by substituting spurious jewelry.

PETE, n.—A safe.

PETERMAN, n.—One who breaks into safes; also called "yegg."

PHONY, adj.—Fraudulent, spurious.

PICKUP, n.—An arrest on suspicion.

PIGEON-DROP, n.—A confidence game; same as "drop the poke."

PINCH, v.—Arrest; n.: arrest.

POINT-OUT, n.—The part of a confidence game in which one member of a mob is pointed out and described as a person of great importance.

POKE, n.—Pocketbook.

PRAT, v.—To push gently, especially by backing into a person; n.: hip pocket.

240

PUSH GRIFT, *n.*—Theft in a crowd by pickpockets.

PUT ON, *v.*—To steal from; originally meant to steal from a person while putting—i.e., helping—him on a streetcar or other conveyance.

PUTUP, *n.*—An opportunity for theft reported to a mob of thieves for a commission or other consideration.

RAP, *n.*—Criminal charge.

RAW-JAW, *adj.*—Unhampered, unafraid, without caution.

RIGHT, *adj.*—Safe.

RIP-AND-TEAR, *adj.*—Without caution; same as "raw-jaw," or "murder grift."

RUMBLE, *n.*—Discovery; suspicion.

SCORE, *n.*—Successful theft, referring to the value of the stolen property.

SEND, *n.*—The act of sending a prospective victim of a confidence game to his home to secure money.

SHADE, *v.*—Cover, conceal.

SHAKE, *n.*—Extortion in connection with homosexuality and other illegal activities.

SHED, *n.*—Railway station.

SHORT CON, *n.*—Confidence games designed to reach completion in a relatively short time and to secure only the money the victim may have on his person.

SHOT, *n.*—Injection of narcotic drugs; an attempt; an important person.

SHOW, *v.*—Produce; reveal; result in.

SHOWUP, *n.*—Lineup of suspected persons in the police station for purposes of identification by witnesses or victims.

SICK ENGINEER, *n.*—A confidence game.

SLANT, *n.*—Aspect, element, part.

SLAVE, *n.*—A workingman, wage-earner.

SLUM HUSTLER, *n.*—One who sells cheap jewelry or other articles under the representation that they are stolen.

SMACK, *n.*—A racket involving fraud in matching coins.

SMALL-TIME, *adj.*—Theft on a small scale, involving simple preparations and small prospective stakes.

SNATCH-AND-GRAB, *adj.*—Same as "raw-jaw."

SNEAK, *n.*—The racket of stealing by sneaking; a sneak thief.

SNITCH, *v.*—To inform on a criminal; *n.:* one who informs.

SPOT, *n.*—Location.

SPRING, *v.*—To secure a release of an arrested person from a police station or prison.

SQUAWK, *v.*—To inform on a criminal; *n.:* a complaint.

SQUEAL, *v.*—To inform on a criminal.

STALL, *n.*—A member of a mob of thieves; the name is applied to all members of a pickpocket mob except the hook or wire; on the boost the stall is one who watches or keeps a lookout.

STAND, *v.*—Suffer, undergo, experience.

STEAL TO ORDER, *v.*—Steal articles which have been ordered in advance by prospective customers.

STEER, *v.*—Direct, guide, especially in confidence games; *n.:* a member of a confidence mob who makes the first contact with the prospective victim and guides him to the inside man; also used as "steerer."

STICK UP, *v.*—Rob with a gun; *n.:* one who robs with a gun.

STING, *n.*—Opportunity for theft.

STINGAREE, *n.*—A confidence game involving short change.

STIR, *n.*—Prison, penitentiary.

STOCK MARKET, *n.*—An elaborate confidence game; one of the methods of the pay-off.

STOOL PIGEON, *n.*—One who informs.

STORE, *n.*—A fake gambling club or brokerage office used in the pay-off racket; also called a "joint."

STRAIGHTEN OUT, *v.*—Remove difficulties; especially to induce a victim to refuse to prosecute or make complaint.

STRAP, *n.*—A confidence game.

STRING, *n.*—Same as "strap."

242

STRONG-ARM, *adj.*—Violent, involving use of physical force.

SUCKER, *n.*—Victim; anyone who is not a thief.

TAIL PIT, *n.*—Side pocket of coat.

TAKE OFF, *v.*—Perform, execute.

TAP, *n.*—A confidence game.

THROW, *n.*—A newspaper or other article placed under the chin of the victim of a pickpocket mob to divert his attention and obstruct his vision.

TOOL, *n.*—A member of a pickpocket mob who takes the money from the pocket of the victim; same as "hook," "instrument," "wire."

TOUCH, *n.*—Execution of a theft; the act of borrowing.

TROUPE, *n.*—A group of thieves who work together; same as "mob" or "outfit."

TUMBLE, *n.*—Discovery of a theft; same as "rumble."

TURN IN, *v.*—To inform; report to the police.

TWO RED ACES, *n.*—A confidence game with cards.

WALL, *n.*—Generic name for places in which victims of the pay-off racket are beaten when a "store" or "joint" is not used; the victim is said to be "played against the wall" and is not taken into the fake gambling club or brokerage office.

WEED IN THE GARDEN, *n.*—A stranger or any person regarded with suspicion.

WIPE, *n.*—A confidence game.

WIRE, *n.*—A member of a pickpocket mob who takes the money from the pocket of the victim; a confidence game which is one form of the pay-off racket.

BIBLIOGRAPHY

BIBLIOGRAPHY

ABELS, A. *Verbrechen als Beruf und Sport.* Minden, 1914.

AVÉ-LALLEMANT, FRIEDRICH C. B. *Das deutsche Gaunertum in seiner sozial-politischen, literarischen, und linguistischen Ausbildung zu seinem heutigen Bestande.* 4 vols. Leipzig, 1858–62.

AYDELOTTE, FRANK. *Elizabethan Rogues and Vagabonds.* ("Oxford Historical and Literary Studies," Vol. I.) Oxford, 1913.

BEGER, FRITZ. *Die rückfälligen Betrüger.* ("Kriminalistischen Abhandlungen" herausgegeben von FRANZ EXNER, Heft VII.) Leipzig, 1929.

BENTON, ROGER. *Where Do I Go from Here?* New York, 1936.

BINGHAM, T. A. "The Organized Criminals of New York," *McClure's Magazine,* XXXIV (1909–10), 62–67.

BLACK, JACK. *You Can't Win.* New York, 1926.

———. "A Burglar Looks At Laws and Codes," *Harper's Magaxine,* CLX (February, 1930), 306–13.

BOOTH, ERNEST. *Stealing through Life.* New York, 1929.

BYRNES, THOMAS. *Professional Criminals of America.* New York, 1886.

CAMPBELL, HELEN. *Darkness and Daylight.* Hartford, 1892. (Part III, "Criminal Life and Experiences," by THOMAS BYRNES, pp. 641–740.)

CARPENTER, MARY. *Our Convicts.* London, 1864.

CHAMBERLAIN, HENRY B. "Some Observations concerning Organized Crime," *Journal of Criminal Law and Criminology,* XXII (1931–32), 652–70.

CHANDLER, FRANK W. *The Literature of Roguery.* 2 vols. Boston, 1907. (Esp. chaps. iii–iv and x.)

CLARK, CHARLES L., and EUBANK, EARLE E. *Lockstep and Corridor.* Cincinnati, 1927.

COFFEY, JOHN. "The Autobiography of an Ex-thief," *Outlook and Independent*, CLIV (February–April, 1930), 421–23, 478–79, 502, 519–20, 538–39, 583–84, 598, 620.

COLBURN, J. G. W. *The Life of Sile Doty.* Toledo, 1880.

COLLIER, W. R., and WESTRATE, E. V. *Reign of Soapy Smith.* Garden City, 1935.

CRAPSEY, EDWARD. "Our Criminal Population," *Galaxy*, VIII (1869), 345–54.

———. "Why Thieves Prosper," *ibid.*, pp. 519–27.

CROOK, G. F. *Complete Newgate Calendar.* 5 vols. London, 1926.

CUÉNOUD, C. E. *Les Classes dangereuses de la population.* Paris, 1879.

DOUGHERTY, GEORGE S. "The Public the Criminal's Partner," *Outlook*, CIV (August 23, 1913), 895–910.

———. *The Criminal as a Human Being.* New York, 1924. (Esp. chaps. v–vi.)

DUBUISSON, PAUL. "Les Voleuses des grands magazins," *Archives d'anthropologie criminelle*, XVI (1901), 341.

DUCAMP, MAXIME. *Paris: ses organes, ses functions et sa vie.* 6 vols. Paris, 1869–75. (Esp. Vol. III.)

EDWARDS, MONROE. *Life and Adventures of the Accomplished Forger and Swindler, Colonel Monroe Edwards.* New York, 1848.

FELSTEAD, SIDNEY T. *The Underworld of London.* London, 1923.

FRÉGIER, A. *Des Classes dangereuses de la population dans les grandes villes.* 2 vols. Paris, 1840. (Esp. I, 205–54.)

GARDNER, ARTHUR R. L. *Art of Crime.* London, 1931.

GRASSBERGER, ROLAND. *Gewerbs- und Berufsverbrechertum in den Vereinigten Staaten von Amerika.* ("Kriminologische Abhandlungen," herausgegeben von W. GLEISBACH, Heft VIII.) Vienna, 1933.

GRIMSTAD, LUDWIG F. "Hotel-Room Prowlers, Connivers, and Sneak Thieves," *Saturday Evening Post*, CCVI (June 30, 1934), 30 ff.

GUERIN, EDDIE. *I Was a Bandit.* New York, 1929.

HAGGART, DAVID. *The Life of David Haggart.* Edinburgh, 1821.

HAMBLY, CHARLES R. *Hold Your Money: A Sucker's Handbook— Con Games Exposed.* Los Angeles, 1932.

HAPGOOD, HUTCHINS. *Autobiography of a Thief.* New York, 1903.

HAYWARD, ARTHUR L. (ed.). *A Complete History of the Lives and Robberies of the Most Notorious Highwaymen, Footpads, Shoplifts, and Cheats of Both Sexes* (reprinted from 5th ed., 1719). London, 1926.

HEALY, WILLIAM. *The Individual Delinquent.* Boston, 1915. (Esp. pp. 316–30.)

HEINDL, ROBERT. *Der Berusverbrecher.* 5th ed. Berlin, 1927.

HERZ, HUGO, "Assoziationen im Verbrechertum," *Monatsschrift für Kriminalpsychologie*, III, 544.

HORSLEY, J. W. "Autobiography of a Thief, in Thieves' Language," *MacMillan Magazine*, XL (1879), 500–506.

IRWIN, WILL. *Confessions of a Con Man.* New York, 1909.

JOHN, ALFRED. *Die Rückfallsdiebe.* ("Kriminalistische Abhandlungen," herausgegeben von Franz Exner, Heft IX.) Leipzig, 1929.

JOHNSTON, JAMES P. *Grafters I Have Met: The Author's Personal Experiences with Sharpers, Gamblers, Agents, and Their Many Schemes.* Chicago, 1906.

JOLY, H., *Le Crime: étude sociale.* 4th ed. Paris, 1887.

JUDGES, A. V. *The Elizabethan Underworld.* London, 1930.

KARPMAN, BEN. *The Individual Criminal.* Washington, 1935. (Esp. pp. 278–83.)

KEATS, JAMES H. *The Destruction of Mephisto's Web: Or All Grafts Laid Bare.* Salt Lake City, 1914.

KEY, V. O. "Police Graft," *American Journal of Sociology*, XL (March, 1935), 624–36.

KING, MORT. "The Secrets of Yellow Kid Weil," *Real Detective Tales*, January, 1931, pp. 44–51, 82–88; February, 1931, pp. 58–70.

LANDESCO, JOHN. "Organized Crime," in *Report of Illinois Commission on Criminal Justice*. Chicago, 1929. (Esp. pp. 847, 1065–71, and 1083.)

———. "The Criminal Underworld of Chicago in the Eighties and Nineties," *Journal of Criminal Law and Criminology*. XXV (September, 1934—March, 1935), 341–57, 928–40,

———. "The Woman and the Underworld," *ibid.*, XXVI (March, 1936), 891–902.

LAURENT, J. B. E. *Le Monde des voleurs, leur esprit et leur langue*. Paris, 1862.

LYNCH, D. T. *Criminals and Politicians*. New York, 1932.

MCADOO, WILLIAM, *Guarding a Great City*. New York, 1906. (Esp. pp. 193–226.)

MACDONALD, ARTHUR. *Criminology*. New York, 1893.

MAGGS BROTHERS. *A Gallery of Rogues: Outlaws of Society in Fact and Fiction*. (Catalogue No. 630.) London, 1936. (Publisher's catalogue of early publications on English thieves.)

MAYHEW, HENRY. *London Labour and London Poor*. London, 1864. (Esp. Vol. IV.)

MERRIAM, CHARLES E. *Chicago*. New York, 1929. (Esp. chap. ii.)

MOLEY, RAYMOND. *Tribunes of the People*. New Haven, 1932.

MOORE, LANGDON W. *His Own Story of His Eventful Life*. Boston, 1893.

MOORE, MAURICE E. *Fraud and Swindles*. London, 1933.

MOREAU, WILLIAM B. *Swindling Exposed: Methods of the Crooks Explained*. Syracuse, 1907.

MOREAU-CHRISTOPHE, LOUIS. *Le Monde des coquins*. 2 vols. Paris, 1863–65.

NEW YORK STATE. *Report of Senate Committee on Police Department of the City of New York* (Lexow Committee). Albany, 1895. (Esp. II, 1622–24, 1799–1831, and 2539–2641).

———. *Report of Committee on the Government of the City of New York* (Hofstadter and Seabury Committee). 5 vols. in 2. New York, 1932.

New York Times Index. "Pickpockets," "Confidence Games," etc. New York, 1913———.

NORFLEET, J. FRANK. *Norfleet: The Actual Experiences of a Texas Rancher's 30,000-Mile Transcontinental Chase after Five Confidence Men.* Fort Worth, 1924. 2d ed., Sugar Land, Tex., 1927.

NORTHROP, W. B., and J. B. *Insolence of Office: The Story of the Seabury Investigation.* New York, 1932.

O'CONNOR, JOHN J. *Broadway Racketeers.* New York, 1928.

PENDRILL, CHARLES. *London Life in the Fourteenth Century.* New York, 1925 (chap. viii, "Swindlers and Swindling").

"Pickpocket Trust," *Literary Digest,* XLVIII (April 4, 1914), 768–73.

"Pickpockets in Nippon," *ibid.,* LIII (September 16, 1916), 704–8.

PROAL, LOUIS. *Political Crime.* New York, 1898. (Esp. chap. vii.)

"Professional Thieves," *Cornhill,* VI (1862), 640–53.

PUILARAUD, L. *Les Malfaiteurs de profession.* Paris, 1894.

Report of [Chicago] *City Council Committee on Crime.* Chicago, 1915.

RIBTON-TURNER, C. J. *A History of Vagrants and Vagrancy.* London, 1887.

RICE, GEORGE G. *My Adventures with Your Money.* Boston, 1913.

ROCHLITZ, C. *Das Wesen und Treiben der Gauner, Diebe, und Betrüger Deutschlands.* 1846.

SCHRÄDER, T. *Das Verbrecherthum in Hamburg.* 1879.

SEABURY, SAMUEL, *Final Report in the Matter of the Investigation of the Magistrates' Courts.* New York, 1932.

SHAW, CLIFFORD R., and MCKAY, HENRY D. "Social Factors in Juvenile Delinquency," in *Report of the National Commission on Law Observance and Enforcement*, No. 13, Vol II. Washington, 1932. (Esp. pp. 232–39.)

STEFFENS, LINCOLN. *The Autobiography of Lincoln Steffens*. New York, 1931.

STODDARD, WILLIAM L. *Financial Racketeering and How To Stop It*. New York, 1931.

STOKER, BRAM. *Famous Impostors*. New York, 1910.

"Technical School for German Pickpockets," *Literary Digest*, XCIX (December 8, 1928), 16.

"Thieves and Thieving," *Cornhill*, II (1860), 326–44.

TOZER, BASIL. *Confidence Crooks and Blackmailers*. Boston, 1930.

TRUMBLE, ALFRED, *Famous Frauds: Or the Sharks of Society*. New York, 1883.

TUFTS, HENRY. *The Autobiography of a Criminal*. Ed. from the original ed. of 1807 by EDMUND PEARSON. New York, 1930.

TURNER, G. K. "The City of Chicago," *McClure's Magazine*, XXVIII (1907), 575–92.

VAN CISE, PHILIP S. *Fighting the Underworld*. Boston, 1936.

VIDOCQ, P. *Les Voleurs*. Paris, 1837.

WERNER, M. R. *Tammany Hall*. Garden City, 1928.

WHITE, FRANK M. "New York's Ten Thousand Thieves," *Harper's Weekly*, L (December 29, 1906), 1892–93.

WHITE, GEORGE M. *From Boniface to Bank Burglar*. New York, 1907.

WILLARD, JOSIAH FLYNT. *The World of Graft*. New York, 1901.

———. *My Life*. New York, 1908.

WULFFEN, ERICH, *Gauner- und Verbrecher-Typen*. Berlin, 1910.

ZIMMERMAN, C. W. *Die Diebe in Berlin*. Berlin, 1847.

INDEX

INDEX

Anderson, V. V., cited, 49
Argot, 4, 16–20, 200–201
Austin, William B., 106–7
Avé-Lallemant, F. C. B., cited, 223
Aydelotte, Frank, cited, 223, 224

Beger, Fritz, cited, 198
Benton, Roger, cited, 78, 202, 203, 205
Black, Jack, cited, 12
Blonger, Lou, 27, 88, 226–27
Booth, Ernest, cited, 137, 172, 188
Burglary, 3, 4, 10–11, 172, 198
Business maxims, 13–15, 35–38, 145–46, 147–48, 150, 152–53
Byrnes, Thomas, cited, 200
Byrnes and O'Brien, 84

Cantwell, 138
Carr-Saunders, A. W., cited, 215, 216
Chandler, Frank W., cited, 223
Clark, Charles L., cited, 13
Coffey, John, cited, 51
Colburn, J. G. W., cited, 160, 221
Confidence games, 17, 21, 22, 23, 24, 26, 27, 32, 35, 37, 42, 43, 44, 56–73, 76, 83, 88, 96, 108, 109, 143–45, 149, 151, 176–78, 180, 198, 200, 217
Consensus, x, 5–6, 38, 39–42, 202–6, 210
Conwell, Chic, vii–ix, 231
Cooper, C. R., cited, 200
Court, 82, 91–98, 115–16, 119–20, 131–34, 220–22
Crisis, 23, 213–14
Crowe, Pat, cited, 222

Diamond smuggling, 66–67
Differential association, x, 4, 206–9

Disgrace, 15
Distinction, 13–14
Drugs, narcotic, 30, 38–40, 42, 112, 116, 160–62, 215
Duke, 57, 68

Erbstein, C. E., 138
Ersine, Noel, cited, 200
Estate frauds, 63–64
Ethics, x, 4–12, 31, 35–38
Eubank, Earle E., cited, 13
Extortion, 21, 31, 43, 78–81, 217

Fall-dough, 31, 35–36, 111
Fence, 25, 145–47, 164, 214
Finkelstein, Louis, 82
Fisher, Richard, 25
Fix, 3–4, 7–8, 13, 25, 38, 39, 82–118, 119, 144, 214, 218–22
Footrace, 57, 68
French, Jackie, 143
Furey, Joe, 154, 184

Glim-drop, 69
Gondorf Brothers, 61
Gondorf, Fred, 177
Goodney, Joseph, 78
Grassberger, Roland, cited, 49, 198
Grimstad, Ludwig F., cited, 55
Guerin, Eddie, cited, 183

Haggart, David, cited, 37, 137, 146, 160
Hangout, 158–61, 180
Hapgood, Hutchins, cited, 8, 25, 26, 37, 104, 110, 111, 117, 135, 137, 154, 160, 174, 199
Harrison, Carter H., cited, 219
Hartzell, Oscar M., 63
Heindl, Robert, cited, 23, 109, 157

255

Hollingshead, A. B., 208
Hotel prowl, 22, 43, 54–55
Hype, 73, 74

Income, 141–45
Informer, 10–12, 203–4
Integration, 181–92, 204–6, 231
Irwin, Will, cited, 69, 118, 142, 177, 184
Isolation, 15–16, 163–68, 205–9

Jackson, Eddie, 11, 82, 83, 84, 96, 97, 99, 107, 108, 117, 120, 136, 142–43, 154
John, Alfred, cited, 198
Johnson, Alec, 25–26
Judges, A. V., cited, 223

Karpman, Ben, cited, 38, 45
King, Mort, cited, 146, 179

Landesco, John, cited, 25, 83, 97, 99, 107, 118, 120, 135, 136, 142, 143, 155, 158, 159
Law, attitude toward, 8, 119–39, 158, 180–82
Lawyer, 85, 92, 137–39, 164
Leadership, 28, 30, 33–35, 107–8
Lemon, 57, 68
Lepreuil, Mimi, 109
Levin, Yale, cited, 223
Lindesmith, Alfred R., cited, 223
Lustig, Count Victor, 82

McKay, Henry D., cited, 11, 23, 45
Marital relations, 30, 31, 112–13, 154–56, 190–91
Mead, W. E., 144
Merriam, C. E., cited, 179, 219
Mob, 10, 12, 14, 18, 24, 27–42, 213
Mobility, 3, 29, 88–89, 149–52, 155–56, 210
Money machine, 57, 66

Moore, Langdon W., cited, 221
Moore, Maurice C., cited, 74
Mouse, 34–35, 78–80

Nelson, Victor, cited, 12–13, 193
Norfleet, J. Frank, cited, 56, 58, 59, 70, 72, 108, 109, 118, 143, 154, 184
Northrup, J. B., cited, 219
Northrup, W. B., cited, 219

O'Connor, John J., cited, 16, 21, 56, 66, 74, 78
Organization, x, 209–11, 214, 224–25
Organized crime, 26, 209–10
Origin, 21–24, 32

Paper Laying, 14, 43, 75–77
Parole, 136–37
Pay-off, 35, 56–62
Pay-off joint, 27, 35, 59, 61
Pennyweight, 21, 43, 54
Pickpocket, 5, 9, 11, 17–18, 21, 24, 25, 27, 37, 44–48, 82–83, 87, 96, 104–6, 110, 111, 143–44, 149–50, 175–76, 179, 198, 217
Pigeon drop, 67–68
Police, 42, 82–85, 89–90, 114–15, 119–31, 165
Politics, 98–100, 110, 219–22
Predatory control, 208–9, 219–22
Prison, ix, 96, 134–36, 184–89
Profession, ix–x, 3–26, 197–226
Putup, 4, 9, 35

Recognition, x, 211, 214, 230
Residence, 156–58, 206, 224–26
Right grift, 29, 117–18
Robbery, 3, 5, 21, 87, 198

Scaffa, Noel C., 128
Seabury, Samuel, cited, 219
Security, 217–22
Selection, 24, 32, 211–13

256

Shaw, Clifford R., cited, 11, 23, 45

Shea, Pete, 82, 118

Shoplifting, 5, 6, 7, 22, 24, 32–33, 35, 39, 42, 43, 48–54, 149, 175–76, 217

Sick engineer, 69

Skidmore, Billy, 87

Slum hustler, 68, 148–49

Smack, 21, 63–66

Sneak thief, 6, 22, 23, 39, 40, 42, 43, 48–54, 100–102

Social disorganization, 222–26

Spanish prisoner, 64

Specialization, 42, 199–200

Stall, 29, 31, 33

Status, ix–x, 4, 43, 169–71, 198, 200–206, 210

Steffens, Lincoln, cited, 219

Stock market, 31, 56, 61

Stoddard, William L., cited, 63

Stool pigeon, 20, 25, 130–31

Tap, 73–75

Techniques, ix, 3, 43–81, 197–200, 210, 218

Thomson, Basil, cited, 71

Tozer, Basil, cited, 71

Train, Arthur, cited, 177

Tully, Jim, cited, 13

Tutelage, x, 14–15, 23, 32, 211–15, 218, 230

Underworld, ix, 15–21, 121, 204

Van Cise, Philip S., cited, 10, 27, 56, 70, 88, 108, 109, 144, 204, 226–28

Victim, 69–73, 83, 85–86, 90–95, 97–98, 102–6, 173–78, 218

Ware, Caroline F., cited, 220

Weil, Joseph, 37, 57, 62, 63, 144, 145, 179

Weston, John C., 221

White, George M., cited, 160, 222

Willard, Josiah Flynt, cited, 21, 109, 118, 125, 141, 144, 204

Wilson, P. A., cited, 215, 216

Wipe, 73–75

Wire, 31, 56, 57–61

PHOENIX BOOKS
in Sociology

P 7   *Louis Wirth:* The Ghetto

P 10   *Edwin H. Sutherland,* EDITOR: The Professional Thief, by a professional thief

P 24   *B. A. Botkin,* EDITOR: Lay My Burden Down: A Folk History of Slavery

P 28   *David M. Potter:* People of Plenty: Economic Abundance and the American Character

P 71   *Nels Anderson:* The Hobo: The Sociology of the Homeless Man

P 82   *W. Lloyd Warner:* American Life: Dream and Reality

P 92   *Joachim Wach:* Sociology of Religion

P 117   *Herbert A. Thelen:* Dynamics of Groups at Work

P 124   *Margaret Mead and Martha Wolfenstein,* EDITORS: Childhood in Contemporary Cultures

P 129   *John P. Dean and Alex Rosen:* A Manual of Intergroup Relations

P 138   *Frederic M. Thrasher:* The Gang: A Study of 1,313 Gangs in Chicago (Abridged)

P 162   *Thomas F. O'Dea:* The Mormons

P 170   *Anselm Strauss,* EDITOR: George Herbert Mead on Social Psychology

P 171   *Otis Dudley Duncan,* EDITOR: William F. Ogburn on Culture and Social Change

P 172   *Albert J. Reiss, Jr.,* EDITOR: Louis Wirth on Cities and Social Life

P 174   *Morris Janowitz:* The Military in the Political Development of New Nations

P 183   *Robert E. L. Faris and H. Warren Dunham:* Mental Disorders in Urban Areas

P 204   *Allison Davis and Burleigh and Mary Gardner:* Deep South (Abridged)

P 205   *E. Franklin Frazier:* The Negro Family in the United States

P 214   *Charles S. Johnson:* Shadow of the Plantation

P 219   *Eileen Younghusband,* EDITOR: Casework with Families and Children

P 226   *Harry Elmer Barnes,* EDITOR: An Introduction to the History of Sociology (Abridged)

P 242   *Morris Janowitz,* EDITOR: W. I. Thomas on Social Organization and Social Personality

P 244   *Bernard R. Berelson et al.:* Voting

P 245   *Harold F. Gosnell:* Negro Politicians

P 253   *Ernest W. Burgess and Donald J. Bogue,* EDITORS: Urban Sociology

P 262   *Manning Nash:* Machine Age Maya

P 263   *Morris Janowitz:* The Community Press in an Urban Setting

P 271   *Robert Blauner:* Alienation and Freedom

P 272   *George H. Mead:* Mind, Self, and Society

P 274   *Louis Schneider,* EDITOR: The Scottish Moralists on Human Nature and Society

P 275   *Ralph H. Turner,* EDITOR: Robert E. Park on Social Control and Collective Behavior

PHOENIX BOOKS
in Anthropology

P 20   *Kenneth P. Oakley:* Man the Tool-Maker
P 31   *Peter H. Buck:* Vikings of the Pacific
P 32   *Diamond Jenness:* The People of the Twilight
P 45   *Weston La Barre:* The Human Animal
P 53   *Robert Redfield:* The Little Community *and* Peasant Society and Culture
P 55   *Julian A. Pitt-Rivers:* People of the Sierra
P 64   *Arnold van Gennep:* The Rites of Passage
P 85   *William R. Bascom and Melville J. Herskovits,* EDITORS: Continuity and Change in
        African Cultures
P 86   *Robert Redfield and Alfonso Villa Rojas:* Chan Kom: A Maya Village
P 87   *Robert Redfield:* A Village That Chose Progress: Chan Kom Revisited
P 90   *Eric Wolf:* Sons of the Shaking Earth
P 105   *Sol Tax,* EDITOR: Anthropology Today: Selections
P 108   *Horace Miner:* St. Denis: A French-Canadian Parish
P 139   *Everett C. Hughes:* French Canada in Transition
P 173   *John F. Embree:* Suye Mura: A Japanese Village
P 175   *Edward B. Tylor:* Researches into the Early History of Mankind and the Develop-
        ment of Civilization
P 176   *James Mooney:* The Ghost-Dance Religion and the Sioux Outbreak of 1890
P 197   *Lloyd A. Fallers:* Bantu Bureaucracy
P 211   *Lewis H. Morgan:* Houses and House-Life of the American Aborigines
P 218   *William Stanton:* The Leopard's Spots
P 227   *W. E. LeGros Clark:* History of the Primates
P 262   *Manning Nash:* Machine Age Maya
P 273   *Émile Durkheim and Marcel Mauss:* Primitive Classification

PHOENIX BOOKS
in Archeology

P 2   *Edward Chiera:* They Wrote on Clay
P 11   *John A. Wilson:* The Culture of Ancient Egypt
P 88   *John R. Willey and Philip Phillips:* Method and Theory in American Archaeology
P 125   *George Steindorff and Keith S. Seele:* When Egypt Ruled the East
P 133   *Alexander Heidel:* The Babylonian Genesis
P 136   *Alexander Heidel:* The Gilgamesh Epic and Old Testament Parallels
P 225   *N. A. Nikam and Richard McKeon,* EDITORS: The Edicts of Asoka